The Knitter's Palette

The Knitter's Palette

A Workbook of Color
and Texture Techniques
and Effects

KATE HAXELL

Creative Publishing
international

First published in the United States of America by
Creative Publishing international, Inc., a member of
Quayside Publishing Group
400 First Avenue North
Suite 300
Minneapolis, MN 55401
1-800-328-3895
www.creativepub.com
Visit www.Craftside.Typepad.com for a behind-the-scenes peek at our crafty world!

Conceived, designed, and produced by
Quid Publishing
Level 4, Sheridan House
114 Western Road
Hove BN3 1DD
England

ISBN: 978-1-58923-730-8

10 9 8 7 6 5 4 3 2 1

Printed in China

For Luise, a friend indeed.

Contents

9   Introduction

10   How this book works

1   Understanding color

14   *Palette 1:* The color wheel

16   *Palette 2:* Color families

18   *Palette 3:* Cool and warm colors

20   *Palette 4:* Complementary and analogous colors

22   *Palette 5:* Color values

24   *Palette 6:* Personal colors

28   Creating a color notebook

2   Color and texture through yarn

32   *Palette 7:* Variegated yarns

34   *Palette 8:* Self-striping yarns

36   *Palette 9:* Self-patterning yarns

38   *Palette 10:* Tweed yarns

40   *Palette 11:* Color-effect yarns with stitch patterns

42   *Palette 12:* Textured yarns

44   *Palette 13:* Combining textured and plain yarns

46   *Palette 14:* Textured yarns with stitch patterns

3   Embroidery and beading

50   *Techniques*

58   *Palette 15:* Beading

60   *Palette 16:* Adding color with beads

62   *Palette 17:* Creating color patterns with beads

64   *Palette 18:* Embroidery

66   *Palette 19:* Embroidery accents

68   *Palette 20:* Yarns and threads for embroidery

70   *Palette 21:* Trims and appliqués

6   Intarsia knitting

114   *Techniques*

124   *Palette 37:* Motifs

126   *Palette 38:* Color balances in a motif

128   *Palette 39:* Color-effect yarns and stripes

130   *Palette 40:* Textured yarns

132   *Palette 41:* Stitch patterns

134   *Palette 42:* Beads and embroidery

7   Stranded knitting

138   *Techniques*

146   *Palette 43:* Traditional colors and patterns

148   *Palette 44:* Contemporary colors

150   *Palette 45:* Color balances in a palette

152   *Palette 46:* Color-effect yarns

154   *Palette 47:* Textured yarns and stitch patterns

156   *Palette 48:* Beads and embroidery

8   Aran knitting

160   *Techniques*

172   *Palette 49:* Aran patterns

174   *Palette 50:* Aran in color

176   *Palette 51:* Multicolor Aran

178   *Palette 52:* Aran in color-effect yarns

180   *Palette 53:* Embellishing Aran patterns

182   *Palette 54:* Aran patterns and embroidery

4 Stripes

5 Slip stitch knitting

74 *Techniques*
78 *Palette 22:* Stripe patterns
80 *Palette 23:* Pastels
82 *Palette 24:* Brights and neutrals
84 *Palette 25:* Color-effect yarns
86 *Palette 26:* Stitch and yarn textures
88 *Palette 27:* Embroidery and beads
90 *Palette 28:* Color-mixing with yarns
92 *Palette 29:* More with stripes

96 *Techniques*
98 *Palette 30:* Tweed patterns
100 *Palette 31:* Line patterns
102 *Palette 32:* Block patterns
104 *Palette 33:* Reversible patterns
106 *Palette 34:* Mosaic patterns
108 *Palette 35:* Texture patterns
110 *Palette 36:* Color-effect and textured yarns

9 Stitchwork

186 *Techniques*
200 *Palette 55:* Lace knitting
202 *Palette 56:* Stitch patterns
204 *Palette 57:* Color-effect yarns
206 *Palette 58:* Textured yarns
208 *Palette 59:* Beads and embroidery
210 *Palette 60:* Texture and colorwork

212 Swatching
215 Substituting yarn
216 Yarns
218 Resources
220 Abbreviations
221 Yarn standards and conversions
222 Index
224 Acknowledgments

Introduction

A visit to a local yarn store or a quick browse online will make it obvious to any knitter that there's a vast number of different yarns out there. But you don't have time to try even half of them, and many of them won't be any good for all sorts of techniques, and experimenting with lots of them will cost a fortune: Which is where this book comes in. *The Knitter's Palette* explores yarns in a huge variety of colors and textures across a wide range of knitting techniques, just so that you don't need to undertake doomed experiments.

When I was asked to write this book I was completely delighted; it was just perfect for me. Along with many little girls of my generation, I was taught to knit by my grandma: I laboriously looped stitches from one slightly sticky needle to another, using yarn that became increasingly grubby and matted with handling and unraveling. I loved knitting, and I especially loved the actual yarn. I wasn't allowed to play with most of grandma's yarn, but when I grew up and could afford my own yarn, I very quickly developed a stash. Now I know all knitters have stashes, but mine was a daft stash. To start with, there was very rarely more than one ball of any yarn, and there are really not many projects that only need one ball. And a significant number of the balls were green: I was definitely in a color rut.

When this finally dawned on me I did make a real effort to expand and develop my colors (turn to page 28 for thoughts on how to do this), but that didn't help me with my one-ball tendency. And the reason for the one-ball thing is because I simply like yarn. I don't need to do anything clever with it in order to enjoy it; just reveling in its color and texture is often enough. So an opportunity to revel for a living was ideal in every way.

In creating *The Knitter's Palette* I've chosen a huge variety of types of yarns (see pages 216–17 for a listing), explored all the color knitting techniques, and used a representative selection of the myriad texture patterns to create a treasure chest of swatches to inspire and inform your own choices. Plus, every chapter has comprehensive

illustrated step-by-steps for the techniques it explores, so as long as you can do the basics (cast on, knit and purl, and bind off), everything else you need to know is explained. So whether you are just browsing for interesting ideas, wanting to learn a new technique, hoping to finally knit up an unusual yarn that's been in your stash for years, looking for inspiration to add detail to a plain but much-loved sweater pattern, trying to expand your knitting horizons by being a bit more adventurous with a technique, or planning to knit your own swatch library of favorite colors and textures for future reference, there will be plenty in these pages to inspire you. I hope you enjoy using this book as much as I enjoyed writing it.

Kate Haxell

How this book works

A lot of thought and planning—as well as a good deal of knitting—has gone into creating this book, so to get the most from it do read through this section. Some of the information is completely straightforward, but it might help you navigate the book and construct themes that you want to explore further in your own knitting.

In addition, most chapters start with step-by-step illustrations of pertinent techniques, so as long as you have the knitting basics (casting on, knit stitch, purl stitch, and binding off), all the skills you need to knit your own swatches are taught in this book. The technique illustrations have been specially drawn and the accompanying instruction text includes tried-and-tested tips and professional advice to help you master each and every technique.

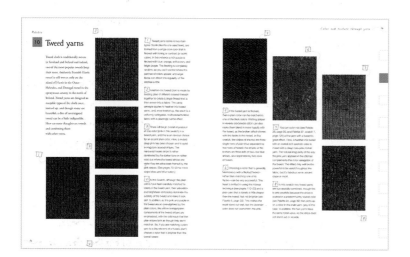

WHAT'S ON THE PAGES

The Knitter's Palette is designed to be an extensive resource for all aspects of knitting with color and texture. It is divided into nine chapters, each one centered on a particular aspect or technique, and each chapter is further subdivided into a number of palettes, each one of which contains individual knitted swatches, all especially designed and worked for this book; there are over 400 swatches in total. Each swatch is captioned with notes on yarn/s, construction, color balances, stitches, methods—whatever is appropriate to understand its role in the book.

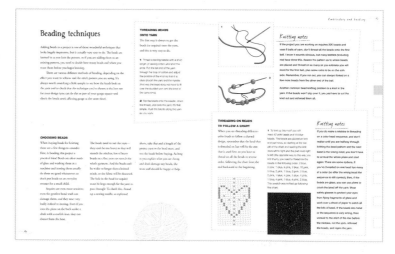

Knitting notes

Plus, palettes contain Knitting Notes that highlight tips, advice, themes, techniques, or warnings that are relevant to the swatches shown.

THE CHAPTERS

Chapter 1 is called "Understanding color" and it gives an overview of all the aspects of this surprisingly complicated topic that are relevant to the knitter. Plus, if you are lacking in color confidence, there are thoughts and advice on developing your color sensibilities. If exploring color is a new adventure for you, do read through this chapter, even if your fingers are itching to start knitting, as it's full of useful information that'll help you later on.

The next chapter looks at achieving texture and color patterning through yarn alone; not using any color knitting techniques and concentrating on plain stockinette stitch. If you are a novice knitter and are rather dismayed by what seem like complicated techniques, then this chapter is a wonderful place for you to start. You'll learn about different types of color-effect and texture yarns, and what you can achieve by just using them with simple knitting.

Subsequent chapters explore different types of knitting—beading and embroidery, striping, slip stitch knitting, intarsia, stranded knitting, Aran knitting, and texture knitting. The palettes within each chapter look at how the techniques can be developed using the understanding of color gained in Chapter 1, and skills and ideas learned and developed in other chapters.

For example, in the textured knitting chapter you'll find a palette looking at how you can use these traditional stitch patterns with embroidery and beading techniques; in the striping chapter there's a palette on texture in stripes; and in the beading and embroidery chapter there's a palette on creating pattern with beads, including stripes. Palettes relate to one another across the chapters as appropriate, but they don't repeat, and there are lots of cross references to help you make your own links for ideas that please you.

DEVELOPING THEMES

It may well be that you have no particular knitting agenda and are happy to potter along through this book, reading what catches your eye and knitting a swatch or two as you please. If so, I am rather jealous and wish you many pleasurable hours. However, you might have more of a mission in mind and want to make the most of one particular color or texture theme. If so, then—once you have digested Chapter 1—turn to the chapter you want to concentrate on; let's say that it's intarsia knitting (see pages 112–35).

The first two palettes in this chapter look at motifs in relation to intarsia techniques (thus supporting the comprehensive ten-page techniques section), and color balances in intarsia (relating to information in Chapter 1).

Then there's a palette on using color-effect yarns and stripes in intarsia (see page 128); different color-effect yarns are used, so you might want to look at Palettes 7–10 (see pages 32–39) in Chapter 2 to find out a bit more about those. And then you could look at Palette 25 (see page 84), which looks at stripe patterns made using color-effect yarns, and go on to look at the whole striping chapter (see pages 72–93). The striping with beads and embroidery palette (see page 88) might lead you back to intarsia to explore Palette 42 (see page 134), which looks at beading and embroidery in intarsia.

I hope that whatever ideas or themes catch your interest, you'll be able to explore them in a similar way, moving between related palettes in the book and gathering ideas from each of them to inspire your own knitting.

One theme you will notice is the heart shape that I've used as a motif throughout this book. I wanted a simple, universally understood symbol that I could use to illustrate color or texture effects that could then be compared across palettes without wondering what effect, if any, different motifs were having on the topic discussed. If you like this little heart you'll find a chart for it on page 114.

1 Understanding color

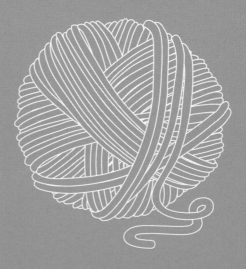

While we are surrounded by color in all aspects of our lives, it's not something we tend to think about very often. We might deliberate over the purchase of a new dress in a color we don't often wear, or worry that newly painted walls are too bright, but we rarely analyze color more than that. And yet color can actually be a very complicated thing indeed (square tetrad color harmony, anyone?).

Color is a natural phenomenon; it is a product of light. The colors of the rainbow are the colors of light, or at least, the part of the light spectrum that our eyes can see. Humans have relatively unsophisticated eyes compared to other animals, and a surprisingly large number of us have physical conditions that further affect our color vision: sometimes for the better, sometimes for worse. And that's before our brains get involved in processing what our eyes are seeing.

As knitters, we won't stray too far into the more technical aspects of understanding color, because most of us will have our choices limited by the commercially available yarns. (Obviously those crafters who dye their own yarns have a clear advantage here, but that is a different story.) However, within these limitations, it is worth understanding the major aspects of color more fully, as the more you understand, the more informed your choices will be, and the more likely your color knitting will be to turn out just the way you wanted it to.

1 The color wheel

Most of us will be familiar with what a color wheel looks like, even if we don't really understand how it might help us. A color wheel is made up of the three primary (first) colors—red, yellow, and blue; secondary (second) colors that are made by mixing primaries together; and tertiary (third) colors that are made by mixing primaries and secondaries. So primary red and primary blue mix together to make secondary violet. Then violet and blue mix together to make tertiary blue-violet.

There are a total of 12 colors on a standard pigment color wheel: blue, blue-violet, violet, red-violet, red, red-orange, orange, yellow-orange, yellow, yellow-green, green, and blue-green. This knitted wheel contains the best versions of these colors that I could find in a single type of yarn (turn to page 216 for a list of the yarns I used).

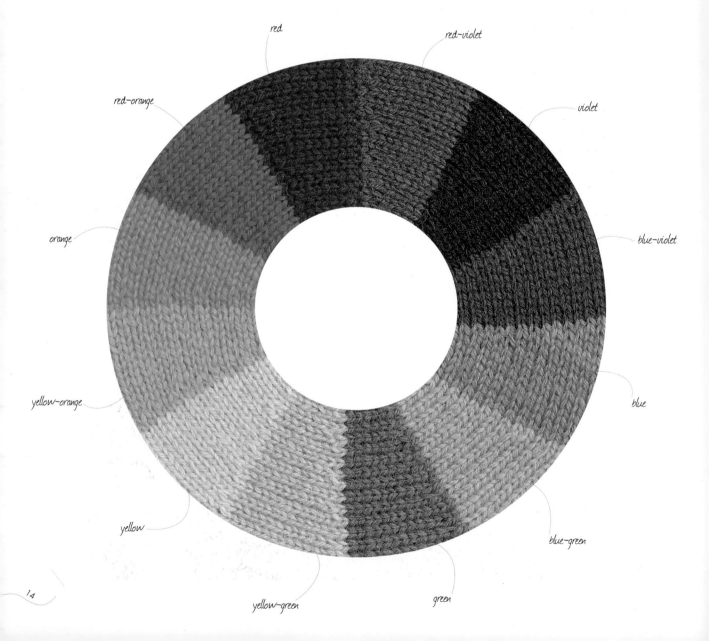

red

red-violet

red-orange

violet

orange

blue-violet

yellow-orange

blue

yellow

blue-green

yellow-green

green

There are other possible color wheels—some based on a different sort of color, and some containing more or fewer colors—but the pigment color wheel is the one most relevant to the world of yarn.

There are relationships between the colors on the wheel, and Palettes 3 and 4 (see pages 18 and 20) explore the most important of these.

Color words

Maybe the first step toward understanding color is to understand some of the words associated with it. Hue and color are, for our purposes, synonymous. The various versions of a color—for example, azure, powder blue, navy blue, cyan, royal blue—are all members of the same color family. For more on color families, turn to Palette 2 (see page 16).

Color saturation

The saturation of a color refers to how bright or dull it is. Primary bright blue is the most saturated version of the blue hue family. Adding white to saturated blue makes it both lighter and less saturated, and this is called tinting. A pastel color is a tint of a saturated color. Adding neutral gray to saturated blue won't necessarily make it darker (that depends a bit on the shade of gray), but it will make it less saturated, and this is referred to as toning. Adding black to saturated blue will both darken and desaturate it, and this is called shading. So, a light version of a color is called a tint, a dull version is a tone, and a dark version is a shade. If you take the study of color very seriously, it is more complicated than that, but we don't need to know more to be able to explore and enjoy color.

Color values

Colors also have values and these are as important to the way a selection of different colors work together in a design as the actual hues are. For more about color values, turn to Palette 5 (see page 22).

1 We can refer to darker versions of a color as shades. These may not be entirely true shades of the blue-green on the color wheel, but they are reasonable enough given yarn availability.

2 Pastel versions of a color can also be called tints. Again, these pinks are not precisely what you would get if you mixed the color wheel red with white, but they give a good idea of pink tints.

2 Color families

All the versions of a single color, whether they be tints, tones, or shades (see page 15), are part of the same color family, so the range of colors in every single family is huge. If you create a design using colors of just one family, that is called a monochromatic design, but you can't just pick any members of a family: Some of them won't get on at all. This is because as well as tinting, toning, and shading colors, you can mix other colors on the color wheel into your chosen color family to create undertones.

All of these samples are from the red color family. These have been narrowed down to pinks, and by absolutely no means at all do we have all—or even most—of the possible pinks. However, this palette does give you some idea of the range of a single aspect of a color that is open to you, even within the fairly limited world of commercially available yarns.

All knitters have been in the position of trying to find the "perfect" green to go with an already purchased orange (or whatever your personal favorite combo is), and sometimes the trick is to try and look at the undertones. Squint at the color: Does your green have a blue undertone, or is it nearer to a yellow undertone? If it's yellow then you're looking at a warm undertone, and you should look for a very warm orange to complement it. If it's blue, then an orange with more yellow in would look better. Yellow is warm, but closer to blue on the color wheel than red is. To understand more about warm and cool colors, turn to Palette 3 (see page 18). For more on colors that are neighbors on the color wheel, go to Palette 4 (see page 20).

1 and **2** These swatches are pink tints, pastel-pinks. Swatch 1 is what you could get if you mixed red with cream, while swatch 2 is closer to red with white mixed in.

3 and **4** Still pink tints, but a little gray has been added to swatch 3, while swatch 4 has been tinted with brown, which, like gray, is a neutral (see also Palette 24, page 82), but will warm up a color it is mixed into.

5 and **6** These versions of pink have some orange in them to send them off toward salmon pinks. If you were mixing paint to try to match these, you'd need to add a slightly yellowish orange to match swatch 5 and a burnt orange to match swatch 6.

7 and **8** These are tones of pink, so mixed with gray. Swatch 8 has more gray mixed in than swatch 7 so the color is less saturated, but the values (see Palette 5, page 22) are very similar.

9 and **10.** These are quite saturated versions of pink. You would not need to mix much white or cream with red to create either of these colors. Swatch 9 has an additional slightly warm undertone of orange, while swatch 10 has a slightly cool undertone of blue.

11 and **12** These pinks have distinctly blue undertones, making them much cooler than the orangey pinks of swatches 5 and 6.

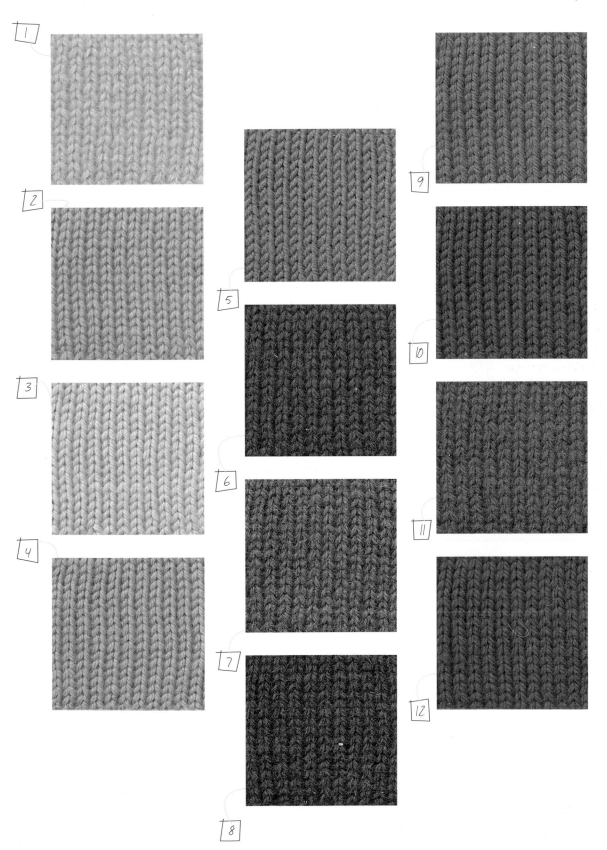

3 Cool and warm colors

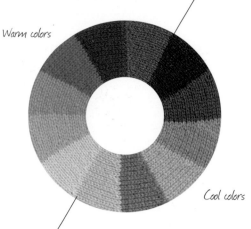

Warm colors

Cool colors

You can split the color wheel in half into two groups: the cool colors and the warm colors. The warm colors are red-violet, red, red-orange, orange, yellow-orange, and yellow, and the cool colors are yellow–green, green, blue-green, blue, blue-violet, and violet.

Visually, warm colors pop forward and stand out, while cooler colors recede. This holds true even when there is a much smaller amount of a warmer color than a cooler one in a design. So if you want a color palette that features both fairly equally, then you'll need to give over a larger area of the project to the cool colors if they aren't going to be completely dominated by the warm colors.

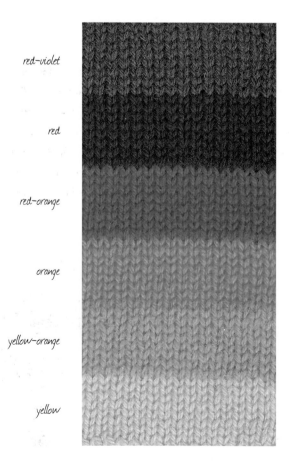

red-violet

red

red-orange

orange

yellow-orange

yellow

yellow–green

green

blue-green

blue

blue-violet

violet

In this swatch the red is so much stronger than the blue that the eye sees the two hearts differently. The red heart really stands out against the blue background, while the blue heart almost reads as a void, a negative shape in the red.

It's quite a common perception to see yellow as cool and purple as warm, maybe because we tend to associate yellow with green—which is cool—and purple with red-violet and red, which are warm. But put yellow and purple together and the reality is much more obvious.

In the swatch on the left, the two very narrow yellow stripes actually stand out in a sea of purple, while the purple stripes have to rely on their darker value to help them hold their own on any level. For more on color values, turn to Palette 5 (see page 22).

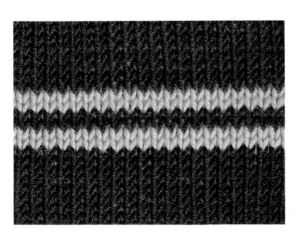 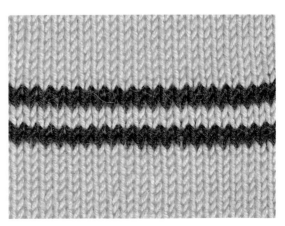

4 Complementary and analogous colors

Complementary colors are those that lie opposite one another on the color wheel, while analogous colors lie next to one another. These two relationships will profoundly influence any color palette.

Analogous colors

These are colors that lie close to one another on the color wheel. Wider analogous groups extend across whole color families, so you're not just looking at direct neighbors, but also other colors analogous to those neighbors. However, you need to be careful if you pick two colors that between them contain all three primaries, because the pairings can start to become unsettled.

1 You can pair up all sorts of shades of blue and green, as long as you steer away from blue-violet, because then you would be introducing red as the third primary into colors based on blue and yellow.

2 This red and red-violet are immediate neighbors and make for a rich combination as both are dark in value (see Palette 5, page 22) and saturated in color (see Palette 1, page 14). However, the red is much warmer than the red-violet, so you'd need to be careful that the cooler color wasn't over-whelmed in a big project.

3 Yellow and orange are the lightest two value colors (see Palette 5, page 22), so they don't fight one another, and they are both well within the warm side of the color wheel, so they don't fight on that level either.

All colors—not just the primaries—have a complementary; it'll be the one 180 degrees around from it on the color wheel. All complementary pairs will contain between them all three primary colors. So the complementary of yellow-green is red-violet, and yellow-orange has blue-violet as its complementary.

Complementary colors

As well as sitting directly opposite one another on the color wheel, another way to think of the complementary colors of the primaries is that each one is made from a mix of the other two primaries. So, the complementary of primary blue is secondary orange (mixed from red and yellow). Red is complemented by green (blue and yellow mixed), and yellow is complemented by purple (red and blue mixed). There are some interesting relationships to look at in these pairings.

1 Red and green are very happy together. They are both mid-tone in value (see Palette 5, page 22), and these shades are similarly saturated, so they don't clash at all. Indeed, red and green are colors that are usually the hardest for people who suffer any degree of color blindness to tell apart.

2 Violet and yellow are at different ends of the value spectrum (see Palette 5, page 22), so in their saturated states they are not comfortable together. The warmth of the yellow is offset by its paleness, while the coolness of the violet is bolstered by its dark value. Too many tensions in this pairing.

3 This blue-and-orange pairing is far more successful, even though, like the yellow and violet pair, the saturated colors are a long way apart in value and warmth. This is because these are tinted versions of the colors; they have been desaturated by gray having added to them (see Palette 1, page 14). Calming colors down like this can improve relationships considerably.

5 Color values

Every color has a value; this is nothing to do with the color itself, but is a comparison of that color to a gray scale. It's a bit like watching snooker in black and white: The balls would all be shades of gray instead of colors.

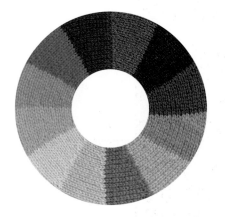

The value of a color is given as a number, and this is signifies the percentage of black that has to be mixed with white to achieve that color's value. The lightest value color is yellow, with a number of 10, signifying that only ten parts of black have to be added to 100 parts of white to make the gray equivalent of yellow. At the other end of the scale, 70–80 parts of black have to be added to 100 parts of white to produce the value of violet.

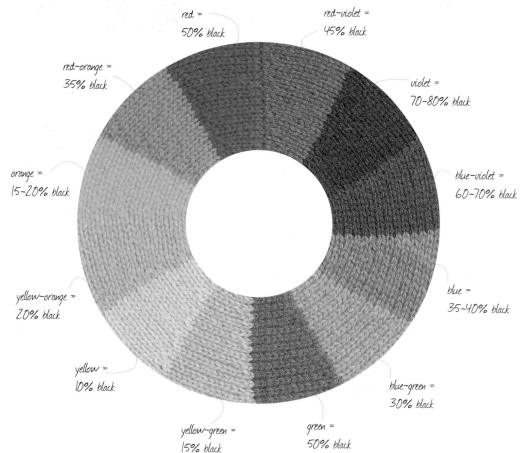

red =
50% black

red-violet =
45% black

red-orange =
35% black

violet =
70-80% black

orange =
15-20% black

blue-violet =
60-70% black

yellow-orange =
20% black

blue =
35-40% black

yellow =
10% black

blue-green =
30% black

yellow-green =
15% black

green =
50% black

yellow

yellow-green

red

blue

violet

yellow =
10% black

yellow-green =
15% black

red =
50% black

blue =
35-40% black

violet =
70-80% black

The value of a color is important because that's actually what the eye registers for the longest time. You might think that fuchsia pink stands out because it's bright, but the dark value of the color contributes as much as the warmth (see page 18) and saturation (see page 15) of the color. Indeed, it can be difficult at first to assess the value of a bright, pure color as the level of saturation can deceive the eye into thinking that the color is lighter than it actually is.

When you are putting together colors for a design, aim for a palette that has an overall balance of color values. So you want one light color, one dark color, and two or three mid-tones for a really harmonious palette. You can check the balances in a palette by wrapping the yarns around a strip of card and taking it to a copy shop to have it photo-copied in black and white. Or, if you have a computer with a built-in camera and photo software, you can either photograph the wraps with a

camera and turn the picture black and white on the computer, or do as I do and just hold the balls of yarn up together in front of the screen and get the computer to take the photo.

6 Personal colors

Getting your colors done is big business, and it can be quite a major procedure. At its simplest level, a color consultant will pick colors from a "season" that is deemed to suit your hair and eye colors and your skin tone. Shown here are just a smattering of colors from each season: If you get your colors done professionally you usually have plenty to choose from.

Spring

These people are pale-skinned, possibly with pink, peach, or pale golden tones. Hair color is generally light, and a lot of redheads are Springs. Eyes are mainly blue or green. As you can see from this small selection, a Spring person's colors contain lots of pastels. There are lots of pinks, peaches, and light, warm browns in the palette, with very few lilacs and greens, though quite a few blues.

Summer

Beige and pink-skinned people with white, light, and light-brown hair and usually blue or green eyes are likely to be Summers. This palette features quite a lot of more muted colors, including lots of rosy pinks and soft blues and greens, with some stronger grays and browns and occasional splashes of bright color to give it some punch.

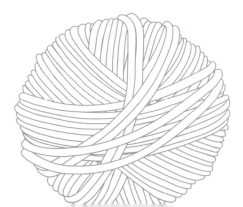

6

At more complex levels the colors can be assigned "personalities" and you undergo an extensive interview to ensure that your personality and those of your colors will gel. More esoteric aspects, such as astrology, can have a role to play. While you might not feel comfortable with the more complex levels, chosen by an expert that really do suit your colorings can be both very liberating (less fretting in changing rooms), and encouraging.

Autumn

Pale and golden-skinned people with red, honey-colored, or brown hair, and brown or blue eyes will probably be Autumns. The palette is a predominantly warm one— although not a bold one—with colors including plenty of rich oranges and muted greens, some softer browns and tans, gentle pinks, and a touch of mauve.

Winter

Those who suit the Winter palette
have very pale or sallow skin, gray or
dark hair, and brown, gray, or blue
eyes. Their palette is the boldest of
the four seasons, with a range of
colors including grays in various
warm tones, strong pinks and blues,
vivid purples and greens, and quite
a few very dark colors.

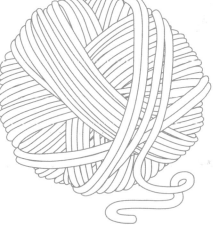

Creating a color notebook

We all have a favorite color, or colors, and this can be very obvious in knitters because their stash will betray them. All those must-have balls will more often than not build up into an impressive collection of shades of one color. This isn't necessarily a problem, but it's a good idea to try and expand your color horizons a bit, if only as an excuse to expand your stash. Here, I tell you how I fill and use my color notebook, but you can take a different path to developing your own book if that feels better to you.

Starting your notebook

If you find that in a clothes store you only really look at garments in a particular color, and in a yarn store you just pick up the balls in your favorite shade, then keeping a color notebook is an easy and efficient way of developing your color sense. Your notebook will be completely personal to you, so you should be open-minded if the book is going to be really useful. If the colors that interest you come from a child's toy advert, then stick the advert in your book, no matter how ridiculous it is.

Your book can be any format: Some people like a traditional notebook (I do), while others find a loose-leaf binder better as you can take out and swap around pages at will. (It's that very ability that I don't like about binders: I like to see how my color choices develop and don't want the temptation of reordering my thoughts.) I use thick, lined notebooks that I can write in as well

as keep clippings and samples. The only thing I would advise is not to use a very small book, because there literally won't be room on the pages for much exploration.

Filling your notebook

You can stick or clip anything into your book—the more variety of inspiration the better. And you can arrange references in whatever ways please you. I tend to work on several double-page spreads at a time, with different things happening on each of them. I often start with clippings from magazine pages and I'll glue these onto pages in groups that feel happy together. I also look out for paint swatch cards and scraps of fabric, but at this stage I usually ignore yarns. This part of the process is very instinctive: I don't analyze what I'm doing very much, I just put things together as I think right at the time. Sometimes I'll cut a particularly attractive bit of colored

pattern into more than one bit so that I can stick bits on different pages and try out a variety of companion clippings.

It's important to try to completely ignore your current color preferences. Don't think, "That's a pretty flower, but I hate pink." If you think the flower is pretty, then stick it in your book: On some subconscious level you relate to that particular shade of pink, or you wouldn't have been attracted by the flower. Likewise, if you tend to wear mainly blue, then make a real effort to look at lots of other colors.

Once I've got a few bits of pattern and color working together, if I like the results then I might move on to looking at some yarns. If I don't like the results then I don't tear the page out, I just move on to another page. Sometimes I quite like the way a page is working, but if it's not saying anything new to me then I'll move on for the time being.

Often, when I flip back through the book, old pages present fresh opportunities: A selection might come together much better mixed with a new clipping. (One thing you will need is lots of bookmarks!)

Using your notebook

You may well find that your notebook starts to grow beyond the original brief of expanding your color horizons. Now I don't want to curb your creativity, but I do urge you to follow these diverging paths in a different notebook and to keep one book just for exploring color. If you expand the remit of your color book too far, you risk losing sight of where it's taking you.

I don't carry my notebook around with me, for a few reasons. Firstly, it's just too precious to me: I'd be terrified of leaving it on a bus. Secondly, it's quite big and even though I like capacious purses, I'll put my shoulder out if I'm always hauling around a few pounds of book. And thirdly, and most importantly, that's not how I use my book. I do always have a beady eye out for anything that might be worth sticking in it, and I take snaps with my cell phone camera (people's clothes, leaves, flowers, furniture…) that I review and print out later, but the composition of the pages happens at home. The only time I take my book out is when I want to match yarns to a collaged page.

Developing color palettes

When putting different quantities of colors together to see how a yarn palette might develop, tapestry wools are great. They come in lots of colors, are inexpensive, and are widely available. Take your notebook with you when you pick wools: No matter how good your "color memory," it's best to go back to the source of your inspiration to pick colors. You might end up picking a shade slightly different to your original reference, but that's a conscious decision rather than a mistake.

If you've got a yarn in your stash that you desperately want to use, but you want to put other colors with it, then it's a good idea to knit a small swatch (see page 212) and match other colors to that. You can stick the swatch in your notebook, too—it's easier to judge the results of color combos that way. Incorporating the swatch into a collection of clippings will give you a good basis for choosing colors for a palette.

Sometimes a palette comes together very quickly, and at other times you might be very unsure about a collection. The answer is not to push it. Just turn the page and let everything sit and stew for a few days, then look at it again. As you grow in color confidence you'll become braver with your experiments and more decisive about the results. Just remember that it isn't a competition; it's not about winning.

Choosing yarns

Once you've put together a potential palette, it's time to look at yarns. This for me is the most fabulous bit of the whole process, but it can also be the most frustrating. It's easy to spend hours, days, months, hunting for the ideal shade of lilac, a perfect match to the tapestry wool palette in your book. And sometimes that just doesn't exist and you need to choose a different shade, or even a completely different color. Sometimes while you are hunting for one color you come across another that you hadn't considered and that is better than your planned color. Whatever the circumstances, try not to stress about it. Go with the flow, roll with the punches, and if necessary, consign a partly fulfilled palette to a bag in your stash to await another day when the design gurus who decide on the colors we are wearing each season come into line with what you are looking for.

If you're planning to knit a particular project, first look at the recommended yarn and examine the color options available in it. If these don't suit you then you need to look at substitute yarns. There will be some practical limitations on what you can choose for your palette and before you commit to buying many balls of something gorgeous, please do swatch carefully (turn to pages 212–15 for information on swatching and substituting yarns).

Chapter

2 Color and texture through yarn

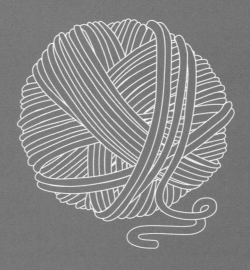

Myriad yarns are available to knitters and there are many that will take the hard work out of knitting color patterning or texture. Yarns that create color patterns through plain stockinette stitch knitting are known as color-effect yarns, while those that produce texture are often called novelty yarns. Some of these yarns have been developed for specific purposes (see Palette 8, page 34 and Palette 11, page 40) and can present problems if used for other tasks, while others are cheerfully and usefully multipurpose. However, do take to heart the old motto "buyer beware" when it comes to color-effect and novelty yarns, as what can seem deeply attractive in a tactile ball or elegantly twisted skein can look distinctly odd when knitted up. This chapter offers advice on how to decide whether a fancy yarn is fit for purpose, and ideas for making the most of the easy ways these yarns can add color and texture detail to plain knits.

7 Variegated yarns

A dictionary definition of the word "variegated" is "exhibiting different colors, especially as irregular patches or streaks" and that is precisely what these yarns do. They are sometimes called space-dyed yarns, but this is misleading because space-dyeing is a specific technique and not all variegated yarns are made using it (it's rather like referring to all yarn as wool). Basically, a variegated yarn is dyed in patches of different colors—or variations of one color—along its length, and when knitted up the colors appear as "irregular patches or streaks," sometimes to surprising effect. The way in which the patches and streaks fall is often called "color pooling," and pooling that is very regular or symmetrical can jump out in a finished project.

2 ...that is knitted over 55 stitches, and the neat two-row stripe instantly disappears. This might seem obvious, but most knitters have at some point knitted up a swatch and missed the obvious. What replaces the gauge-swatch pattern might be nicer—or it might be vile. The lesson is to work a swatch (see page 212) the intended width of the project (though you usually only have to work about 15 rows to assess the color pooling) before buying multiple balls of the yarn. And remember that with a sweater the pooling on the arms and body won't be the same, and that on a hat such as a beanie the pattern will change as the stitch count reduces. These effects may well be part of the yarn's charm for you, but it is worth checking.

3 Gently variegated yarns use variations of one color to often lovely effect. The color transitions are subtle and the overall slightly distressed, well-worn effect can be absolutely perfect for knitting up patterns with a vintage look. This is a four-ply yarn, so the little stitches make the effect especially subtle. With yarns like this it's still worth knitting up a full-width swatch, but the effect is unlikely to be terribly different to that of a standard gauge swatch.

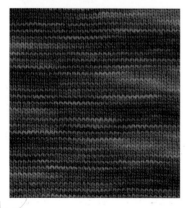

1 This is a gauge-swatch of a green-and-purple variegated yarn, and knitted straight off the ball over 30 stitches, it produced this beautifully neat two-row stripe pattern. You can see the streaks of lighter and darker tones along the rows, but the transition from green to purple is well-defined. And this is the danger of variegated yarns and gauge swatches: You knit a swatch and then believe what you see. And so you start a scarf...

4 This yarn is effectively the same as that in the previous swatch (a variegated yarn in one color), but it's brighter and is a worsted weight. The thicker weight means larger stitches and so a less subtle effect. Lots of different greens—from lime to mint, kelly to olive—are happily mixed, a convincing display of how colors in a single hue family (see Palette 2, page 16) can be harmonious.

5 Variegated yarns usually stripe up very well, though you have to choose the other color/s carefully. Here, the yarn used in the previous swatch is knitted in single-row stripes with a plain green yarn of the same weight. You definitely need to swatch the stripe pattern as yarns that look good together in balls can look unbalanced when knitted up in rows. (See pages 72–93 for more stripe ideas and information.) This is a great way of making an expensive color-effect yarn go further.

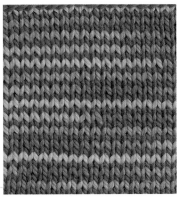

Knitting notes

A good yarn store will often offer a scheme whereby they will sell you one ball of yarn, but set aside for an agreed time the number of balls you'll need for the whole project. This means you can go home and thoroughly swatch a variegated yarn before committing to a whole project: Ideal.

6 Another way of making an expensive yarn go further is to use it just for details, and variegated yarns are great used this way. In this swatch the gently variegated yarn used in swatch 6 is worked in seed stitch as an edging on stockinette stitch in plain yarn: a really lovely collar, cuff, or front band detail on a cardigan or jacket. (See Palette 11, page 40 for more ideas for using color-effect yarns with different stitch patterns.)

7 This variegated yarn also supplies some texture when knitted up in plain stockinette stitch (see Palette 12, page 42, Palette 13, page 44, and Palette 14, page 46, for more on knitting with textured yarns). It's a ribbon yarn divided lengthways into a shiny and a matte stripe, which adds yet more variation to the color and texture. This particular yarn also has a stretch, so keeping an even gauge is not easy, though the color and texture are forgiving of a rather uneven fabric. This yarn could be a nightmare or a dream; it really does depend on personal taste.

8 Self-striping yarns

These color-effect yarns are dyed in a similar way to variegated yarns (see Palette 7, page 32), but the length of yarn in each separate color is such that when the yarn is knitted up a stripe pattern is produced. Obviously, the number of stitches in the project will affect the depth of the stripes, so swatching (see page 212) to the full width of the project is vital if you want to know what the stripe pattern will actually look like. And, as with variegated yarn, if elements of the project are different widths, the stripe pattern will vary. You can adjust the pattern by looping yarn at the sides, cutting the loops, then sewing the ends in later, but this does result in bulky seams and wouldn't be recommended in a garment. (See pages 74–93 for more stripe knitting ideas.)

Knitting notes

In my experience it is completely impossible to knit a self-striping yarn over any stitch count and have the stripes begin and end at the same place on the rows. I've tried and tried and tried… However, it usually looks okay to have stripes starting wherever they want, so best not to worry about it.

1 This self-striping yarn is designed for knitting socks, and over about 64 stitches in the round it knits up to this neat pattern (see Palette 9, page 36, for more on knitting with sock yarns). With narrow stripes you won't always achieve the same result by knitting back and forth over the same number of stitches (the colors may well start to pool in places—see Palette 7, page 32), so if you want to use a sock yarn in a flat project, then don't be led astray by any accompanying photo of stripy socks.

2 A yarn that produces wider stripes can usually be successfully knitted back and forth, even if it is designed for knitting in the round. The pattern might be marginally less successful, with stripes being wider at one end than the other by two rows, but an overall stripy, rather than patchy, effect will be produced. This swatch shows the full stripe repeat top to bottom, and you can see where the stripes fade in and out on the rows.

3 Also a sock yarn, this produces a pattern of wider and narrower stripes. It's worth swatching a full stripe repeat on these yarns to decide how you want the stripes to appear in the project. For example, it would look unbalanced to have the narrow orange and white stripes at the top of a sock; better to start with one of the wider stripes.

3

4

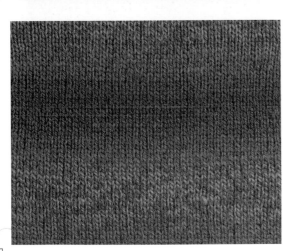

5

4 The stripes this yarn creates are wide and softly blended rather than distinct. The effect is not dissimilar to the results that can be obtained from color-mixing yarns (see Palette 28, page 90), but here the yarn does the whole job for you. Again, the number of stitches will obviously affect the stripes, but the blended effect is more forgiving of varying stripes in different parts of a project.

5 This yarn is marled (composed of two plies of different colors) and both plies change color, but are different colors at different intervals; it's as though you were knitting with two self-striping yarns held together. Again, the effect is of a blended stripe sequence, but the flecking created by the two plies is quite distinct and so you don't get the gentle color transitions seen in the previous swatch.

6 Though not actually knitted, pom-poms are one of the staple trims in any knitter's repertoire, and color-effect yarns make for truly magnificent pom-poms. This one was made using a self-striping yarn that would have produced quite short stripes, which results in a flecked pom-pom. A wider stripe yarn (such as that used in swatch 2) wound carefully and evenly can produce a striped pom-pom, although the stripes will not be as distinct as in the knitting.

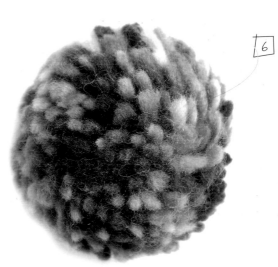

6

9 Self-patterning yarns

Similar in nature to self-striping yarns, these clever sock yarns have some sections dyed different colors in very short lengths so that only one or two stitches are worked before the color changes. The result is a flecked pattern that is supposed to resemble Fair Isle. In truth, one has to view the pattern from a distance, and suspend a bit of disbelief, to see it as Fair Isle, but the effects are generally attractive and do allow you to knit patterned socks very easily indeed. As these yarns are designed especially for knitting socks (I've never found one that wasn't), all the samples shown (other than swatch 2) were knitted over 64 stitches in the round then pressed flat, so you are seeing just one side of each sample.

1 The stripe and fleck pattern isn't precise in the way that genuine Fair Isle is, but the overall effect is colorful. These yarns are great if you are a novice sock knitter, as they allow you to concentrate on the shaping rather than the patterning, and the multicolored result effectively disguises any minor gauge or technique flaws.

2 This swatch is knitted over the same number of stitches as the previous swatch, but worked back and forth. You can clearly see that although the underlying stripes have worked out well (they are reasonably wide, see also Palette 8, page 34), the flecks are unevenly distributed, and so an almost impossible amount of disbelief would have to be suspended to allow the result to be seen as Fair Isle.

Knitting notes

Producing a matching pair of socks from self-patterning (or self-striping, see Palette 8) yarn is easy; just start each sock at the same place in the yarn pattern. However, I've always liked a pair of socks knitted in the same yarn but with the pattern positioned differently on each one; a detail that's quirky, but not silly.

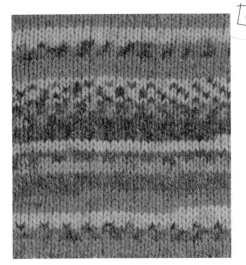

3 A variation on the theme, this self-patterning yarn offers a more complex stripe pattern and softer flecks. The overall effect is even less "Fair Isle" than swatch 1, but the stripe pattern is more interesting. As with self-striping yarns (see Palette 8, page 34), it's worth working out how you want the stripe sequence to be positioned on the sock.

4 This is a double-knitting weight self-patterning yarn, though it's still designed for socks. Using just blues and grays, and with more random flecking than other yarns, it produces an overall patterned effect, though the sense of "Fair Isle" recedes still further over the horizon.

5 Although this yarn uses the flecked dyeing principle, the patterning is restricted to distinct stripes rather than a faux Fair Isle, and the result is very successful. Also, notice the color intensity in the band of patterning between the dark gray stripes compared to the same pattern band between the pale gray and pink stripes; for more on how neutrals affect color stripes turn to Palette 24, page 82.

6 One thing to note when using self-patterning yarns in socks is that the ribbed cuff rarely does the yarn any favors. This yarn is generally very successful (the charcoal and white bands are really quite good faux Fair Isle), but once you get to the rib section it stops working so well. So it might be best to choose a sock pattern with very short rib to use with such a yarn.

10 Tweed yarns

Tweed cloth is traditionally woven in Scotland and Ireland and indeed, two of the most popular tweeds keep their roots. Authentic Scottish Harris tweed is still woven only on the island of Harris in the Outer Hebrides, and Donegal tweed in the eponymous county in the north of Ireland. Tweed yarns are designed to resemble types of the cloth once knitted up, and though many are beautiful, a diet of unmitigated tweed can be a little indigestible. Here are some thoughts on tweeds and combining them with other yarns.

1 | Tweed yarns come in two main types: Some (like the one used here), are formed from a single core color that is flecked with toning or contrast (or both) colors. In this instance a rich purple is flecked with blue, orange, soft brown, and bright purple. The flecking is completely random, so you can't control where the patches of colors appear, and larger flecks can distort the regularity of the stitches a little.

2 | Heather-mix tweed cloth is made by twisting plies of different-colored threads together to create a single thread that is then woven into a fabric. The same principle applies to heather-mix tweed yarns, and, once knitted up, the result is a uniformly variegated, multicolored knitted fabric with a pleasingly subtle effect.

3 | There will be an overall impression of one color (pink in this swatch) in a tweed yarn, and this is an obvious choice for an accent plain color. Here, a muted deep pink has been chosen and is used in irregularly spaced stripes. The narrowest tweed stripe is rather dominated by the darker tone on either side, but where the tweed stripes are wider they are attractively framed by the pink stripes. (See pages 72–93 for more stripe ideas and information.)

4 | In this swatch, although the plain colors have been carefully matched to colors in the tweed yarn, their saturation and brightness completely dominate the subtlety of the tweed and make it look dull. In addition, as the pink and purple in the tweed are so overwhelmed by the plain colors, the yellow/orange/green components of the tweed stripes are emphasized, with the odd result that the plain stripes look as though they don't match in. So, if you are matching a plain yarn to a tiny element of a tweed, don't choose a color that is brighter than the overall tweed.

5 If the tweed yarn is flecked, then a plain color can be matched to one of the fleck colors. Knitting stripes in reverse stockinette stitch can also make them blend in more happily with the tweed, as the broken effect chimes with the flecks in the tweed. In this swatch, the stripes at the top are three single rows of plain blue separated by two rows of tweed; the stripes at the bottom are three sets of two-row blue stripes, also separated by two rows of tweed.

6 Choosing a color that is generally harmonious with a flecked tweed—rather than matching one of its flecks—can be very successful. This heart is knitted in using the intarsia technique (see pages 112–23) and a plain yarn that is tonally a little deeper than the tweed, but not brighter (see Palette 5, page 22). This makes the motif stand out well, but the lavender color does not overwhelm the pink.

7 You can color-mix (see Palette 28, page 90, and Palette 37, swatch 7, page 124) a fine yarn with a tweed to great effect. Here, a heather-mix tweed with an overall soft lavender color is mixed with a deep rose-pink mohair yarn. The natural irregularity of the way the pink yarn appears in the stitches complements the color variegation of the tweed. The effect may well be too powerful to be used throughout the fabric, but it's fabulous as an accent stripe or motif.

8 In this swatch two tweed yarns are successfully combined, though this is only possible because the stripe is worked in a predominantly neutral color (see Palette 24, page 82) that picks up on a color in the main yarn: gray in this case. In addition, the two yarns have the same tonal value, so the stripe does not stand out or recede.

11 Color-effect yarns with stitch patterns

Many projects will include a simple stitch pattern—for example, rib on a cuff, seed stitch on a collar, or garter stitch for a reversible scarf—and the combination of such patterns and color-effect yarns can be unexpected. If the stitch pattern is just a small element, then even if it does the yarn no favors it probably won't detract from the finished project, but if the stitch pattern is a large or central element, then do swatch it (see page 212) with your yarn to judge the effect. It's often possible to match a plain yarn to a color in the patterned yarn and knit the stitch pattern section in that. (See Palette 36, page 110, Palette 52, page 178, and Palette 57, page 204, for more ideas on using color-effect yarns with different types of knitted stitch patterns.)

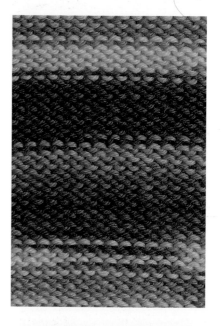

1 Reverse stockinette stitch is often referred to as "the wrong side" of its more popular relation, stockinette stitch, and this is a pity as it's a useful and attractive stitch in its own right. Most commonly used as a background for cables (see Palette 49, page 172, Palette 50, page 174, and Palette 51, page 176), it can look really good with color-effect yarns. Here, a variegated yarn works particularly well; as the color transitions are always split across a stitch, the blended effect is increased. See swatch 6 for another way of using this yarn.

2 Garter stitch, the simplest of all stitch patterns, is great for collars, cuffs, and bands because it doesn't curl, and ideal for scarves as it is reversible. The ridged surface will obscure the fleck detail on self-patterning yarns (Palette 9, page 36), and color transitions are split across a stitch (on one side or the other), but the latter can be effective. This is a self-striping yarn and you can see the split color transitions, but they don't adversely affect the overall look of the knitting.

3 Rib is a hugely popular and very useful stitch pattern, but one that can be tricky with some color-effect yarns as the vertical ridges obscure detail (see swatch 6, Palette 9, page 37). Also, on the purl stitches color transitions will be split across a stitch and this can look a bit chaotic with very distinct or contrasting stripes. However, a rib pattern presents no problem at all with this gently blending self-striping yarn.

4 Seed stitch is another excellent choice for edges that don't curl, or reversible items, and it has an endearingly vintage appeal. However, generally it's not much of a friend to color-effect yarns, as you can see from this swatch. This yarn is used in swatch 3, Palette 9, page 37, with mixed results, but here even its more interesting stripe pattern is blurred. Color transitions are split over the alternating purl stitches, distorting the edges of stripes, and the flecks of color look entirely random; any semblance of a pattern is lost.

| 3 |

| 5 |

5 | Double seed stitch offers a
more intricate-looking pattern,
although it is entirely straightforward
to knit. The textured surface presents
all the problems for self-patterning
yarns that the previous swatch showed,
and the way color transitions will split
over alternating pairs of purl stitches
won't do a lot for self-striping yarns
with distinct stripes. However, this
color-effect yarn is both a flecked
tweed (see Palette 10, page 38) and a
gently blending self-stripe and it looks
good with the pattern; proof that
combinations of more intricate patterns
and complex color yarns can work.

6 | I-cords are a staple trim
for knitters; useful for drawstrings,
handles, appliqué, edgings, and more.
They generally work well with both
variegated and self-striping yarns,
but not with self-patterning ones.
This yarn is the one used in swatch 1,
and even over just 5 stitches you
can see the difference in color
transitions when it is knitted in
stockinette stitch—and it makes for
a really attractively patterned cord.

| 4 |

| 6 |

Knitting notes

Making trims such as the I-cord shown here and the pom-pom on page 35
from the same yarn as the main part of a project can give a sophisticated,
coordinated look, but it can also be a missed opportunity for an accent color.
Do swatch your trim idea in the color-effect yarn (make a small bundle of loops
and cut the ends for a pom-pom swatch), and try out a contrast of toning
color as well; it only takes a little yarn and a short time.

12 Textured yarns

Sometimes called "novelty yarns," textured yarns allow you to create surface effects with plain stockinette stitch in the same way that color-effect yarns allow you to create color effects (see Palette 7, page 32, Palette 8, page 34, Palette 9, page 36, and Palette 10, page 38). However, the effects can be more than a little overwhelming if used across a whole project. In addition, many textured yarns need to be knitted on quite large needles to make the texture show up well, and the resulting loose gauge can easily stretch and cause problems with the finished piece. There are many, many textured yarns available, and it is always vital to work a swatch (see page 212).

1 Probably the most popular textured yarn is mohair, and one of the main reasons it is so popular is because the texture is light and soft, making it friendly to both your hands and stitch patterns. Most mohair yarns are very fine, but work well knitted up on thicker needles, as the swatch on the left shows. Knitted on very fine needles, the fabric is lovely, though it'll take a while to "grow."

2 Slubbed yarns are loose twist yarns with soft nubs and irregularities along their length, created for deliberate effect rather than by accident. As they are designed to look uneven, they are naturally forgiving of varying gauge, but the loose twist means that it's quite easy for the needle to pierce the yarn rather than go through the stitch, making them not the best choice for a novice knitter. Worked to a fairly firm gauge, the effect can be pleasingly haphazard.

3 Bouclé yarns are made up of two (or more) plies, spun together with one core ply under tension and the other looser so that it forms loops along the length of the resulting yarn. The loops can be large or small, the yarn smooth or fluffy. Bouclé is another yarn whose nature makes it forgiving of uneven gauge, but it's very easy to put the needle through a loop rather than a stitch, so best not used when knitting in front of the television. This is a fairly thick bouclé with loops of varying sizes, knitted to a firm gauge, and you can easily see how much more textured it is when used for reverse stockinette (bottom half of swatch) than for stockinette stitch. (See Palette 14, page 46, and Palette 58, page 206, for more on using textured yarns with stitch patterns.)

1

2

3

4 This is another bouclé yarn, but the core ply is very fine and the loops thin and soft. Knitted on relatively large needles, the fabric is both tactile and uneven. It is, and is intended to be, entirely impossible to knit bouclé yarns with a completely even gauge, so if you find the texture unattractive, then these soft, fine bouclés simply aren't the yarns for you.

5 This is also a bouclé yarn, but one that produces a very different fabric from the previous ones (see swatches 3 and 4). The twisted plies are the same thickness, with a smooth texture, and when knitted up with a fairly firm gauge, the result is barely identifiable as a knitted fabric. This is quite a thick fabric, so not great for small garments, but makes a lovely, and reversible, scarf.

6 Rather astonishingly, this is a knitted yarn. Designed especially for making scarves, the ruffled effect (which is completely reversible) is created by knitting through just the top edge of a wide, loosely woven ribbonlike yarn. I read the instructions for using it and entirely failed to understand them, but once I started knitting it was obvious how it worked, and it was easy to do.

7 Fur yarns are available in varying degrees of hairiness, with this one firmly at the hirsute end of the range. They are made from a core ply with fine strands coming out from it; when these strands are sparser the yarn is sometimes called "eyelash" yarn. The fine strands do get trapped in the stitches, but gently stretching the fabric and running your fingers over it a few times will free many of them and bring the fabric to its full furriness.

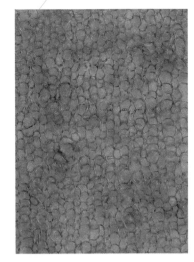

4

5

6

Knitting notes

Textured yarns can look remarkably different knitted up on different-sized needles. If you do fall in love with a textured skein and the first swatch is disappointing, don't immediately abandon it, but try knitting it with both larger and smaller needles to see if the results improve.

7

13 Combining textured and plain yarns

A very good use of textured yarns, particularly the more heavily textured ones, is as accents on an otherwise plain project. A furry cuff or fluffy collar can lift a sweater design and are easy to work. However, one problem that may well arise is gauge: It is highly likely that the textured yarn will require a different gauge to the plain one, making it almost impossible to simply change yarns, and potentially tricky to pick up and knit. Knitting separate pieces and sewing them on is usually the safest and easiest solution. Another possible issue is laundering: When combining any two yarns, do ensure that they can be laundered together, although careful hand-washing will usually overcome any problems (see also page 214).

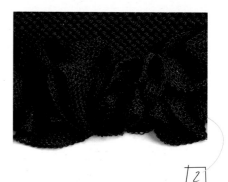

1 A dense eyelash yarn makes a great furry edging. In this instance the main yarn was chunky enough for the eyelash yarn to be knitted straight off it. The main yarn is worked in stockinette and the eyelash yarn in reverse stockinette to make the most of its furriness (see swatch 1, Palette 14, page 46). In addition, the slightly mottled color of the main yarn complements the way the light reflects off the strands of the fur, giving the latter a two-tone appearance even though it is actually a single color.

2 This wide ribbon yarn is specifically sold for making ruffled scarves, but it looks good as a trim. As you knit the ribbon by only picking up a few threads of the top edge of it, I was—after a bit of experimentation—able to knit the main yarn off the top of a couple of rows of ruffle. However, it would be just as easy to knit the ruffle as a separate piece and sew it on.

3 Chenille yarn produces this velvet texture that almost completely blurs the shape of the knitted stitches, especially if worked with a firm gauge. The plain yarn is a double knitting/light worsted weight and while the chenille stripes are quite firm, the plain yarn ones are at the loose end of desirable. The combination does work, but maintaining gauge over a larger piece of knitting would take concentration.

4 Doubled up, the mohair yarn used to knit this intarsia motif was almost the same weight as the main yarn, so no major problems here. If you are new to intarsia—or just not great at it—lightly textured yarns can be your friend as they can hide uneven stitches very effectively. (See Chapter 6, pages 112–15 for more ideas and techniques for intarsia knitting.)

5 An easy and effective way of introducing a very chunky yarn is by weaving. You simply bring the chunky yarn forward between the needles, knit a couple of stitches, then take it back again, leaving a bar of chunky yarn on the front of the knitting. You can do this on a knit or a purl row, on successive rows, and in patterns. However, it does affect the drape of the fabric a bit and can affect gauge (depending on how thick the weaving yarn is and how much you weave it in), so quite a large test swatch (at least 10 x 10in/25 x 25cm) is a good idea.

6 There's no particular reason why you shouldn't use two textured yarns together, if your knitting nerves can take it. This swatch boasts stripes of a thick angora-mix yarn worked in reverse stockinette combined with a variegated ribbon yarn worked in stockinette; a real multiplicity of texture and color.

Knitting notes

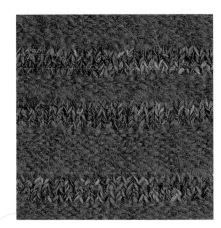

If you want to pick up and knit a fancy yarn from a plain one, then knit a swatch of the fancy yarn on the needle size that produces the best results. Measure the swatch and the plain edge and count the number of stitches in the swatch. Work out how many stitches of the fancy yarn are needed to fit along the plain edge, then knit a swatch with that many stitches to check it fits. Use safety pins to divide the plain edge into quarters (or smaller sections if it's a long edge) and pick up a quarter of the required fancy yarn stitches evenly from each marked section. Very furry or ruffled yarns are fairly forgiving of slightly uneven picking up, so you don't have to be too precise.

14 Textured yarns with stitch patterns

As will be obvious from the swatches in Palette 12 (see page 42), many textured yarns will not be suitable for knitting anything other than stockinette, because the texture will conceal the patterning. However, lighter textures and simpler patterns can be good bedfellows (see Palette 58, page 200, for ideas for using textured yarns with stitch patterns). Be aware that a textured yarn can need quite a loose gauge to show it off to best effect, and stitch patterns often look best with a fairly firm gauge to make the most of the varying stitch shapes. As always with textured yarn, a swatch (see page 212) will definitely be needed to see if your dream yarn is, in fact, a nightmare.

Knitting notes

You can have huge problems with furry or fluffy yarns if you try to unpick them after making a mistake. The fibers interlace surprisingly firmly when knitting even simple stitch patterns and unpicking, even done carefully, can result in rather bald sections of yarn. In addition, the texture makes it quite hard to see the stitch loops, so pulling out rows and then trying to pick up the stitches can be harder than it usually is. If you do have to unpick textured yarn, it's best to be slow but sure and unpick stitch by careful stitch.

1

2

3

1 Reverse stockinette stitch comes into its own with textured yarns: It isn't just the wrong side of stockinette, it really does have something different to offer here. The relatively long loops (compared to the Vs of stockinette) allow fluffiness and furriness to reach full potential. Even the light fluff of mohair yarn benefits from reverse stockinette.

2 I-cords can be worked in reverse stockinette and this one really shows off the short tufts and furry strands of this heavily textured yarn: It looks a bit like an exotic caterpillar. Work the cord in exactly the same way as usual, just purling every stitch instead of knitting it. (See Palette 13, page 44 for more ideas on using textured yarns as accents.)

3 This is a version of a slubbed yarn, spun so that it is different thicknesses along its length. Unlike some slubbed yarns, it does not have added nubs (see Palette 12, swatch 2, page 42), but the difference between the thick and thin sections is quite extreme. It looks lovely worked in garter stitch, the irregularity of the yarn working well with the wriggling rows of stitch loops. There's always the problem of piercing the yarn with the needle, rather than going through the stitch, but if care was taken with that, the most novice knitter could use this yarn without fear of uneven gauge ever being an issue.

4 This is a stretchy ribbon yarn, but when knitted up into this double rib pattern the edges of the yarn curled in and the effect was almost that of a chunky yarn, knitted slightly unevenly. I tried knitting this yarn on larger needles to give the ribbon structure more room to expand, but the looser stitches did not benefit the double rib pattern. This is a classic example of something more-or-less working, but the yarn is inherently unsuited to the stitch pattern.

5 Two firmly twisted individual plies were twisted together to make this yarn; the result looks rather like thin, wooly cable or rope. It's a very light texture that's enhanced by the plies being slightly different shades of orange, and one that makes this seed stitch pattern look even more attractively knobbly than it usually does. The heavy and firm twist means that every stitch is clearly defined in a way that is more often seen with cotton yarns than with wool ones.

Chapter

3 | Embroidery and beading

I've grouped these two embellishment methods into one chapter because, although they use different materials, are worked in very different ways, and at different stages in a project, they both offer a simple way of adding detail, color, and decoration to even the plainest knitted item.

Many knitters will know the slip stitch beading method (see page 52), as this is the most popular type of beaded knitting, but there are other methods, and indeed my favorite is knitted-in beading (see pages 52–53). This is equally easy to learn, easier to tension correctly, and though the beads are a bit trickier to manage on the stitches, any errant ones can easily be guided back into place once the knitting is complete.

There are a few practical considerations to bear in mind (see Choosing beads, page 50, and Palette 19, Page 66), but usually none of these techniques will affect your gauge, so you can simply add them to a pattern you already have and love. Having said that, a practice swatch (see page 212) is, as always, never a waste of time.

Beading techniques

Adding beads to a project is one of those wonderful techniques that looks hugely impressive, but is actually very easy to do. The beads are knitted in as you knit the pattern, so if you are adding them to an existing pattern, you need to decide how many beads and where you want them before you begin knitting.

There are various different methods of beading, depending on the effect you want to achieve and the stitch pattern you are using. It's always worth swatching a little sample to see how the beads look on the yarn and to check that the technique you've chosen is the best one for your design (you can do this as part of your gauge square—and check the beads aren't affecting gauge at the same time).

THREADING BEADS ONTO YARN

The first step is always to get the beads (or sequins) onto the yarn, and this is very easy to do.

1 Thread a sewing needle with a short length of sewing cotton and knot the ends. Put the tail end of the yarn through the loop of cotton and adjust the position of the knot so that it is clear of both the yarn and the needle (that way the bead does not have to fit over the doubled yarn and the knot at the same time).

2 Slip the beads onto the needle, down the thread, and onto the yarn; it's that simple. Push the beads along the yarn as you work.

CHOOSING BEADS

When buying beads for knitting there are a few things to consider. First, is beading this project a practical idea? Beads are often made of glass and washing them in a machine and ironing them usually do them no good whatsoever; so don't put beads on an everyday sweater for a small child.

Sequins are even more sensitive; even the gentlest hand wash can damage them, and they react very badly indeed to ironing. Even if you iron the piece on the back under a cloth with a coolish iron, they can distort from the heat.

The beads need to suit the yarn—they can't be too heavy or they will stretch the stitches; lots of heavy beads on a fine yarn can stretch the whole garment. And the beads can't be wider or longer than a knitted stitch, or the fabric will be distorted. The hole in the bead (or sequin) must be large enough for the yarn to pass through: To check this, thread up a sewing needle, as explained above, take that and a length of the project yarn to the bead store, and test the beads before buying. As long as you explain what you are doing and don't damage any beads, the store staff should be happy to help.

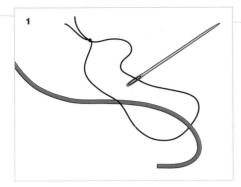

Knitting notes

If the project you are working on requires 300 beads and uses 8 balls of yarn, don't thread all the beads onto the first ball. I know it sounds obvious, but many knitters (including me) have done this. Assess the pattern as to where beads are placed and thread on as many as you estimate you will need for the first ball, plus some extra to be on the safe side. Remember, if you run out, you can always thread on a few more beads from the other end of the ball.

Another common bead knitting problem is a knot in the yarn. If the beads won't slip over it, you just have to cut the knot out and rethread them all.

THREADING ON BEADS TO FOLLOW A CHART

When you are threading different-color beads to follow a charted design, remember that the bead that is threaded on last will be the one that is used first, so you have to thread on all the beads in reverse order, following the chart from the end backward to the beginning.

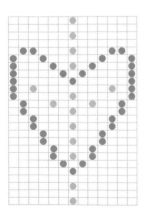

1 To knit up this motif you will need 42 pink beads and 15 blue beads. The beads are placed on knit and purl rows, so starting at the top left of the chart and reading the knit rows left to right and the purl rows right to left (the opposite way to the way you knit them), you need to thread on the beads in the following order: 2 blue, 2 pink, 1 blue, 8 pink, 1 blue, 10 pink, 2 blue, 2 pink, 1 blue, 2 pink, 2 blue, 2 pink, 1 blue, 4 pink, 1 blue, 4 pink, 1 blue, 4 pink, 1 blue, 4 pink, 2 blue. This swatch was knitted up following this chart.

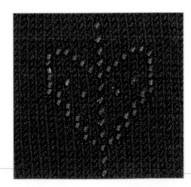

Knitting notes

If you do make a mistake in threading on a color bead sequence, and don't realize until you are halfway through knitting the bead pattern and the next bead is the wrong color, you don't have to unravel the whole piece and start again: There are some options. If you've threaded on one bead too many of a color (so after the wrong bead the sequence is still correct), then, if the beads are glass, you can use pliers to crush the bead off the yarn. Wear safety glasses to protect your eyes from flying fragments of glass and work over a sheet of paper to catch all the bits of bead. If the beads are metal or the sequence is very wrong, then unravel to the start of the row before the mistake, cut the yarn, rethread the beads, and rejoin the yarn.

SLIP STITCH BEADING

This is the most often used beading technique, and it is simple to work. However, beads can only be placed on every alternate stitch and row, though those can be either knit or purl rows. This technique is best worked on stockinette stitch and will usually not affect gauge at all.

1 On a knit row, work to the position of the bead. Bring the yarn forward between the needles, then slide a bead down the yarn so it sits right against the knitting. Slip the next stitch purlwise (see page 96).

2 Take the yarn back between the needles, making sure the bead stays on the front. Knit the next stitch as firmly as possible. The bead is lying on a strand of yarn running across the base of the slipped stitch.

3 On a purl row, work to the position of the bead. Slide a bead down the yarn so it sits right against the knitting, and slip the next stitch purlwise. Purl the next stitch as firmly as possible.

Knitting notes

As the strand of yarn carrying the bead runs across the base of the slipped stitch, the bead sits in a straight line in relation to the stitch, but rather low on the row. If you want to place a bead very precisely in a motif (for example, as an animal's eye), it can be necessary to place it on the row above where you think you want it in order for the end result to look right.

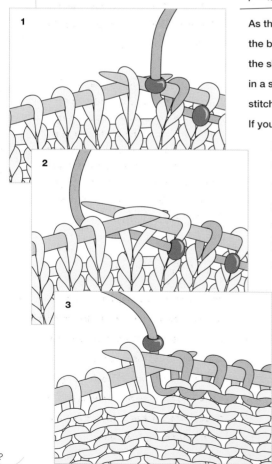

KNITTED-IN BEADING

This method allows you to have a bead on every stitch on every row, but you need to work with a tight gauge for the technique to be successful. Also, if you add a lot of beads to the knitting it can affect both the gauge and the way the project hangs. This technique works best on stockinette stitch.

1 On a knit row, work to the position of the bead. Slide a bead down toward the needles, then put the tip of the right-hand needle into the stitch. Wrap the yarn around the needle in the usual way, adjusting the bead position so that it's just above the needle.

2 Draw the loop of yarn through to knit the stitch, making sure you draw the bead through with it. Tighten the stitch.

Knitting notes

This technique can be frustrating, particularly if you are placing beads on every row, as the beads will try their hardest to wriggle through the knitting to the wrong side. To help prevent this, when you've completed a row, push all the beads down to the base of the stitches before starting the next row. Work carefully to try and keep as many beads on the right side as possible, but if odd ones do escape, don't panic. When you've completed the beaded section, ease any wrong-side beads through by sliding them along the yarn to follow the path of their stitch back to the right side.

3 On a purl row, work to the position of the bead. Slide the bead down the yarn, put the right-hand needle into the stitch and wrap the yarn around the needle in the usual way. Adjust the position of the bead so that it's just above the needle.

4 Draw the loop of yarn through to purl the stitch, making sure you draw the bead through with it, but that the bead stays on the right side of the knitting. Tighten the stitch.

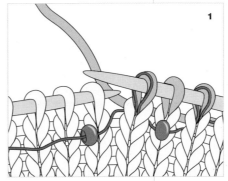

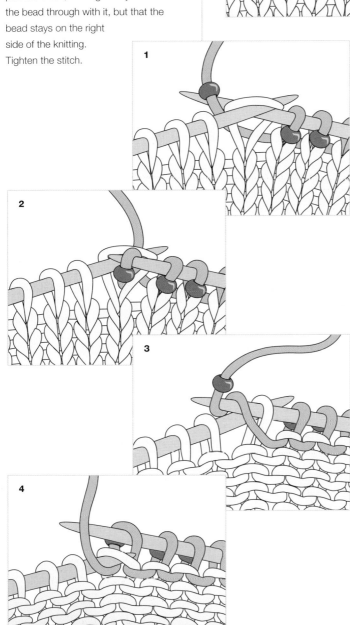

BEADING WITH TWO YARNS

If you desperately want to use a bead with a hole too small for your yarn to go through, you can use a second, finer yarn to carry the beads and place them using a variation of the slip stitch method (see opposite). The bead can be placed on either a knit or a purl row; it's shown here on a knit row and the same principles apply for a purl row. If the color of the second yarn matches the main yarn well, then this will look like ordinary slip stitch beading. If the second yarn is a different color, then a color-mixing effect can be produced in addition to the beading.

1 With both yarns held together, work to the position of the bead. Split the two yarns, leaving the main yarn at the back of the knitting and bringing the fine yarn between the needles to the front. Position the bead and knit the next stitch with the main yarn, then take the fine yarn to the back again. Using both yarns, knit the next stitch.

Knitting notes

You can use a second finer yarn to carry beads for all other beaded knitting techniques, but if the beads are small the results are usually not very successful. The gauge the thicker yarn requires allows the small beads to slip through the stitches to the wrong side of the knitting far too easily.

BEADING BETWEEN STITCHES

This technique works best on garter stitch and beads can be placed between every stitch on every row if desired, making a more or less reversible beaded fabric. It's a quick, easy technique to use, but note that you are adding the beads on the side of the knitting facing away from you.

1 Knit to the position of the bead. Slide a bead down the yarn to sit next to the last stitch, then knit the next stitch. That's all there is to it.

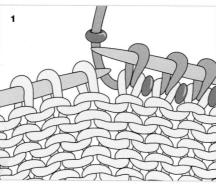

Knitting notes

As garter stitch is particularly elastic, adding a lot of beads can cause the knitting to stretch considerably, which not only looks bad, but also gives the beads the opportunity to wriggle through the stitches.

PLACING SEQUINS

Sequins are placed using the slip stitch method (see page 52). Shown here is a sequin placed on a knit row, and the same principles apply for a purl row. On a knit row, purling the stitch that follows the slipped stitch helps to stop the edge of the sequin that the yarn lies over from tucking into the fabric.

1 Knit to the position of the sequin. Bring the yarn forward between the needles, then slide a sequin down the yarn so it sits right against the knitting. Slip the next stitch purlwise (see page 96).

2 Purl the next stitch. Then take the yarn back between the needles to continue knitting.

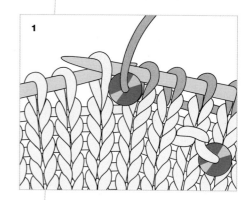

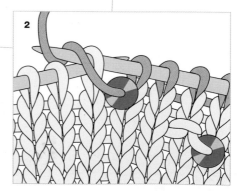

Knitting notes

If you don't like the bump the purled stitch makes next to the sequin, just take the yarn back between the needles after slipping the stitch and knit the next stitch.

Embroidery stitches

Knitted stitches form a natural grid that helps make it easy to work almost any embroidery stitch. However, the open structure of knitted fabric—as opposed to woven cotton fabric—and the fact that you can't stretch it in a frame, makes it tricky to tension embroidery stitches neatly, so the simpler stitches do work best. Always use a blunt-pointed knitter's sewing needle or a tapestry needle and try to work between stitches rather than splitting yarn, as that can damage the knitting, sometimes irreparably. It's best to add embroidery after the knitting has been blocked, but, if possible, before pieces are sewn up. Press the finished embroidery lightly for best results.

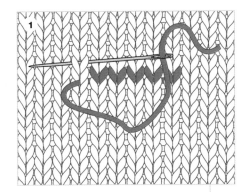

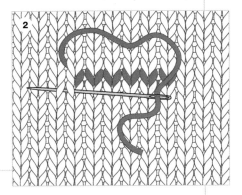

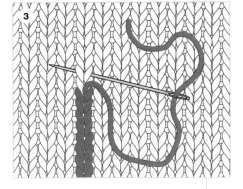

SWISS DARNING

This is an embroidery stitch specific to knitting. It matches the stitches on the right side of stockinette stitch and is both an excellent way of adding small amounts of color without using intarsia (see pages 112–35) or stranded knitting (see pages 136-57), and the perfect way to disguise any small mistakes made when working either of those techniques. Use yarn that is the same weight and texture as that used to knit the project for the neatest results.

1 To work a horizontal row of Swiss darning, work across the knitting in whichever direction feels most comfortable. From the back, bring the needle through at the base of a stitch. Then take it under the two loops of the stitch above, being careful not to split the yarn with the needle.

2 Pull the yarn through so that it lies flat over one "leg" of the stitch. Take the needle back through the base of the lower stitch where it came out and pull the yarn through. Do not pull the yarn tight or it won't lie neatly over the knitted stitch. Bring the needle to the front again through the base of the next stitch along.

3 Work a vertical row of Swiss darning from bottom to top. Bring the needle through the base of a stitch and take it under the loops of the stitch above. Take the needle back through the base of the stitch. Bring it to the front again through the base of the stitch above.

RUNNING STITCH

Undoubtedly the simplest embroidery stitch there is, running stitch works very well on knitting.

1 Take the needle in and out of the fabric, going over and under knitted stitches to make running stitches the required length.

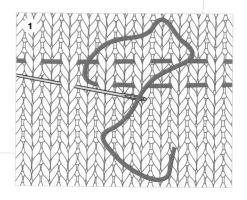

CROSS-STITCH

A naively charming stitch that works well on knitting, cross-stitch can be worked in rows, as a motif, or as single stitches.

1 Bring the needle through and make an upward-slanting stitch the required length. Bring it out again directly below where it last went in and make another diagonal stitch to complete the cross. When working a series of cross-stitches, always have the top stitch sloping in the same direction.

BLANKET STITCH

Traditionally used along an edge, blanket stitch can also be used within that fabric to embroider motifs and decorate buttonholes.

1 From the back, bring the needle through between two stitches, the required number of rows away from the edge. *On the same row, take it back through one or two knitted stitches farther along but do not pull that thread through. Take the needle under the edge and through the loop of the working thread, then tension the stitch by pulling gently. Repeat from * across the edge. The principle is the same when working within the fabric, just bring the needle up through the knitting the required distance away—rather than under the edge—and take it through the loop of the working thread.

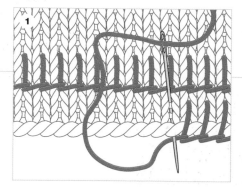

CHAIN STITCH

This versatile stitch is great for outlining shapes and for creating flowing lines.

1 Bring the needle through at the start of the line and pull the working thread through. *Take the needle back into the fabric where it came out and make a straight stitch the required length of a chain loop. Loop the working thread under the point of the needle before pulling the needle and thread slowly through to form a loop. Repeat from * to make a linked line of stitches. Anchor the last chain in the line with a tiny straight stitch over the end of the loop, as in lazy daisy (see below).

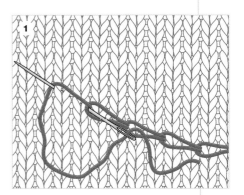

LAZY DAISY

These are just single chain stitches that are placed to form a simple flower motif.

1 *Make a single chain stitch (see above), tying down the loop with a tiny straight stitch over the end. Bring the needle up where the stitch started and make another. Repeat from *, fanning the stitches around to make the flower.

FRENCH KNOT

These neat little knots can be scattered decoratively, or grouped into clusters. They make excellent centers for lazy daisies (see above).

1 Bring the needle through where the knot will be and pull the working thread through. Holding the needle close to the fabric, wrap the thread two or more times around the needle, as shown. (The more times you wrap the thread around, the larger the knot will be.) Holding the wraps in place with your thumb, pull the needle and thread slowly through them and pull the knot taut. Take the needle back down where it came out, or half a stitch away for a larger knot.

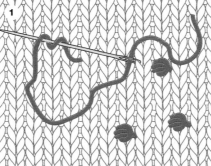

15 Beading

Pages 52–54 show you how to work four different beading techniques and how to knit in sequins, and these swatches show you what the techniques look like translated into embellished knitted fabric. Be aware that sliding beads along yarn can cause wear and tear, and if you have to unpick and start again, the wear and tear is doubled. If you've unpicked more than once—and just once with delicate yarn—discard the used section as the damage can show in the finished knitting.

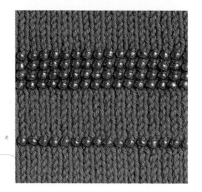

|1| This swatch shows slip stitch beading (see page 52 for technique), where the beads lie straight across the base of a stitch. The bottom row has single beads placed on every alternate stitch, the closest they can be using this method. The middle row has beads on subsequent rows, with those on the purl row placed between those on the knit row. As the top row shows, one advantage of this method is that you can use quite chunky beads, though they can't be longer than the knitted stitch is wide or they will distort the fabric. You can also thread other things onto the yarn—dangling beads, buttons, charms such as the flower used here—and place them with a slip stitch, but if they are heavy they will in time drag down the strand of yarn holding them and distort the stitches on either side.

|2| In knitted-in beading (see page 52 for technique) the beads lie at an angle on one "leg" of a stitch. With round beads the angle isn't really obvious, but a column of beads with flat ends can look quite wriggly (see swatch 3, Palette 17, page 62). The four rows of beads together show how, if you pick the right-size bead, you can almost completely obscure the yarn. If you are knitting several beaded rows, the determination of the beads to wriggle through can be completely exasperating (see page 52). A good trick is to push them down to the base of the stitches, then press a length of masking tape over them to hold them there while you work the next row. Low-tack tape will peel off again easily without leaving sticky residue.

|3| A lace-weight yarn in a slightly lighter tone than the main yarn carries the small beads in this swatch (see page 53 for technique). Both yarns were used held together for the whole swatch, hence the slight color variations where the lighter yarn is at the front of the stitch (See Palette 28, page 90, for more on working with two yarns.) Beads can only be placed on alternate stitches, but because the main yarn isn't being slipped, they can be placed in columns on adjacent rows. Keeping the gauge even can be a problem with this method, and you need to be especially careful to keep the fine yarn taut after placing a bead, or you end up with droopy beads and loops of fine yarn.

|4| Beading between stitches (see page 54 for technique) is the method that works really well on garter stitch. Because the beads are sitting on curved loops of yarn, they don't all lie neatly at the same angle, and on this swatch this is particularly noticeable on the top row of square beads. Be aware that it is quite easy to knit two beads in at the same time with this method.

[5]

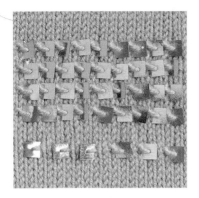

[5] Depending on the size of sequin you use, slip stitch-knitted sequins (see page 54 for technique) will overlap slightly, covering the yarn almost completely. You can flip the sequins to lie to one side or the other, so that the purled stitch does or doesn't show. On the bottom left the sequins are flipped over to hide the purl bump, though that does then raise them up a little.

[6] You can easily bead a cable cast-on; it makes for a lovely decorative edge to a project. Simply use the knitted-in beading technique (see page 52) to put a bead onto every cast on stitch. The beads lie right along the bottom of the cast-on and are visible from both sides, so this method also works for a reverse stockinette project. Obviously, you can use this for garter stitch, but a thumb cast-on (see swatch 7) is a better match for that stitch.

[7] A thumb cast-on is easy to bead using the same principle as beading between stitches (see page 54 for technique). Push the beads down past the position of the slip knot, then just push one up against the knitting after each cast on stitch. The beads show a bit more on one side of the knitting than the other, so the right side will be row 1.

[8] You can also bead a bound-off edge, and there are two ways of doing this, both of which used the knitted-in technique (see page 52). Knit two beaded stitches, then pass the first stitch over the second and wriggle the bead on the second stitch up through the first stitch; fiddly, but entirely possible. Continue in this way, so that all the beads sit on the edge of the knitting, as on the right of this swatch. Alternatively, don't wriggle the beads up through the stitches, then they sit just under the bound-off edge, as on the left of the swatch. Remember, if you are going to bead only the bind-off in a project, don't thread all the beads onto the last ball of yarn and push them all the way along it. Instead, when you get to the bind-off row, cut the yarn leaving a tail at least four times the width of the knitting, and then thread on the beads.

Knitting notes

The only problem most knitters encounter when they start bead knitting is getting their gauge right. Although, once you've got the hang of them, the techniques themselves don't alter gauge, it can take a while to get used to handling the beads. At first you'll be constantly dropping the yarn to move the beads and then retensioning it around your fingers, adjusting the yarn gauge across slipped stitches, tweaking knitted-in bead stitches taut…But as you do more bead knitting your fingers will be come familiar with the beads on the yarn, and you'll be flicking them into place with your thumbs and tensioning stitches perfectly.

[6]

[7]

[8]

16 Adding color with beads

The principles that apply to mixing colored yarns (see Chapter 1, pages 12–29) apply equally well to placing colored beads on colored yarns. In addition the shiny surface of beads can enhance their color when set against a matte yarn. Seen on their own, sparkling in a jar, beads will look beautiful, but on the wrongly colored yarn they can become dull—and make your yarn look dull—so always work a swatch to check that you're making the most of the bead color. Shown here are four swatches with different-colored beads on one color of yarn, and four with one color of bead on different colors of yarn.

1 Green beads on green yarn might not add extra color, but they do add delicious sparkle. Using beads that match a yarn is always a safe option and is a lovely way of adding subtle detail. This doesn't mean that you can use any green beads with any green yarn; kelly and lime will never make very happy neighbors.

2 Yellow is analogous to green (see Palette 4, page 20), so the beads work well with the yarn. As warm colors advance visually (see Palette 3, page 18), the cool green of the yarn emphasizes the warmth of the golden yellow beads, making the beads dominate the swatch. Even used sparingly, these beads would be a strong feature of a project in this yarn.

3 Blue is also analogous to green, but both are cold colors and this blue and green are very similar in value (see Palette 5, page 22). So, even though the beads are bright and very shiny, the colors of beads and yarn are balanced; one does not dominate the other. Such shiny beads also reflect light, and their color, onto the yarn, making little dappled patches that attractively wink in and out.

4 This swatch shows how two colors can do one another no favors. Although these two are not precisely opposite each other on the color wheel (see Palette 1, page 14), they are in opposite camps and so almost complementary (see Palette 4, page 20). However, although some shades of green and purple can look lovely together, but this warm violet does not sit happily on this cool green: The beads look dull and the yarn murky.

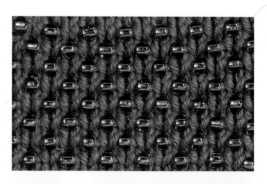

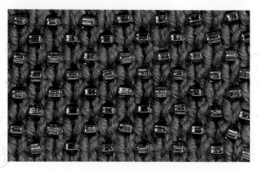

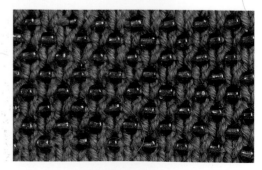

5 Orange is a close cousin of pink, and though at first sight the two colors together rather jar the nerves, they are actually fairly harmonious. However, this pink is a little too blue to sit completely comfortably with the rich orange, so if you wanted to use these beads a slightly more salmon tone of yarn would work better.

6 Blue and orange are true complementary colors, and the coolness of this slate blue makes the orange beads positively glow. Even though the beads are little spots on a background, they spring forward visually. As with swatch 2, you would not need many of these beads to make a statement on this color yarn.

7 This is not a successful relationship. The intense purple yarn sucks all the red out of the orange beads, turning them almost brown. Yarn this color would be best paired with red or pink beads, though the vibrant results would certainly not please knitters who like subtle color schemes.

8 Neutral gray is friendly enough to these orange beads as both have about the same value. The warmth of the bead color is still enough to make them stand out from the background, but they look nowhere near as vibrant as they do in swatch 6. The turquoise beads from swatch 3 would be better with this yarn.

Knitting notes

Beads come in various materials and finishes, and these can affect their perceived color. All the beads used here are glass (the most common material) and are shiny. The light reflecting off them draws the eye and makes them more of a feature than a knitted stitch in the same color would be. But if you use matte ceramic beads, then there is no sparkle and they rely on just their color and shape. This isn't necessarily a problem, and matte beads are lovely to use, but you can't substitute matte beads for glass beads—even if they are the same color—and get exactly the same effect.

5

6
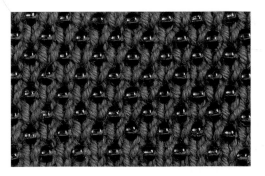

7

8
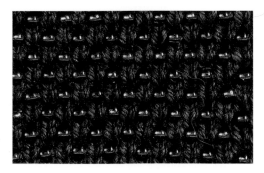

17 Creating color patterns with beads

If neither intarsia (see Chapter 6, pages 112–35) nor stranded knitting (see pages 136–57) are your thing, then consider using beads—and the occasional easy-to-work stripe (see Chapter 4, pages 72–93)—to add all sorts of color patterning to your projects. Because small numbers of beads won't affect gauge, you can add motifs or panels to any project. Even if you are working an all-over bead pattern, unless it is very dense you should encounter no problems.

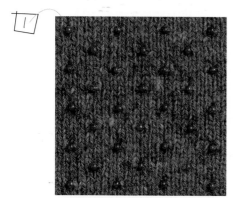

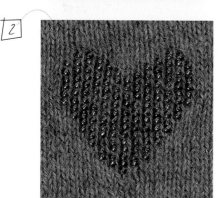

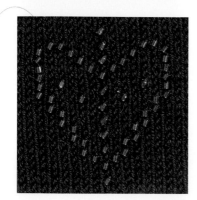

1 These beads are placed in a diamond grid pattern using the slip stitch technique (see page 52). You can work out a repeat on graph paper to suit the number of stitches you need to cast on for your project. The beads all came from the same packet, but are slightly different shades of pinks and oranges, adding further interest to the simple pattern.

2 Knitted-in beading (see page 52) was used to work this heart motif (turn to page 114 for chart). The same motif is featured throughout this book (for example, Palette 39, page 128), but here each square is filled with a bead. As the beads are small, the motif weighs very little and doesn't drag at all on the yarn. Knitted into the side of a cap or the front of a sweater, this is a lovely way of adding pretty detail to a project.

3 This is the same heart motif as the previous swatch, but with some additional blue beads, and worked as an outline with knitted-in beading. The tubular beads clearly show how they are lying at an angle on the stitches. To work this motif, turn to page 51 for a chart and the order in which the beads need to be threaded on to the yarn.

4 This deceptively complex tartan design is actually just horizontal knitted stripes with vertical and horizontal rows of knitted-in beads. Plan a design on a piece of graph paper to make sure it's clear in your mind as to what you are doing, but once you get underway, it is very easy to work. Also, a slightly sparkly yarn complements shiny beads perfectly.

5 This is actually a self-striping yarn; look at the top and bottom of the pink band and you can see where the colors transition. I sampled to work out how many rows of each color there would be over the number of stitches, then decided on how many bead clusters I wanted per stripe. I threaded on five beads for each cluster and just positioned them randomly. Of course, you could use one color of bead and chart the positions, or, place them on just one stripe of the yarn.

6 Sequins of different sizes, and indeed different shapes, can be successfully knitted in. Though you can't use solid sequins with a radius of more than a stitch, the snowflake sequins work because the yarn can slip between the spokes. The metallic yarn is an equal match for the glitter factor of the sequins, but as a garment it might all be a little too much.

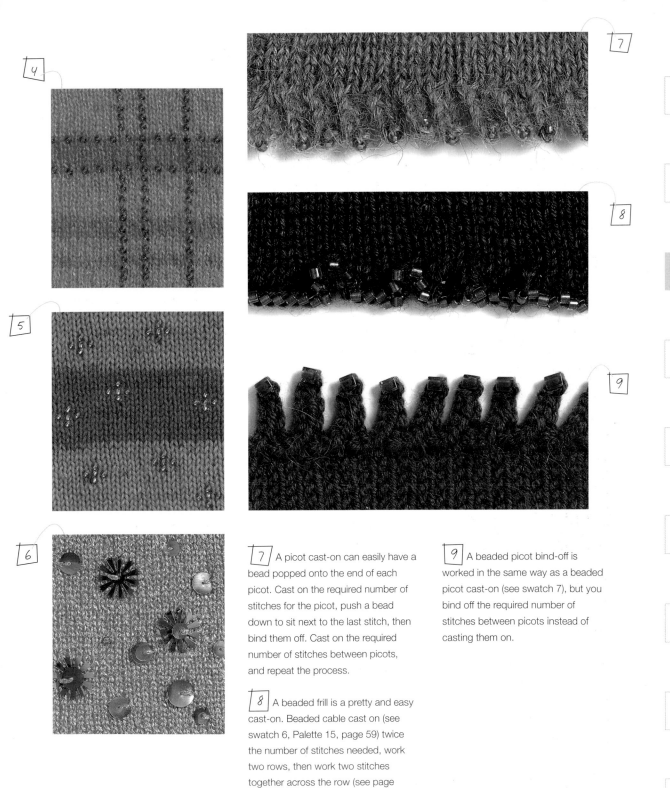

7 A picot cast-on can easily have a bead popped onto the end of each picot. Cast on the required number of stitches for the picot, push a bead down to sit next to the last stitch, then bind them off. Cast on the required number of stitches between picots, and repeat the process.

8 A beaded frill is a pretty and easy cast-on. Beaded cable cast on (see swatch 6, Palette 15, page 59) twice the number of stitches needed, work two rows, then work two stitches together across the row (see page 191). Working more straight rows before the decrease row will produce a deeper frill.

9 A beaded picot bind-off is worked in the same way as a beaded picot cast-on (see swatch 7), but you bind off the required number of stitches between picots instead of casting them on.

18 Embroidery

The stitches shown on pages 55–57 are all easy to work, but—even if you are an experienced fabric embroiderer—you do need to practice embroidering on knitting as it requires a different way of working. Because you can't stretch or tension the fabric in a frame, you need to work carefully to make neat stitches. Pulling the embroidery yarn tight in an attempt to neaten the stitches will just pucker up the yarn; it's a gentle, even tension that you're looking to perfect. Work two or three small squares in the project yarn and, using the project embroidery yarn, practice the stitches you want to use until you've got them just right.

1 Swiss darning (see page 55 for technique) is worth perfecting as it is so useful. Not only can you embroider motifs that look like they have been perfectly color-knitted, you can also use this stitch to correct any mistakes in intarsia (see Chapter 6, pages 112–35) and stranded knitting (see pages 136–57), and to add detail to intarsia motifs (see swatch 6, Palette 37, page 125, and swatch 1, Palette 42, page 134). Use a yarn that is the same weight and texture as the background yarn if you want to imitate color knitting.

2 Running stitch (see page 56 for technique) has a naive charm that never fades, and it's so simple to work. However, it is very easy to pull the stitches too tight and then when the project is worn or used and the knitted fabric stretches, the running stitches snap. Use a looser tension that you think is desirable, and then be prepared to loosen it some more for the stitches to look and feel right.

3 The only issue with cross-stitch on knitting (see page 56 for technique) is that if you use the natural grid of whole stitches and rows, because a knitted stitch is wider than it is high, your cross-stitches will not form square blocks. So be it: The stitch still looks lovely.

4 Blanket stitch (see page 56 for technique) is traditionally used for edging, but also makes beautiful motifs. Fan the stitches in and out to create flowing curves, and vary the length of the stitch "legs" if you wish (see swatch 2, Palette 19, page 66). Tension this stitch especially carefully because you are pulling in two directions at the same time: I find it best to tension the horizontal stitch first, then go back and adjust the "leg."

1

2

3

4

5

6

7

5 Chain stitch (see page 57 for technique) is very versatile and works equally well in straight lines and quite tight curves. Pulling the loops too tight not only risks puckering the knitting but also spoils the shapes of the stitches, so make them only gently taut. The loops of the stitch complement the shape of knitted stitches rather well, and chains look good on stockinette, reverse stockinette, and garter stitch.

6 Lazy daisy stitches (see page 57 for technique) are most often used to create little flowers, but single loops can be useful, too. As with chain stitch (see swatch 5), pulling the loop too tight spoils the soft curve of the stitch. Spacing the petals of a flower equally can take a bit of experimentation, but fortunately they look good even if they aren't completely regular; after all, real flowers aren't uniform.

7 A French knot (see page 57 for technique) takes a bit of practice to get right, and still more practice if you want to make a group that are all the same size, but once you've got the hang of it, this is a very useful stitch. The only problem can come in fastening off, as if it's a single knot then you have to stitch into the back of the tiny knot, and that's not easy to do without spoiling it. Better by far to fasten off in the back of another embroidery stitch close by.

Knitting notes

No matter how careful you are with embroidery, you're bound to make a mistake at some point, and then you need to become super-careful because unpicking can damage your patient knitting. Very often, unpicking will irreparably spoil the embroidery yarn, so if you are taking out a whole section, start by cutting off the unused yarn and be prepared to abandon what you unpick. Use a blunt-pointed knitter's sewing needle to gently ease out the embroidery stitches one at a time, being sure not to push the needle into any knitted stitches or pull on them. If embroidery stitches are stubborn and you have to cut them out, work in a good light, use a pair of slim-bladed embroidery scissors, and be VERY, VERY careful; it's ridiculously easy to cut a knitted stitch.

Embroidery accents

As well as embroidering motifs on a project, you can use embroidery to highlight a detail, such as an edging or buttonband. However, do be aware that embroidering along an edge will more or less stop it stretching, so don't embellish a hem or neckline that needs to expand very much in order for you to get the garment on. And take good note of laundering requirements: If you embroider a cotton garment with wool yarn and then wash it, the wool can shrink though the cotton won't.

1 A traditional use for a classic stitch, but one that doesn't lose its appeal. Blanket stitching (see page 56 for technique) around the edge of a collar neatens the look of the selvage, adds a touch of color, and provides decoration, all in one go. As always, remember that the difference in stitch width and length will make the spacing along row ends and bound-off edges slightly different, unless you abandon the natural grid and start piercing the knitted stitches. Personally, I think that varying spacing is the better—and better-looking—option.

2 Eyelets (see page 186 for technique) for cords or decoration look particularly cute edged with blanket stitch (see page 56 for technique). Making the "legs" of the stitches different lengths not only removes the problem of trying to keep them all even on a varying grid, but also has a vintage style appeal.

The closely packed inner edge of the stitching is very firm and will stop the eyelet stretching, so this isn't a good option for eyelet buttonholes. However, oversewing the edges of the eyelet, either with doubled yarn (middle eyelet) or single yarn (top eyelet), provides color and a neat edge, and still allows for some stretch.

3 The join between the row end and first picked-up row of a feature such as a buttonhole band can be a bit noticeable, depending on your gauge and the stitch the band is worked in. A line of chain stitch (see page 57 for technique) will quickly and decoratively cover any irregularities; work it in a contrast color for added decoration, or in the main yarn for subtle detail. Edging the buttonholes in the same stitch may seem an attractive option, but do try just one first and check that the button will still fit through. If it does, then it will look good either buttoned or unbuttoned.

4 A line of bright color highlights this sewn-on rib buttonhole band. It's just two lines of different-colored running stitches (see page 56 for technique), one set of shorter stitches fitting into the gaps between longer ones, but it's very effective. Again, using the same colors to edge the button-holes (this time in blanket stitch) looks good, but do check that the buttons still fit through.

5 A pocket full of flowers: How cute would this look on a little girl's cardigan? But do make sure your design is practical and that small fingers won't get caught in the stitches while trying to put treasures in the pocket. It's easiest to do the embroidery before sewing the pocket lining into place.

Knitting notes

Because of the issues of unpicking stitches (see Knitting Notes, page 65), do plan and swatch embroidery ideas before embarking on embroidering a garment that has taken months to knit. If it's possible, do the embroidery on the project pieces once they have been blocked, but before you sew up. (Obviously, if you are embroidering, for example, a hem, this won't be possible.) A quick and light press before sewing up will "set" the embroidery stitches.

Yarns and threads for embroidery

Other than for Swiss darning, there is no reason why you should embroider a project using the same type of yarn it is knitted in, as long as you can overcome any potential laundering problems. The two main issues will be colorfastness and shrinkage. Test for colorfastness by dipping the proposed embroidery thread in warm water and rubbing it firmly in a scrap of white cotton cloth. If any of the thread color appears on the cloth, then the thread is not colorfast. You can test for shrinkage by embroidering a swatch and washing it: Measure the swatch carefully before and after washing to see how much it reduces by (see also page 214).

Careful hand-washing will get around many laundering issues, but do test your threads before embroidering a project that has taken many hours to knit.

|1| Stranded embroidery floss is the staple of most embroiderers working on fabric, and it works perfectly well on knitting. Being able to separate the floss into groups of strands is a distinct advantage when it comes to embroidering fine knits, and useful for creating motifs of different sizes on any knitted fabric. This swatch uses two shades of red, both the full thickness of the floss (six strands), for the central flower and one thickness of one shade for each of the smaller flowers. Everything else is stitched in one thickness of thread. These threads are widely available and come in a simply enormous selection of colors.

|2| Tapestry wools are usually 100 percent wool and so ideal for embroidering knitted woolen fabric. However, they are surprisingly chunky and so best used on fabrics of worsted weight and above. This swatch is knitted in sport weight yarn and while the flowers look fine, the rest of the embroidery is really just a bit too chunky for the fabric. These wools are widely available and the color selection from major companies is very good.

Knitting notes

If you want to place an embroidered motif exactly, you can mark the stitches on the knitting with a dressmaker's fading marker. Choose an air-soluble one rather than a water-soluble one, so that you don't have to dampen the knitting. Do test the marker on your gauge swatch to make sure that it does fade away completely.

3 Crewel wools are also usually 100 percent wool and are much finer than tapestry wools, though they can be rather uneven in weight. In this swatch the wool is used doubled for the flowers and single for everything else. Crewel wools are available from specialist embroidery suppliers, often online, and can be found in a great variety of colors, as subtle shading is an important feature of traditional crewel embroidery on fabric.

4 You can find all sorts of fancy embroidery yarns at specialty stores and online, including vintage threads such as those used on this swatch. The flowers are stitched in a 1970s rayon thread and the stems in a very fine chenille thread. Do be slightly cautious with vintage threads—if they haven't been stored carefully (and sometimes even if they have) they can be rotten and will break easily.

5 Cotton perlé, or pearl, threads are another hand-embroidery staple and are great for working on knitting. They can be found in various thicknesses (though none are very thick) and a great array of colors, including variegated colors such as those used here. All this embroidery is stitched with doubled thread, thus increasing the color variations, although if you wanted to lessen that effect you could cut two lengths of thread from the same point in the color sequence— so that they match along their lengths— and then thread two ends through the needle.

6 Fine knitting yarns often work well as embroidery yarns, though obviously the color selection is more limited. However, you can exploit lightly textured and fancy yarns. Here, the flowers are knitted in mohair with a metallic strand in it, and the stems in one stand of bouclé mohair (see swatch 3, Palette 12, page 42) and one strand of plain mohair. The flowers have a bead sewn on in the center, rather than the French knots of the previous swatches.

21 Trims and appliqués

There are a variety of trims that you can knit to decorate projects, lace being maybe the most obvious (see Palette 55, page 200). The laundering issues described in Palette 19, page 66, will apply, and you will also need to be careful about compromising the knitting's elasticity: Sewing a nonstretchy trim around a neckline that needs to expand to get the garment on is a seemingly obvious, but surprisingly easy, mistake to make.

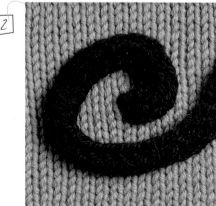

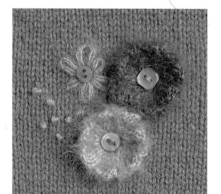

1 I-cords can make great trims— as well as ties and handles: This example is knitted in variegated mohair and just sewn onto a piece of plain stockinette knitting with sewing thread. You can knit an enormous length and wind and coil it over a project, or knit measured lengths to trim specific areas or to use as button loops.

2 An alternative to I-cord is French knitting. When I was small we used to do this on a wooden cotton reel with four nails hammered into the top, but now that cotton reels are plastic, you can buy "knitting dollies" especially made for French knitting. The cord produced is squarish rather than round like I-cord, but you can use it in just the same way. Take the tail left at the beginning and end through the background knitting and sew it down on the wrong side for a neat finish.

3 There are many patterns for knitted flowers in books and on the Internet and they are an excellent way of using up small amounts of lovely yarns left over from previous projects. Sew them onto projects as decoration, but be aware that you might need to take them off for laundering: In my experience knitted flowers don't take to being washed terribly well. Here, an embroidered lazy daisy flower (see swatch 6, Palette 18, page 65) complements the three-dimensional flowers. Little buttons work well as flower centers.

4 This is a different flower pattern knitted in two types of yarn and with a cluster of tiny beads sewn on in the center. Using multiple yarns can add interest to any simple flower shape.

5 Pretty buttons make practical fastenings, but don't discount them as decorations in their own right. This stylized flower is made from a mismatched selection of vintage pearl buttons sewn on with fine woolen embroidery floss. Use a line of buttons to edge a jacket collar or cuff or to trim the top of a pocket. Have them mismatched or matching the buttons used to fasten the garment. There are literally thousands and thousands of styles of buttons available and myriad ways of using them.

6 When sewing on flat appliqués such as this heart, you might find it easier to pin the knitting out on an ironing board or blocking board—without stretching it—and then pin or baste the appliqué in place. However, even if you make the knitting as flat and even as possible this way, it's still tricky to sew on a flat appliqué without the knitted background puckering or distorting a little bit. Do the best you can and accept that a little unevenness is part of the nature of the technique.

7 You can also sew fabric appliqués onto knitting, and making them from the same fiber as the yarn will help when it comes to laundering. You can felt pure woolen knitting by washing it in hot water with plenty of detergent, so you could knit a square, felt it, and cut an appliqué from that. This heart was cut from an old, felted, wool fabric blanket.

Knitting notes

Do bear practicality in mind when embellishing a knitting project. It's easy to get carried away with lovely trims and notions, and then realize that some of the trims are chunky enough to distort the knitting, you can't launder the item, and it's so heavily decorated it'll be uncomfortable to wear anyway.

4 Stripes

The simplest form of color knitting (so simple that some people are surprised that it counts, though it certainly does), striping is both easy to do and open to many more creative possibilities than you might at first think. Above and beyond the knitting basics (casting on, knit stitch, purl stitch, and binding off), the only techniques you need to learn are how to join in a new color yarn correctly, how to carry colors not in use up the side of the knitting to where they are needed again, and how to darn in ends of yarn when the knitting is completed. Generally, stripes in yarns of the same brand and weight won't affect gauge, so you can add stripes to any project, though, as always, please do knit a swatch (see page 212) to make sure.

Creatively, stripes have a lot to offer. Stripe patterns, color palettes, yarn textures, stitch patterns, other color techniques, and embellishments can all be combined in a single glorious burst of striping (see Palette 29, page 92 for some examples of creative striping), or you can choose just a couple of elements at a time to experiment with. Either way, you'll quickly discover that there's a lot more to stripes than the staple scarf.

Stripe techniques

Striping is the first type of color knitting that most of us learn as it's so very simple; if you can knit then you can work stripes. However, joining in new yarns in the right way will make a difference to the finished knitting, as will carrying the yarn up the side of the knitting tidily. And once you've finished your project, you'll need to darn in the loose ends of yarn, though if you've joined in and carried the yarn correctly, there won't be many of those.

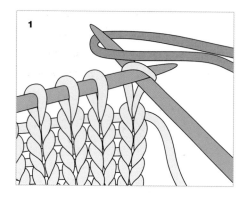

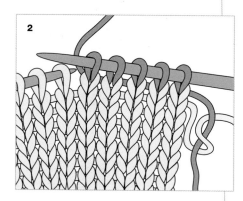

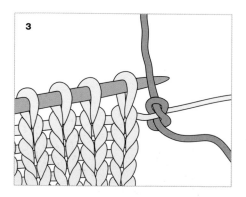

JOINING IN NEW YARN

The method of joining in a new yarn color for a stripe can also be used for joining in a new ball of the same color yarn on a large project. Always join in new yarn at the start of a row; it's shown here on a knit row, but you can join in on a purl row using the same principle.

1 Have the new color yarn ready with a tail of yarn pulled out. Insert the right-hand needle into the first stitch as if to knit it. Loop the new yarn over the needle and knit the stitch with it, leaving a loose 4in (10cm) tail.

2 Knit the first row in the new color. Then pull on the loose tails of the new and old color yarns to tighten the stitches, and tie the two ends together in a double knot. If the edge is not going to be seamed to another piece, then make the knot firm but not tight, as you'll need to unpick it later.

3 Alternatively, tie the end of the new color yarn in a single knot around the old color yarn, leaving a 4in (10cm) tail. Slide the knot up tight against the last stitch, then start knitting with the new yarn.

CARRYING YARN UP THE SIDE OF THE KNITTING

You don't have to join in yarn for every separate stripe, just carry the yarn(s) not in use up the side of the knitting, catching them in at the start of every alternate row, until they are needed again. If you are working with a lot of colors, the bundle of yarn running up the side can become very thick.

1 If you are working a two-row stripe pattern with two colors of yarn, then just swap the colors for every third row.

2 If the stripes are wider, then you need to catch the yarn not in use against the side of the knitting at the start of every second or fourth row to prevent long, loose strands running up the edge of the knitting. At the start of the row, take the working yarn (white) under the yarn not in use and then knit the first stitch, catching the loose yarn against the stitch.

Knitting notes

Catching in the yarn in this way also makes it easier to tension it correctly when it comes to knitting with it again. You need to get the right balance between the new yarn being taut enough to knit the first stitch neatly, but not tight enough to pucker up the edge of the knitting. Take the time to get this tension right; if it's wrong the stripes will look distorted at the edges.

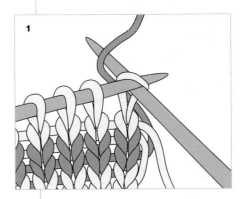

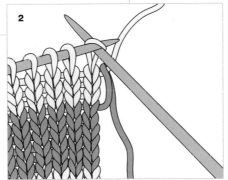

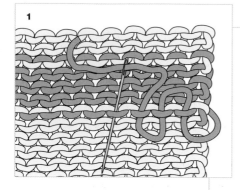

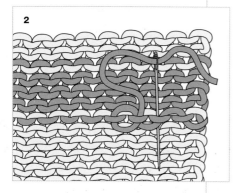

DARNING IN YARN ENDS

Once the knitting is complete you need to darn in the loose tails to secure them and stop the knitting from ever unraveling. If the edges of the project are going to be seamed, then you don't need to unpick the knots joining new yarns to old.

If the edge is to remain visible, then carefully unpicking the knots before darning the ends in will make the edge smoother.

1 Thread a blunt-tipped knitter's sewing needle or a tapestry needle with a tail of yarn. On the back of the knitting, take the needle in and out of three or four stitch bumps of the same color. Here, the loops are shown loose for clarity, but you should pull the yarn gently taut as you go.

2 Work back along the bumps in the same way, but taking the yarn in the opposite direction to form loops, as shown. Cut the end short.

3 Alternatively, darn the ends into the selvage. Take the yarn up through the stitch bumps of three or four rows, then, skipping the last bump, take it back down through them again. Be careful not to pull the yarn tight and pucker the edge.

Knitting notes

The same principles apply for darning in ends on intarsia (see chapter 6, pages 112–35) and stranded knitting (see chapter 7, pages 136–57). Always darn ends into the bumps of stitches in the same color to prevent colors appearing in the wrong places on the right side of the knitting.

You can leave long ends when casting on or binding off and sew up the seams with those, giving you fewer ends to darn in. Many knitting books advise against this, but I'm never sure why as, assuming the yarn is suitable for sewing up, then that's what you'll use, and if you make a mistake and have to unpick a seam, even if you damage the sewing-up yarn you can just cut it short without compromising the knitting.

MANAGING MULTIPLE BALLS OF YARN

Firstly, it's always best to pull the yarn out from the center of a ball—this stops the balls rolling around and tangling up more than need be. First, find the visible outer end, which will usually have been tucked into the center of the ball. Pull this out or it'll tangle horribly with the center end when you start to knit. Just tuck it well under some outer wraps of yarn to keep it out of the way.

To find the center end, use your fingers to fish around in the hole in the ball on the opposite side to the side the outer end was tucked into, searching for the loosely wound section; you'll become familiar with the feel of this in time. Pull out this section and, with a bit of luck, you shouldn't have to pull out too much yarn before the end appears. If rather a lot does come out, just wind it loosely around the outside of the ball and it'll get used up very quickly.

If you are using just two colors of yarn, then if you turn the knitting one way—say clockwise—at the end of a knit row and the other way—counterclockwise—at the end of a purl row, then the yarns won't get twisted around one another. It takes a while to get into the rhythm of turning like this, as we all tend to turn the knitting in just one direction at the end of every row, but if you can establish this alternate turning as a habit you'll save yourself a lot of time and the aggravation of untangling twisted balls of yarn, particularly when you are using more than two colors.

If you are knitting with several colors—say five—then there are a few ways of managing the yarns. If you are working just short lengths of color, then you can make bobbins, see page 117. If not, then you can either place each ball in a separate jar and arrange the jars around you in the order the yarns are being used, or put the balls in a box. If you have

a smallish box that will hold the balls snugly, then just pop them in in the order they'll be used. If you have a shoe box, then punch holes in the lid, put the balls in the box, thread a yarn though each hole, and start knitting. The disadvantage of the last method is that you can't move the balls around in the box without cutting the yarn, but it does stop them tangling as long as you turn the knitting in alternate directions, as explained above.

If the yarns do twist, then stop and untwist immediately before the problem gets worse. Having said all of this, some knitters are entirely happy to knit along and tangle up the yarns, then stop occasionally when no more yarn will pull free and sort out the knots. This is only an inadvisable method if you are using delicate yarns, or textured yarns such as mohair, where the fuzz can knot the strands inextricably together.

Stripe patterns

There are myriad stripe patterns to choose from, and a huge part of the fun of striping is choosing the arrangement of rows of color. Shown here are some basics and some variations on those, but they are just a taster of the stripe opportunities open to you. Always swatch a stripe pattern (see page 212), preferably across the full width of the proposed project, and work at least three repeats to see properly how your pattern will develop.

I've chosen a palette of two cool and two warm colors (see Palette 3, page 18) and colors that are complementary and analogous (see Palette 4, page 20), in a balanced range of color values (see Palette 5, page 22). Further palettes in this chapter explore other color combinations.

1 This swatch is a classic four-row stripe repeat. The colors are placed so that the analogous pairs are separated by their complementaries, but it is the warm orange and pink colors that jump out. They are so much bolder that at an initial glance it's easy to think that the cool green and blue stripes are actually narrower, but that's just a trick of the eye that you should be aware of when planning a stripe pattern.

2 While you don't look at this pattern and actually think the warm color rows (two-row stripes) are the same width as the cool color rows (four-row stripes), the effect is more balanced. However, although the colors are repeated in the same order as the previous swatch, because the value of the green is darker than the blue (see Palette 5, page 20), the eye tends to read this pattern as green stripes edged with warm bands on a blue background. This swatch perfectly demonstrates why it's worth swatching several repeats of a proposed stripe pattern, as this effect wouldn't be apparent with just one repeat.

3 One-row stripes are knitted on a circular needle or a pair of double-pointed needles. Just knit a row, then slide the knitting to whichever end of the needle you need to make the next color yarn available. Interestingly, when the stripes are so narrow the warm colors are less dominant, as the whole effect is so much busier. While you might not want an entire garment in this pattern (visual chaos?), one-row stripes are a useful tool in a stripe pattern, not least because they allow you to carry yarns up different sides of the knitting (see page 75), making for less bulky seams.

4 Dropping the pink—the lighter in value of these two warm colors—and using the orange as a one-row accent stripe produces a far more sober effect. The cool blue and green stripes dominate and the orange neatly divides them, though there is still a tendency for the eye to see green stripes edged with orange, in a similar way to swatch 2.

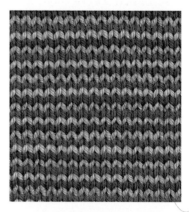

5 If you have a confident eye for color and a relaxed attitude to knitting, random stripes can be very effective in balancing colors in a scheme. Just knit away, adding stripes as you see fit. It's a good idea to periodically hang the knitting up (I drape mine over a picture frame on the wall) and step back to evaluate from a distance how the stripe pattern is growing.

6 A single stripe or stripe sequence can make for a great accent on an otherwise plain project. Do be aware of where you position a stripe, especially on a garment: A stripe across the middle of your chest could be distracting to say the least, while if you are not as svelte as you'd like to be, then a stripe around the widest part of your tummy won't do you any favors.

7 Chevron stripes are not difficult to knit, though you'll need to add basic increases and decreases to your repertoire of knitting skills (see pages 190–97). There are lots of patterns available for these stripes, but be aware that unlike straight-line stripes, chevrons can affect both gauge and drape, so you can't just introduce them into a project. Also, these stripes tend to make the knitting less elastic, and as the top and bottom edges will both zigzag, you need to decide how to treat those.

8 You might think that vertical stripes require stranding or intarsia skills, but in fact there are two simple ways of achieving them. The first is to rotate the knitting 90° (for a scarf, cast on one long edge rather than one short end), and the second is to use slip stitch knitting, as here. This only works over quite narrow stripes (four stitches at most) and in two colors, but it is effective and easy to do. (For more slip stitch ideas turn to pages 94–111.)

Knitting notes

When planning a stripe pattern, do think about how many yarn colors you'll need to carry up the side of the knitting. A sequence using six colors might look fabulous, but the edge of the fabric will have a bulky bundle of yarns along it. One-row stripes can move a yarn to the opposite edge of the fabric (see swatch 3) to distribute the bulk, or if you really do want lots of colors and the stripes are quite wide, you can darn in all the ends (see page 76), though on a large project that would be a real labor of love.

23 Pastels

Pastels are basically saturated colors mixed with white (see Palette 1, page 14). Here, I've picked a simple palette of ice-cream colors to clearly illustrate the points I want to make, but adding tiny amounts of other colors—usually brown or gray—can tint pastels to create more sophisticated colors that move away from the usual associations with babies. So even if you think that you aren't a "pastel person," don't dismiss the whole pastel family because some members of it will be useful in many color schemes.

1 Pastels used just on their own can look rather washed out and insipid, even for a baby. In this swatch the color values (see Palette 5, page 22) of all three stripes are almost the same, making it bland: I photographed this swatch in black and white and it was almost impossible to discern the stripes.

2 Adding a single row in a darker version of just one of the pastels adds some punch to the stripe pattern, but also dominates it: The eye sees the narrow darker pink rows before fully acknowledging the pastel stripes. This may not be a bad thing, but it is a visual effect to be aware of.

3 Here, adding a darker version of each of the pastel colors both enlivens and balances the stripe sequence. It will usually be impossible to find both pastels and darker versions of them—darker versions of similar values to each other—within the same brand of yarn, so lots of shopping with samples, cautious buying, and careful swatching will be the orders of the day if you want to create a stripe pattern like this one.

4 When you are using one-row stripes of darker colors, as in swatch 3, you can get away with the colors being not quite true versions of each other, but if you use equal amounts of them, as in this swatch, the inconsistencies do show. You'd have to add a lot more white to the dark blue to make its pastel than you'd have to add to the pink to make its pastel; and no matter how much white you added to the green, you'd never get the pastel I've placed it with. This is where as a knitter you have to relax about color theory, accept the limitations of yarn colors, and just knit with colors you like in sequences that work for you.

5 Adding a darker stripe of a different color to the pastels you are using is a great way of punching up a pastel stripe pattern. You've avoided the issue of inconsistent versions of colors, and if you choose a cool color for the contrast stripe, it won't completely dominate the palette. I've used a two-row stripe because when I tried a one-row it looked too insignificant; you just wondered what it was doing there.

6 Striping with one pastel and a darker version of the same color can produce classy-looking stripes: You keep the simplicity of the pattern of equal-width bands, but take away the multiple colors that can distract the eye. For this to work well, the two colors do need to be fairly true to one another—if you added white to that darker pink then you could achieve the pastel.

7 The two colors used in swatch 6 are used here in a random stripe sequence to good effect. As with swatch 5 in Palette 22 (see page 79), if you have a confident eye for color you can just knit away, placing stripes as you work and periodically checking from a distance that the pattern is developing in a way you like. If the idea of this horrifies you, but you like the random look, then just a little time, some graph paper, and colored pencils will give you a pattern to work to.

Knitting notes

If you are struggling to assess whether darker yarn and a pastel are true to one another, old-fashioned paints can help. Use a child's inexpensive paint box to mix a color as close as you can to the darker yarn, then add some white and see where the pastel goes. You may well not be able to match the pastel perfectly, but you should be able to see if it's more or less right.

Brights and neutrals

There's a real allure to bright stripes: Their exuberance and clarity are simple and joyful. But they can be completely visually overwhelming and what started out as a fun idea can be a chaotic finished project. One way around this is to introduce neutral colors into stripe sequences; they can calm down brights without unduly influencing them. At the bottom of most of these swatches you'll see rows of the stripe colors butted up to help you judge the effect the neutral is having on the pattern.

Neutral colors are white, black, creams, grays, and browns, and the last three can be made cool or warm by adding tiny amounts of other colors to them. This versatility makes neutrals very useful indeed, despite the often almost pejorative use of the word "neutral."

3   Black is a neutral that should be used with caution: It can make muted colors look drab, and even clear brights won't necessarily benefit from it. The stripes at the bottom of this swatch show how these three analogous, warm colors (see Palette 4, page 20) sit happily next to one another, but once black is introduced as a dividing line, they lose some of their harmony.

1   Primary red and yellow are of very different values (see Palette 5, page 22; yellow is pale in value, while red is dark), but they are both warm colors (see Palette 3, page 18), so the red is less dominant than you might imagine from a description. Adding a single row of brilliant white alleviates the density of the colors, giving a breezy, seaside feel to the pattern without creating another color relationship, in the way that introducing a different color would.

2   If your stripe colors are muted, then choose a cream as the neutral rather than brilliant white, which could simply make your colors look dirty. Varying the width of the color stripes but keeping the cream to a single row changes the emphasis the neutral has, varying the visual density of the stripe pattern.

Knitting notes

Do be aware that white isn't always white: What might be billed as "white" (or "snow" or "polar," or some such white-sounding name) in a yarn collection will very often be cream or off-white, and these can really throw your stripe colors. So take the color yarns with you when shopping for white; don't rely on the yarn label.

4

5

6

4 This warm gray gives the eye somewhere to rest in a strong color palette, and as it's warm, it sits happily with the yellow and orange colors (see Palette 3, page 18). If you wanted to use a color palette of, for example, green and violet, then a steel gray with its blue tinge would be a good choice for a neutral.

5 If you are using brown as a neutral then—as in swatch 4—choosing a warm version complements a warm color scheme, and vice versa (see Palette 3, page 18). Varying the width of the neutral stripes can be interesting and brings the neutral further into play as a feature in the stripe pattern. For the logical extension of this, look at the next three swatches.

6 Neutrals can be pressed into service in their own right as a color in a scheme, rather than just as a divider between other colors. Here, a cool gray is used with a warm orange; the contrast between warm and cool (see Palette 3, page 18)—as well as the equal-width stripes—helps push the gray into its role as a true color.

7 In this swatch the neutral stripe is wider than the orange color stripe, but the orange still stands out. As both colors are warm (see Palette 3, page 18) they are harmonious. As an aside, these yarns are both from one designer's collection and you will sometimes find that colors in a collection sit particularly happily together, especially when they are the choice of a single designer.

8 And if you follow the direction swatches 6 and 7 are pointing in, eventually you end up with a stripe pattern composed entirely from neutrals, at which point you really have to start thinking of them just as colors. And so you should, as brown and gray especially are delicious and versatile colors that deserve to be used in their own right.

7

8

25 Color-effect yarns

This might seem counterintuitive; after all, isn't the point of most color-effect yarns to create stripes of some sort? Indeed it is, but using them with plain colors in stripe patterns can produce gorgeous, and unexpected, results.

I must say that it is a bit pointless to use short-stripe self-striping yarns and self-patterning yarns (see Palette 8, page 34, and Palette 9, page 36) in this way—as I found out when I swatched for this palette—but variegated yarns (see Palette 7, page 32), tweeds (see Palette 10, page 38), and yarns that self-stripe over a longer distance all work well.

You do need to spend time choosing a plain yarn/s to combine with the color-effect one: See Knitting Notes for more on this.

The first four swatches all use the same yarn combination, but with quite different results.

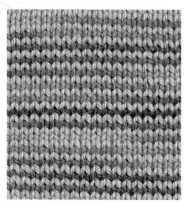

1 In this swatch a variegated yarn and a plain yarn are both knitted in four-row stripes, but because of the color changes in the variegated yarn, the plain stripes look twice the width. Obviously, if this was the back of a sweater rather than a swatch, the effect would be different again (for more on this issue, and to see this variegated yarn as a swatch on its own, see Palette 7, page 32). Here, the plain stripes rather overwhelm the variegated ones and the final effect is dull.

2 These variegated stripes are kept at four rows, but the plain ones are reduced to two rows, and the result is far more balanced than in swatch 1. One great advantage of striping in this way is that you get multiple colors, but only have to carry two yarns up the side of the knitting (see page 75), thus reducing bulk.

3 Maybe the most striking use of this variegated yarn is in one-row stripes: all that color change with just two yarns. If you've not knitted one-row stripes before, they are easy: Use a circular needle or a pair of double-pointed needles (depending on the size of the project), just knit a row, then slide the knitting to whichever end of the needle you need to make the next color yarn available.

4 Reverse stockinette stitch always makes for interesting stripes (see swatch 1, Palette 26, page 86), and the effect works well with color-effect yarns. This is the same stripe sequence as swatch 1, but the interlacing stitch bumps of the first and last row of each stripe move the plain yarn into the color-effect stripes, making the color-effect stripes look wider.

5 A self-striping yarn that changes color over a long distance is mixed here with a tweed yarn, and the result is lovely. The progression of color in the self-stripe yarn shows up well and makes for clear stripes. The self-stripe was chosen to pick up the tiny pink flecks in the tweed, but where the self-stripe is itself pink the flecks in the tweed are rather overwhelmed and they don't really stand out until the self-stripe becomes pale yellow.

6 This yarn is marled (composed of two plies of different colors) and both plies change color, but at different intervals (see swatch 5, Palette 8, page 35 for more on this). The result is that the stripes gradually change color, and I've increased the width of the color-effect stripes by two rows each time to enhance that. The plain color yarn is mohair (see Palette 26, page 86 for more ideas on striping with textured yarns) and picks up one of the ply colors.

7 Flecks in this color-mix tweed yarn have been matched for the three plain stripe colors, with the tweed worked in two-row stripes and the plains in one-row stripes to show off the tweed coloring. Picking out flecks in this way can be trickier than you might think (see Palette 10, page 38 for more on this), but when it works, the effect is good.

8 Very gently variegated yarns make for softly patterned stripes that look best if they are quite wide; here the green stripes are six rows wide. And a neutral, here a cool gray (see Palette 3, page 18), is a good way of dividing the yarn into stripes, without influencing the coloring very much (see Palette 24, page 82 for more on using neutrals).

Knitting notes

Choosing a plain yarn, or yarns, to combine with a color-effect one can be tricky: too good a match with one of the color-effect tones and everything can merge into an amorphous color splodge. Definitely take the color-effect yarn with you when shopping for the plain and collect various potential plain balls, choosing colors that are in the color-effect yarns and others that are complementary and analogous to it (see Palette 4, page 20). One-by-one, place the plains next to the variegated ball, assess the colors, and keep swapping them and discarding the least suitable until just one ball is left: The result might surprise you.

26 Stitch and yarn textures

As well as color you can introduce texture into your stripe patterns. The easiest way to do this is by using textured yarns (see Palette 12, page 42, and Palette 13, page 44, for more on these yarns), but you can also use stitch patterns. I've worked with some quite simple patterns here—and some more complex ones simply wouldn't work at all—but there are hundreds to choose from (see Palette 60, page 210 for a couple of options), so swatching (see page 212) is what's required if you'd like to take these ideas further.

|1| The most obvious stitch pattern is reverse stockinette, and it does rather wonderful things with stripes. This is a pattern of two-row stripes in dark blue, pale blue, white, pale blue, repeated; so a very simple pattern. However, the interlacing stitch bumps mix flecks of color along the edges of the stripes to make them look more intricate than they really are.

|2| Stripes on garter stitch look different depending on the row the colors change on. Some people talk about "right-side" and "wrong-side" color changes, but I think both are equally attractive and prefer not to label them that way. On the bottom of this swatch you can see how the color change looks when the stitch bumps overlap, and at the top how it looks when they don't.

|3| If you want to have clean, straight edges to a stitch pattern stripe, without interlacing stitch bumps (see swatches 1 and 2), then you need to work the first row as a plain knit row if it's on the right side of the fabric, or purl row if it's on the wrong side, no matter what the stitch pattern dictates. Usually this won't show when the patterning is complete. The first row of every gray seed stitch stripe on this swatch is knit only, and, as the purl bumps sit low, the stitches on the row above effectively disguise the "flat" row.

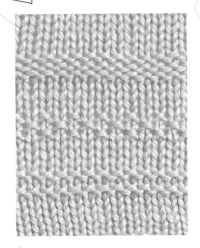

4 | A variation is to knit the stripes in stitch patterns only, no color at all. The result is subtle, but it's pleasing and easy to do. This swatch has stripes of garter, seed, and reverse stockinette, though you could easily use more elaborate stitch patterns as you don't have to worry about flecks of interlacing color from stitch bumps (see swatches 1 and 2). A single band of a stitch pattern makes a good yet subtle highlight for a feature such as a pocket or handle in a project.

5 | Novelty yarns can be far too much used alone, but very effective combined with plain yarns (see Palette 13, page 44, for more on this). In this swatch, stripes of eyelash yarn (with short eyelashes) are combined with stripes of plain wool in a darker shade of blue. The stripes are the same width, but the darkness of the wool means that the plain stripes aren't dominated by the texture.

Knitting notes

A problem you may struggle with using textured and plain yarns together is that of gauge. Very textured yarns often need to be knitted with quite a loose gauge in order to get the best effect, and that means that plain yarn stripes can be too loose. On the other hand, you may have to double up a mohair yarn to match the weight of other yarns in a stripe pattern. Either way, getting and maintaining gauge can be an issue (see page 212), and swatching over a fairly large sample (10 x 10in/25 x 25cm is good) is recommended.

6 | Here, mohair yarn in a neutral off-white (see Palette 24, page 82) divides stripes of two shades of blue knitted in a slightly rough wool. The texture of the wool isn't too strong a contrast with the quite hairy mohair, and the stripe pattern brings the neutral into play as a color in its own right.

7 | If you want to make a textured yarn stand out more, you can either combine it with a very smooth yarn, or knit it in a different stitch pattern, or both, as here. This is a soft mohair yarn—used double—striped with a silk-mix yarn; the mohair stripes are knitted in reverse stockinette to make the most of the yarn's fluffiness (see Palette 13, page 44), and the silk stripes in stockinette.

27 Embroidery and beads

The embellishment techniques described in Chapter 3 (see pages 48–71) can turn the humble (or even not so humble) stripe into a marvellous thing. Embroidery is added once the knitting is complete—or even once the project is sewn up—so you can decide to add stitches if the finished piece isn't quite what you hoped. Beading needs to be worked as you knit, so you'll need to plan for that when working out a stripe pattern. This can be really quite tricky if you want a bead pattern to work over different-colored stripes, as you'll need to thread the beads onto the different yarns in the right order (see page 51 for how to thread on beads to follow a chart). A full graph with all the stripes and the beads colored in will be a must under those circumstances.

1 It's really easy to create a plaid pattern by combining stripes with Swiss darning (see page 55). This is a simple stripe pattern with two lines of vertical Swiss darning, one of which is intermittent. The darning lines are slightly raised and do stiffen that area of the knitting a tiny bit, but not so much as to affect gauge or drape in most projects. I've used just two colors, but with more this would be a great way to make a sweater or scarf to match a specific tartan. (See swatch 4, Palette 31, page 101 for a plaid swatch knitted using the slip stitch technique.)

2 Sticking with just two colors, this swatch features cross-stitches (see page 56) worked on the paler stripes in the darker stripe yarn. The paler stripes are two rows wider than the dark ones to accommodate the stitches and balance the colors. A pattern such as this does need a bit of planning for, but a standard gauge swatch should suffice. Embroidery can be unpicked with a tapestry needle, so you can reuse a swatch to perfect an embroidered pattern.

3 You can introduce more color into a stripe pattern through embroidery. In this swatch, toning shades of crewel wool have been used to embroider lines of chain stitch (see page 57) to separate the knitted stripes. The changing colors of the crewel wools really perk up the plain stripes, and as these wools are available in the most astonishing selections of colors, you're bound to be able to find one or more to suit your project.

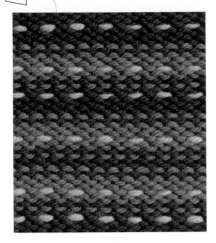

4 Here, the interlacing stitch bumps of reverse stockinette stripes (see swatch 1, Palette 26, page 86) have been supplemented with lines of simple running stitch (see page 56) that echo their flecked appearance. The stripe pattern is irregular and the running stitch doesn't appear at the same place on each stripe (or, indeed, on every stripe), increasing the intentionally random effect.

5 For these stripes, beads were threaded onto different yarns, but only one type of bead on each yarn, so actually the pattern wasn't hard to work out or to knit. The beads were placed using the slip stitch technique (see page 52), so as this makes the bead sit low on the stitch, they were placed on the fourth row of each five-row knitted stripe. Odd-row stripes are knitted on a circular needle or a pair of double-pointed needles in the same way as one-row stripes (see swatch 3, Palette 22, page 78). The toning colors of the beads and yarns make the beads a feature of the stripes rather than stripes in their own right.

6 As in the previous swatch, different beads are threaded onto each yarn. The beads were placed using the knitted-in technique (see page 52) on the last row of each stripe. As they are different colors to the yarns, the beads act as stripes and so you do have to take the colors—as well as the positioning—into account when planning the stripe pattern.

7 Although these beads extend across many stripes, they were only actually placed on the pale stripes—using the knitted-in method (see page 52)—and so only needed to be threaded onto one yarn. Each line of clear beads is topped with a little flower-shaped bead to make a very styliszed motif.

Knitting notes

If you are going to embroider or bead a striped project, do bear the laundering rules in mind. Beads need to be able to be washed by hand (generally, machine-washing beads isn't a great idea), and embroidery threads or yarns should be made of the same fiber as the yarn in case of any slight shrinkage. You can prewash both the yarn/project and the embroidery threads before starting stitching to avoid the latter problem (see also page 214).

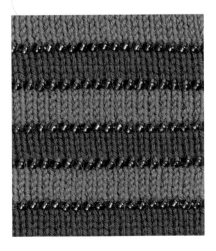

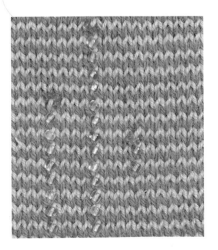

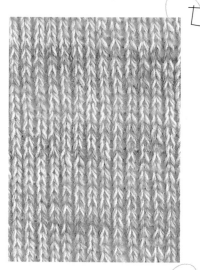

28 Color-mixing with yarns

Painters have the enviable facility of being able to mix colors to create the perfect shade, whereas we knitters must make do with the yarn colors we can buy, which are often dictated by seasonal fashion and are more limited than is desirable. (Obviously those crafters who dye their own yarns have a clear advantage here, but that is a different story.) However, it is possible to knit together strands of different-colored commercial yarns to create blended effects. The technique works best with fine mohair yarns as the fuzziness of the yarn helps to trick the eye into believing the visual color-mixing.

1 Here, lace-weight teal and mauve yarns of the same tonal value (see Palette 5, page 22) are knitted together with cream crochet cotton in a four-row stockinette stitch stripe pattern. The lighter-toned cream stands out as a series of irregular flecks, creating a tweed-like effect, but not actually altering the tints of the yarns or blurring the stripe pattern.

2 The same teal and mauve yarns are knitted together with cream mohair. The fuzz of the mohair yarn softens the flecks and gives an overall paler tint to the two stripe colors. The stripes are still clearly visible, but the effect is softer than in the first swatch. Knitting in mohair is also the way to create a "ghosted" motif on a single-color fabric (see Palette 37, page 124).

3 This swatch shows two stripe patterns combined: the teal and mauve four-row stripes of the first two swatches, knitted together with petrol and cream mohair yarns in a four-row stripe pattern that does not align with the original stripes. The stripe repeat is: two rows teal and petrol, two rows mauve and petrol, two rows mauve and cream, two rows teal and cream. The only strong stripe line is between the cream and petrol mohair yarns, which are so very different in tone. The other colors run gently into each other in soft stripes. To make this effect work you need to choose a mix complementary and analogous colors (see Palette 4, page 20). You will also need to manage the multiple balls of yarn carefully to avoid a terrible tangle (see page 77).

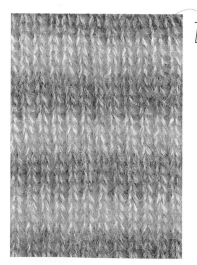

Knitting notes

Knitting with more than one yarn really isn't difficult. You obviously need to ensure that the needle goes through all the strands of a stitch, but generally it will without any extra effort from you. As you knit, the strands naturally twist so different colors appear at the front of stitches; this means that if you do drop a strand on one stitch, you won't notice that there's a missing color in the finished fabric.

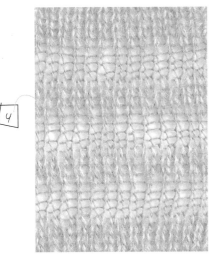

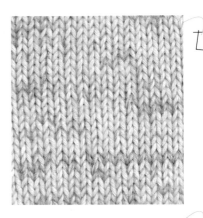

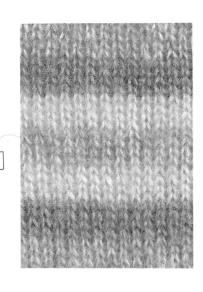

4 | Adding a yarn into a fabric will change its weight and drape, so you always need to swatch effectively (see page 212). Here, a teal lace-weight yarn is knitted in stockinette stitch with four-row stripes of mint mohair knitted in. The mohair bulks out the fabric in the stripes, creating both a color and texture effect at the same time. The stripes blend attractively into the fabric, but it can be hard to maintain a good-looking gauge on both the single-yarn and double-yarn stripes.

5 | Expanding on swatch 4, this sample adds and takes away single strands of fine yarn to create a wide, blended stripe. It starts with a strand of cream crochet thread and a strand of cream mohair, then a single strand of lime mohair is added in. Then the cream mohair is dropped and a second strand of lime added. The crochet cotton is dropped for a couple of rows, then reintroduced. The yarns are added and taken away in the reverse sequence to complete the swatch. Color-mixing like this will certainly affect the drape of the fabric and you need to swatch carefully to check you can maintain gauge (see page 212). However, it's a lovely way of working a border on an otherwise plain project.

6 | Explore the color-mixing possibilities, but avoid the issues of changing drape and gauge by keeping the same number of strands of yarn, but changing the colors. The stripe sequence of this swatch is: four rows in one strand mint and one strand lime, four rows in two strands lime, four rows in two strands mint, four rows in one strand mint and one strand lime, four rows in two strands mint, four rows in two strands lime, four rows in one strand mint and one strand lime. You will need to manage the balls of yarn carefully to avoid knots (see page 77).

7 | You can mix fine mohair yarn and heavier yarn with good results. For this swatch a worsted-weight yarn has stripes of petrol and lime mohair knitted into it. The heavier yarn dominates, but the strength of the mohair color naturally increases and decreases along the rows, adding to the blurred effect. You will probably need to go up one needle size to accommodate the added mohair, but work a swatch to check (see page 212).

8 | Color-mixing works equally well on reverse stockinette stitch. In fact, because of the way stitches are constructed, the loops of reverse stockinette can allow the knitted-in color to show more than it does on the stockinette side. This is a lime sport-weight yarn with four-row stripes of mint and cream mohair knitted in.

29 More with stripes

Stripes are the ideal experimental tool in color knitting; they are easy to work, amazingly versatile, and good-looking in almost every permutation. You can add plain horizontal stripes to any project without altering gauge, though other stripe patterns will need swatching, such as bias stripes (see swatch 2, below), mixed stitch pattern stripes (see swatch 4, below), and multiyarn stripes (see swatch 5, below).

Stripes are an ideal way of using up small amounts of yarn left over from previous projects, or for making an expensive yarn go further, so they can be economical as well as fun. (See Palette 22, page 78 for more stripe pattern ideas.)

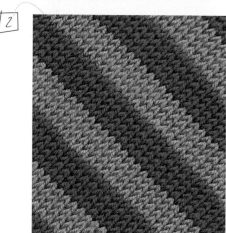

1 You can base a stripe pattern on a mathematical sequence: This swatch uses the Fibonacci sequence, where each number is made up of the previous two numbers added together—1, 1, 2, 3, 5, 8, 13... You could use an arithmetical sequence, where you increase by adding the same number (for example, 3) each time—1, 4, 7, 10, 13, 16... A geometric sequence relies on multiplying by the same number (again, 3) each time—1, 3, 9, 27, 81, 243...though you'd want a large project to make this last sequence work.

2 Bias fabric is knitted by casting on two stitches and increasing at each end of every row until the lower edge is the required width, then increasing at one end of every row and decreasing at the other end until the knitting is the required length. To make stripes, just change colors, carrying the yarn along the edge of the knitting as you would for horizontal stripes (see page 75).

3 Reverse stockinette is all too often just seen as the wrong side of stockinette stitch, but it's actually a marvelous knitted fabric in its own right, and stripes make the most of it. This swatch shows single-row stripes in one color family (see Palette 2, page 16), and the resulting intricate-looking fabric belies how easy it is to make. Any stockinette project can be worked in reverse stockinette without affecting gauge, though you may need to work an extra row in some places to make the right side of the knitting the reverse stockinette side.

4 Adding texture to stripes can be done with textured yarns or stitch patterns, or both (see also Palette 26, page 86). If you want your stripes to have clean edges—without colors splitting across interlacing stitch bumps—then make every new color row a plain knit row if it's on the right side of the fabric or purl row if it's on the wrong side. Work following rows in the chosen stitch pattern and the plain row will usually not show at all.

5 Monochromatic stripes might sound like a misnomer, but they can work beautifully. Here, yarns in the same color family (see Palette 2, page 16) but with different textures make a gorgeous striped fabric. You need to keep the yarns more or less the same weight—so you might have to double up finer yarns—and if you are going to need to launder the project then it's better if all the yarns are made from the same fiber, although careful hand-washing in lukewarm water will usually work well with mixed yarns. A row of beads can be used as sparkly stripes; these ones were knitted in (see page 52).

6 Quite a lot of stranded patterns are essentially stripes with motifs knitted into them (see Chapter 7, pages 136–57), but you can be a bit more free-form than that. This is a simple six-row stripe pattern with spots of green bouclé yarn (see swatch 3, Palette 12, page 42) knitted in at random, using the stranding technique. The thickness and texture of the bouclé has distorted the adjacent plain yarn stitches a bit, but overall the spotty effect works well.

7 The positions of stripes can be used cleverly to accent features of a project. It's usually best to plan these first to be sure that they sit in the right place. Here, the wide pink stripe incorporates the seed stitch pocket edge: You might try stripes that span buttonholes in a cardigan so that when done up the buttons make spots on the stripes.

5

6

7

Slip stitch knitting

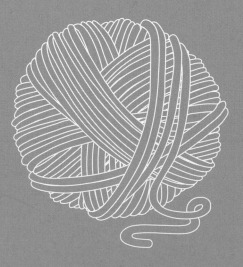

Of all the color knitting techniques, slip stitch is possibly the least well-known and yet, second only to striping, the easiest to do. To work color slip stitch patterns you use only two colors of yarn at a time, and on each row you handle only one color, slipping the stitches that are not in that color on that row and knitting those that are. Then you work back across the row, slipping the same stitches and knitting or purling the others, depending on the pattern texture required. To incorporate a third color you simply swap out one of the existing ones and carry on with the new one.

However, although handling the colors is simple if you are a beginner to color knitting, getting the gauge right can be more of a struggle. You'll often have to go up one or more needle sizes than you'd usually use to knit a particular yarn, and getting the slipped stitches to lie evenly and smoothly can take some practice. I find it best to swatch a pattern more than once, changing needle sizes until I find the most pleasing result.

Also, a lot of slip stitch patterns are given only as charts, and if you are not used to knitting from charts, they can be intimidating until you grasp the logic of them. Having said all of this, if you've never worked slip stitch patterns before, do try the technique as it's actually quite hard to explain how much easier it is to work than it might look, and how very satisfying the results can be.

The fabric slip stitch patterns create is thick, with floats of yarns running across the back, so it may not be ideal for garments but it's great for home decor items such as pillows and afghans, and the wonderful reversible nature of some patterns makes it perfect for scarves too (see Palette 33, page 104).

Slip stitch techniques

Above and beyond knitting and purling, the only technique required for slip stitch knitting is, as the name suggests, slipping stitches. This means just passing them from the left-hand needle to the right-hand needle without knitting or purling them. You'll usually only need to slip stitches purlwise, whether it's a knit or a purl row, so that the stitch isn't twisted. However, there are a few variations that some patterns will ask for.

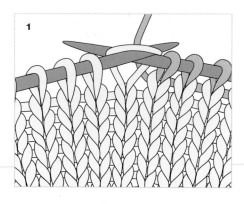

SLIPPING KNITWISE ON A KNIT ROW

Sometimes you may need to slip a stitch knitwise on a knit row in order to twist it.

1 Insert the right-hand needle from left to right into the front of the next stitch on the left-hand needle, as if you were going to knit it, and just slip it onto the right-hand needle.

A stitch can be slipped knitwise on a purl row in the same way: just insert the needle into the front of the stitch from left to right.

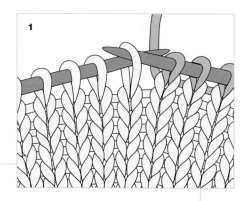

SLIPPING PURLWISE ON A KNIT ROW

This is how to slip a stitch purlwise on a knit row.

1 Insert the right-hand needle from right to left into the front of the next stitch on the left-hand needle, and then just slip it onto the right-hand needle.

SLIPPING PURLWISE ON A PURL ROW

This is how to slip a stitch purlwise on a purl row.

1 Insert the right-hand needle from right to left into the front of the next stitch on the left-hand needle, as if you were going to purl it, and just slip it onto the right-hand needle.

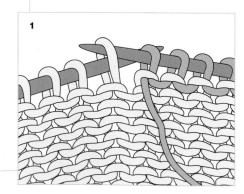

SLIPPING A STITCH WITH YARN IN FRONT

Some slip stitch patterns—usually texture patterns (see Palette 35, page 108)—will ask you to take the yarn to the front when slipping a stitch on a knit row (see also Knitting Notes).

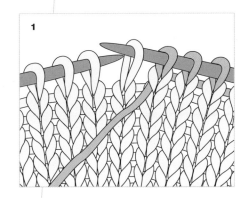

1 On a knit row the working yarn will naturally be on the side facing away from you, at the back of the knitting. Bring the yarn between the tips of the needles to the front of the knitting, then slip the stitch as instructed (here it has been slipped purlwise), then take the yarn between the needles to the back of the work again, ready to knit the next stitch. This leaves a little bar of yarn in front of tho clipped stitch on the right side of the knitting.

SLIPPING A STITCH WITH YARN IN BACK

Some patterns will ask you to take the yarn to the back when slipping a stitch on a purl row (see also Knitting Notes).

1 On a purl row the working yarn will naturally be on the side facing toward you, at the front of the knitting. Take the yarn between the tips of the needles to the back of the knitting, then slip the stitch as instructed (here it has been slipped purlwise), then take the yarn between the needles to the front of the work again, ready to purl the next stitch. This leaves a little bar of yarn in front of the slipped stitch on the right side of the knitting.

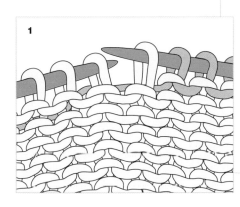

Knitting notes

The instructions for taking yarn back or forward before slipping stitches can be written in two ways. Some patterns will say, "k1, yf, sl 1, yb, k1." So you will knit one stitch, bring the yarn forward, slip one stitch, take the yarn back, knit one stitch. This can also be written as, "k1, sl 1 wyif, k1," with "wyif" the abbreviation for "with yarn in front." Similarly, on a purl row the instruction can be written as "p1, yb, sl1, yf, p1," or as "p1, sl 1 wyib, p1," with "wyib," the abbreviation for "with yarn in back."

Tweed patterns

These patterns are unique to slip stitch knitting and they combine color and texture very successfully. Generally they are small-scale and so can be rather too busy used over a large area, but tweeds are great for smaller projects or used to accent specific areas of something bigger. Choose distinct colors to knit them with or the stitch definitions will be lost and the patterns can be unsuccessful.

Tweeds can be quite slow to knit as many of them have you constantly passing the yarn back and forth between the needles, but the pattern repeats are invariably very short and simple, so you quickly get into the rhythm of the stitches.

1 A basic, classic tweed that uses both color and texture to make up the pattern. Dark blue and cool gray have a strong difference in value (see Palette 5, page 22) while still keeping to a harmoniously cool palette (see Palette 3, page 18). This allows the stitches to be distinct, but the fabric as a whole to be quite subtle. The texture shows up much better on the gray stitches than on the blue, but this just adds another dimension to the pattern.

2 Mixing pale yellow and deep turquoise makes a palette that is different in both value and warmth, and the colors are almost directly complementary (see Palette 3, page 18, Palette 4, page 20, and Palette 5, page 22). The stitch definition in the resulting swatch is clear, but the contrast is perhaps a little too stark and the pattern slightly brash. The tiny horizontal bars are made by slipping a stitch purlwise with the yarn in front, then taking it to the back again (see page 97).

3 This is a garter stitch pattern with distinct color horizontal lines and fainter textural vertical lines that give an almost pleated effect. The gray and teal colors are similar in value (see Palette 5, page 22) but different enough in hue (see Palette 1, page 14) to make the pattern work.

A more elaborate tweed pattern worked just in stockinette, this is very dependent on color for its success, but a difference in yarn fibers will help, too. The light blue is not only lighter in value (see Palette 5, page 22) but it's also shiny, so it reflects light and highlights the stitch pattern beautifully in contrast to the matte darker blue stitches. A very successful yarn combination.

 This is the same pattern as swatch 4, but worked in three yarn colors that alternate up the rows. However, you still only work with one color yarn at a time and the colors not in use are carried up the side of the knitting, as for striping (see page 75). The warm pale yellow (see Palette 5, page 22) dominates the design, knocking the neutral gray right back, and the result is unbalanced; replacing the blue with a lighter color to balance the yellow would get a better result (see swatch 6).

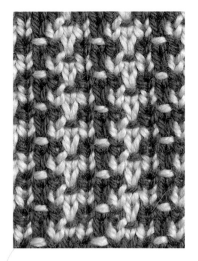

4

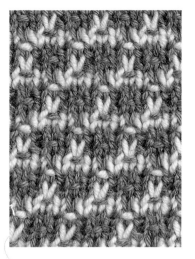

5

6 Here, the cream and yellow balance each other and contrast well with the gray, making the pattern clear. Although the pattern is a slightly larger scale and less complex than swatch 5, the same principles apply and the balance of colors is much better in this swatch.

7 This swatch uses the same colors as swatch 5, but only two are in touch at any time, so the relationships are far more successful. This design is also interesting in that it's not an all-over pattern, though on the rows with the tweed checks the contrast yarn is stranded right out to the edges of the knitting, as in stranded knitting (see pages 136–57).

Knitting notes

Tweed patterns work well knitted in most weights of yarn; the change of scale doesn't detract from the pattern. Try chunky or bulky yarns to make the fabric grow quickly, but be aware that if you're a novice knitter you might find it harder to achieve an even gauge with big needles than you would with smaller ones.

6

7

31 Line patterns

These patterns are, as the name suggests, based on lines of different colors that form designs. The narrow lines of these patterns do need the stitches to lie neatly to define them clearly, so practice and swatch until you get the stitch gauge right. Also, choosing darker and lighter value colors (see Palette 5, page 22) to best advantage is important. Simple texture helps define some patterns, but only stockinette and garter stitch are used here, so no problems for novice knitters.

3 Here, texture helps push the dark lines forward, even though the vertical lines of elongated stitches actually cross over them. The dark lines are worked in garter stitch and the elongated stitches are created by knitting the stitch with the yarn wrapped twice around the needle, and then on the return row the extra loop is dropped, creating the elongated stitch. When knitting the garter stitches on the wrong-side rows you have to bring the yarn forward before slipping the stitches (see page 97) to prevent a bar appearing across the stitch on the right side.

4 This plaid is created with elongated stitches made as described in swatch 3. Other than these long stitches that are slipped over several rows of stockinette, this swatch is made up only of rows of pink garter stitch spaced by rows of cream stockinette. The pink is both physically and visually proud of the neutral background. (For an embroidered plaid pattern, see swatch 1, Palette 27, page 88.)

1 A very simple linear pattern that resembles classic houndstooth check fabric. Worked in a warm dark pink and warm shade of neutral brown, the small shapes are well defined but the overall look is harmonious rather than stark. (For more small-scale patterns, see Palette 30, page 98.)

2 This pattern relies on just clear narrow lines and it is entirely knitted in stockinette, so the colors need to be well differentiated. Black is a harsh neutral to use (see swatch 3, Palette 24, page 82), but a very dark brown is just as effective at defining the lines and more forgiving with the warm rose pink. You may look at this swatch and initially see a pattern of dark lines on a pink background, but squint at it and the pink will move forward to produce a pink pattern with dark shadows.

1

2

3

4

5 Vertical stripes are very easy to knit using slip stitch, and the width of the stripes can be varied, though four stitches is about as wide as you can go. Here, the dark brown stripes are two stitches wide and the pink ones, three stitches wide. The extra width and the warm color (see Palette 5, page 22) make the pink stripes stand out, even though their value is much lighter than the brown stripes. (Variations on this pattern can be seen in swatch 8, Palette 22, page 70, and swatch 7, Palette 36, page 110.)

6 This is a variation on classic slip stitch; the dots are slipped knit stitches and the dashes are created by bringing the yarn forward, slipping some stitches, then taking the yarn back, leaving a bar on the right side of the fabric: This technique is also known as weaving. The two colors are similar in value, but the woven yarn is both a little warmer and more prominent in the knitting.

Knitting notes

Tensioning single slipped stitches can be tricky, especially in a design worked entirely in stockinette. Try not to pull the stitches in any way, just slip them from one needle to the other without stretching them at all. Don't knit stitches either side of a slipped stitch extra firmly (though this might be tempting) as it'll just make the knitting look even more uneven. And make sure you slip all stitches in the direction the pattern asks for; a twisted stitch will always look unevenly tensioned.

5

6

32 Block patterns

These slip stitch designs are based on blocks of color that tessellate together to form patterns. Color is the main component of the swatches shown here, but texture does have a role to play, too, helping to define shapes and outlines. In this type of pattern—and in mosaic patterns (see Palette 34, page 106)—the longer slipped stitches can end up looking a bit baggy and untidy against the more uniform background, but that is part of the nature of the pattern, and while it's good to make the stitches as neat as you can, even experienced slip stitch knitters will end up with some rather loose stitches.

Knitting notes

Block patterns can have quite long floats (loose strands of yarn) across the back between stitches. As with stranded knitting (see pages 136–157), don't pull these too tight or the knitting will pucker up. Spread the stitches out on the needle to help you strand the yarn evenly across the back of the knitting before working the first stitch of a group.

Long floats are not great for small children and babies as tiny fingers can get caught in them, so these patterns are best avoided in garments and blankets for little people.

| 1 | To outline a pattern of blocks such as this one to best effect, choose a color that is a darker value (see Palette 5, page 22) than the filler color: This green is about as light as you could go and still keep the pattern clear. Using a neutral as the filler color has the advantage of not adding a color relationship to the mix, and so not confusing a fairly intricate pattern further (see Palette 3, page 18). You can reverse the color scheme and outline in the paler color, but the results are often unsuccessful.

2 In this swatch a third color is introduced, but if you look carefully you will see that there are still only two colors on any one row. The cool green and the blue alternate up the rows with the warmer yellow as the constant (see Palette 3, page 18), and you just carry the color not in use up the side of the knitting, as you would for a stripe pattern (see page 75). (For more small-scale patterns, see Palette 30, page 98.)

3

4

3 In this pattern some of the olive green stitches are knitted with the yarn wrapped twice around the needle, and then on the return row the extra loop is dropped, creating an elongated stitch: You can see these clearly on the yellow rows in the pattern, and slightly shorter versions on the blue rows. These elongated stitches are an ingredient of many slip stitch patterns, adding texture to color designs.

4 Bands of reverse stockinette create these puffy, three-dimensional brick shapes, which are divided by elongated stitches made as in swatch 3. The warm yellow color (see Palette 3, page 18) helps to push the bricks forward visually. This three-dimensional aspect of slip stitch patterns is often ignored in favor of intricate color-patterning, but actually it's one of the most satisfying aspects of the technique. (See Palette 35, page 108, for a collection of texture-only patterns.)

5 The more intricate the pattern is, the more important it is to differentiate between the colors, especially if it is all worked in stockinette with no textural variety to help clarify the shapes. The very dark value (see Palette 5, page 22) teal blue used to outline these blocks easily dominates the pale yellow filler color and the design is perfectly clear.

6 A larger-scale pattern can get away with less differentiated colors: This honeycomb design is quite happy with an outline color just a little darker in value than one of the filler colors. The outlines are further strengthened as they are worked in garter stitch, so they stand slightly proud of the stockinette hexagons.

5

6

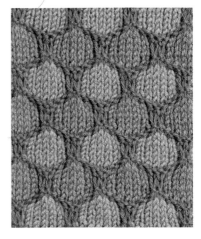

33 Reversible patterns

Quite a lot of slip stitch patterns look attractive on the back as well as the front, and this is a real plus when making throws or scarves, or any project where both sides will be seen. However, it's extremely hard to judge what the back of a pattern might look like—and the result is often not at all what you expect—so you do just need to swatch patterns and see what happens. Some patterns have been specifically designed (by very clever knitters) to be seen on both sides and this fact will usually be advertised in a pattern book.

1 and 2 Four shades of red and orange have been exploited to the full in this pattern. On one side elongated stitches in a color span horizontal bands of other colors and the surface is very textural. On the other side the horizontal bands are clearer and separated by bold dashes of other colors. Very sophisticated use of color in this way takes careful planning, but the results are certainly worth it.

3 and 4 The basic structure of vertical columns appears on both sides of this fabric, but other than that the patterns are very different. With such complex-looking patterns (though they are not necessarily complex to knit), it's better to keep the yarn colors simple and distinct so as not to confuse the eye. Two very different shades of the same color are a perfect palette here.

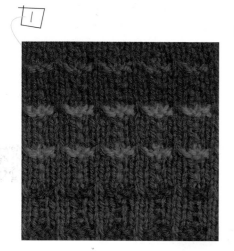

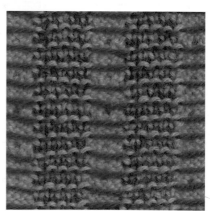

5

6

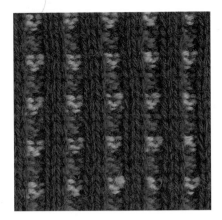

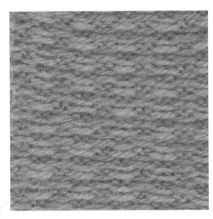

7

8

5 and 6 This is a great example of how unexpectedly different the two sides of a pattern can be: What looks like horizontally striped rib on one side turns out to have bold vertical stripes on the other. This is a basic two-row stripe repeat and essentially a two-by-two stitch rib pattern, with the red stitches slipped on the reverse stockinette side: Looks complicated, is actually very simple to knit.

7 and 8 Even if the back of a slip stitch pattern isn't specifically designed to be seen, it can be attractive enough to display. This vertical stripe pattern (see swatch 5, Palette 31, page 100 for another version) has a definite right and wrong side, but while the vertical three-stitch stripes might be what you're supposed to admire, the interlocking horizontal strands on the other side look good, too. Simple, clearly structured patterns such as this can be knitted successfully in two colors of similar value and warmth (see Palette 3, page 18, and Palette 5, page 22).

Knitting notes

Depending on the yarn you use, you need to be a bit careful when blocking reversible slip stitch patterns, particularly if there are floats of yarn involved. Pure wool yarns that have not been treated for super-wash can felt a bit during steam blocking and this can spoil the effect on the stranded side of the fabric. Either block using the warm water method (soak the knitting in warm water, pin it out and leave it to dry on the board), or pin it out, and spritz it with cool water and leave to dry. Experiment on your gauge swatch to see what works best.

34 Mosaic patterns

This type of pattern is probably what many people envisage when they think of slip stitch knitting: Celebrated knitter Barbara G. Walker was a big fan of slip stitch mosaics—indeed, she coined that name for them—and her enthusiasm did a lot to popularize the patterns. You can form quite complicated patterns using just one color of yarn at a time, although the repeats can be quite long so you have to pay attention for the first of each pair of rows, but then you just copy the pattern when working back across for the second row. As you have to effectively knit each row twice, the knitting is quite slow to grow.

1 Mosaic patterns are often shown worked in stockinette, and in many ways this is the easiest stitch to use as the yarn is naturally always on the right side of the work when you slip the stitches. The pattern shows clearly on the flat fabric and you just need to accept that the longer slipped stitches are intrinsic to the technique, even if you're a beginner knitter and have only just managed to achieve an even gauge on ordinary stockinette.

2 However, mosaic patterns are also very successful knitted in garter stitch. The longer slipped stitches blend into the textured surface better that they do in flat stockinette. Although the texture does also blur the pattern a bit, stick to strongly contrasting colors and the results will be fine (see also swatch 5). When knitting the wrong-side rows, you do need to bring the yarn forward before slipping the stitches (see page 97) to prevent a bar appearing on the right side.

3 A third option is to use a combination of garter and stockinette, and this can have an excellent effect. You can choose either color for either stitch: In this swatch the lines are in garter and the background in stockinette. The textured lines are slightly proud of the flat background, emphasizing the patterning even further.

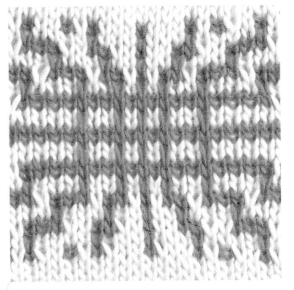

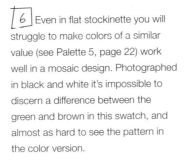

4 When working stockinette mosaics you can choose less contrasting colors and still have the patterns work well. These two shades of green are harmonious for an overall quite subtle effect, but using the darker value color (see Palette 5, page 22) for the lines keeps the pattern clear enough.

5 However, the same palette and pattern worked in garter stitch effectively shows how the texture of the stitch pattern blurs the design. The horizontal garter ridges just confuse the eye and darker lines are much harder to see as shapes than they are in swatch 4. If you're planning a mosaic project, do try swatching your chosen colors in all the stitch combinations as the pattern can look quite different in each.

6 Even in flat stockinette you will struggle to make colors of a similar value (see Palette 5, page 22) work well in a mosaic design. Photographed in black and white it's impossible to discern a difference between the green and brown in this swatch, and almost as hard to see the pattern in the color version.

7 Choice of yarn can make a big difference in mosaic knitting. Lightweight mercerized cotton yarn will highlight (in the worst way) every elongated stitch and will wriggle and twist very obviously if your gauge is anything short of perfect. A good choice is a wool/man-made fiber mix that has reasonable elasticity and a matte finish, and if it is loosely plied, like the yarn used in this swatch, so much the better. While this yarn might not be the simplest to knit with (it's a bit too easy to split the yarn with your needle while forming a stitch), the loose twist means that it fills out the stitch a bit, making the inevitable small gaps less obvious.

35 Texture patterns

Some slip stitch patterns are designed to be knitted in one color, while others have enough texture to make them viable in monochrome. The fabric produced is thick and cozy and, as there are no color changes, most patterns are good-looking on both sides, with no floats—or only very short ones— on the back, making them just perfect for afghans and throws. The stitch repeats tend to be short, so are easy to remember over a lot of stitches, and the texture usually makes the finished result very forgiving of slightly uneven gauge. If you are a beginner knitter and want to explore beyond simple knit and purl patterns, but aren't quite ready to try Aran knitting yet (see Chapter 8, pages 158–83), then have a go at textural slip stitch.

1 Slip stitch rib-lookalikes often have a lovely drape and thick texture and aren't elastic in the way conventional rib is. The well-defined texture means that the stitch definition is clear in darker colors, and looks good in chunky yarn as well as lighter weights. Short and simple row and stitch repeats make these patterns great for larger projects.

2 Slip stitch patterns with small scale and relatively flat texture can be rather overwhelmed by a strong color. Busy patterns like this one are better knitted in paler yarns that show the stitches more clearly, and a yarn with a slight sheen would be a bonus: You could experiment with bamboo yarn to doubtless good effect.

3 One reason that slip stitch texture patterns are maybe not as popular today as they have been in the past is that they are often rather intricate-looking, whereas today's mainstream fashions favor a simpler, more minimal style of knit, with chunky yarns and big stitches as features in their own right. Look out for simpler, well-defined patterns such as this one, which look fresh and modern in bold colors.

4 Elongated stitches are a feature of many textural slip stitch patterns, and they can be made longer than usual by wrapping the yarn twice around the needle when knitting a stitch, then dropping one of the loops when working back across the row. The resulting stitch is long enough to be slipped over several rows without puckering up the knitting. Getting these very long stitches to lie evenly is actually easier than you might think.

5 Slip stitch patterns can be surprisingly three-dimensional. Choose a lighter color value yarn (see Palette 5, page 22) that allows the shadows created in the fabric to show or the effect will be spoiled, and that effect is all that some of these patterns have to offer.

6 Do consider a slip stitch pattern as an edge pattern on a project. Many patterns have the same noncurling, firm characteristics of seed stitch—so often used as a border—and are pretty as well as practical. A little planning can extend a pattern into the main stockinette stitch of a garment without altering gauge; here, stitches have been slipped on purl rows for just a few rows of the stockinette.

Knitting notes

As with all textured stitch patterns, you need to be careful when blocking slip stitch not to destroy the depth of the texture. Don't pull the fabric too taut and don't press it with an iron. You can either pin it out and spritz it with lukewarm water, or you can steam it by holding the iron just above it and generating bursts of steam; it just depends on the yarn fiber, so check the information on the yarn wrapper.

7 The ruching effect that can be created by slipping stitches can make for an attractive slightly scalloped border that is part of a pattern. You could work the pattern over the whole project, or work just a few rows as an edging and then continue in stockinette, or another stitch that complements the slip stitch pattern you have chosen.

8 Woven patterns involve taking the working yarn backward and forward between the needles to create bars of yarn on the right side of the work (see page 97). Where the bars are short, as here, they are quite firmly anchored and are more stable than color floats, but still not ideal for projects for babies or small children, as little fingers can catch in them.

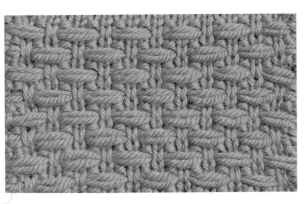

36 Color-effect and textured yarns

If you have looked at Palettes 12 or 14 (see page 42 or 46) you won't be surprised to learn that, on the whole, textured yarns and the subtleties of slip stitch patterns are not a great combination. But they are not completely impossible as long as the texture is quite light. Variegated and self-striping yarns (see Palette 7, page 32, and Palette 8, page 34) can be fabulous with slip stitch as the slipped stitches can carry one color into another in really interesting, if slightly unpredictable, ways.

Knitting notes

As with knitting color-effect yarns in stockinette (see Palette 7, page 32, and Palette 8, page 34), you can't really judge how a color-effect yarn will work with a slip stitch pattern by working a standard 4in (10cm) gauge swatch; you really need to work a swatch that's the full width of the project, though you probably only need to do about 15 rows to evaluate the results.

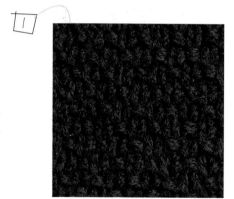

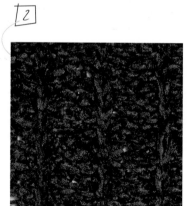

1 A bulky, braid-effect yarn works well with a very clearly defined stitch pattern where the purl bumps and knit Vs are prominent. One advantage of such a thick yarn is that the knitting grows quite quickly, even with notoriously slow-to-grow slip stitch patterns. And the overall texture is quite forgiving of the uneven gauge that is a common problem when knitting with very fat needles.

2 Chenille yarn disguises stitches at the best of times: Plain stockinette tends to resemble a woven fabric as much as it does a knitted one. However, choose a defined pattern (this is the same as swatch 3, Palette 35, page 108), and the way the light reflects off the velvet sheen surface of the yarn will give you some stitch definition, even with such a dark-colored yarn as this one.

3 Mohair yarns render slip stitch patterns almost invisible, but lightly fuzzy yarns are fine. This yarn also has a gentle tweed color effect (see Palette 10, page 38), but the stitch pattern, with its obvious knit Vs, is bold enough to cope with both the color and texture. Although the main pink/purple tone is quite saturated (see Palette 1, page 14), the overall color value is quite light (see Palette 5, page 22), so the shadows in the texture do show up.

4 Self-striping yarns that change color over a long length work well with slip stitch texture patterns as the color change is slow enough not to confuse the eye. If the pattern has stitches slipped over quite a few rows, as here, then where the color change occurs one color stretches up into the next in a lovely way.

5 The short color change in this self-striping yarn is highlighted by the stitch pattern. The lengths of each color cluster into groups and stripes and the elongated stitches show up well as one color is carried over another. The result is a bit busy and confused, but it is certainly interesting.

6 A heather-mix tweed yarn (see Palette 10, page 38) with quite strong colors rather blurs the stitch definition in even a well-defined slip stitch pattern. Some stitch detail is visible, and the overall effect is attractive enough, but the yarn doesn't make the most of the pattern and the pattern doesn't show off the yarn to best effect.

7 The bottom part of this swatch shows pinstripes using a variegated yarn and a plain yarn that is an almost perfect match to one of the colors in the variegated range. The result is that the stripes appear to be interrupted; only the colors that are very different to the plain yarn really stand out. The top half of the swatch uses the same variegated yarn but a contrast plain yarn and the stripe effect is perfectly clear. Both are good-looking, it just depends on the effect you want as to which you would choose.

6 Intarsia knitting

Intarsia is the type of color knitting used to create individual motifs, rather than continuous patterns; the latter are worked using stranded knitting (see pages 136–57). In intarsia, a separate ball, or bobbin, of yarn is used for each area of color, and in complex motifs this can add up to a lot of different yarns to be managed. However, with careful handling and by turning the knitting the right way at the end of each row (see page 77), this can be done more easily than you might initially think.

The vital elements in intarsia are linking the separate areas of yarn properly to avoid holes forming in the knitting (see pages 119–22), and achieving an even gauge on different colored areas. The latter is probably the thing that new intarsia knitters find hardest, and the secret is to be gentle: The harder you pull, the more distorted the stitches are likely to be. If you can find a smooth rhythm to your color changes, your stitches will be more even. But if there are some odd distorted stitches—or even quite a few baggy stitches—there is a fix or two that will cure many problems (see page 123).

The motifs in Palette 37 (see page 124) are designed for you to practice the different techniques for linking separate areas of color, so if you are an intarsia novice do work some of these before starting your first project. If you can perfect the linking then getting the gauge right will be easier.

Intarsia techniques

The secret of success in intarsia is twisting the yarns around one another correctly at the color joins. If you don't twist you will have holes in the knitting, and if you twist too much you will have distorted stitches and lumps. Like many knitters, when I first worked intarsia I was led astray by the word "twist" and I happily spiraled my yarns around one another; better words for the technique might be "linked," or "interlaced," or "interlocked," as it is all about linking one area of colored knitting to a different colored area. However, "twist" is the commonly used word and we'll stick to that to avoid confusion.

Twisting colors isn't at all difficult, you are just bringing one under another, but you need to do this in the right way on every row. Start by knitting a few swatches with very simple shapes (see Palette 37, page 124): a square to perfect straight-edge twisting, a diamond for twisting on diagonal joins, a circle for a combination of twists. Work methodically and you will soon find the rhythm of the twisting.

CHARTS AND HOW TO USE THEM

Color motifs or stranded patterns are nearly always shown as charts in knitting books, and sometimes as both charts and text. Charts are great because you can see exactly what the pattern is supposed to look like and it's easy to keep track of where you are (see Knitting Notes, page 116).

Single heart chart

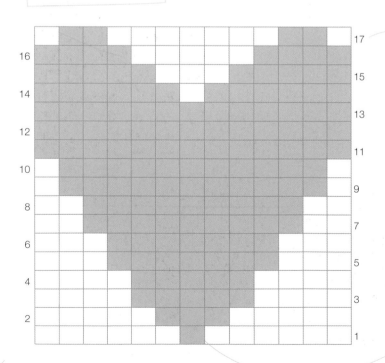

A chart will usually give odd row numbers (starting with 1) running up one side of the chart only, plus the final row will be numbered, even if it's an even-numbered row.

The boxes in this chart are rectangular rather than square in order to show the final motif more accurately; for more on this turn to page 116.

If you are working in rows, then you start reading the chart on the bottom right, at the row marked 1. This is usually a right-side row and you follow across it from right to left. So for this chart you would knit six stitches in the background color, then one in the heart color, then another six in the background color; this would establish the position of the heart in the knitting. Row 2 will be a purl row and you'll follow the chart from left to right: so five stitches in the background color, three in the heart color, then five in the background color. Continue in this way, working every odd-number row as a right-side row read from right to left, and every even-numbered row as a wrong-side row read from left to right.

This heart was knitted following the chart opposite; see palette 13, page 44, for more details of this swatch.

You can work charts in the round, but only with stranded knitting, not intarsia motifs because the yarn will always be at the wrong edge of the motif. For advice on using a chart in the round, turn to page 138.

A chart with a repeated motif will often just show the repeated section and the edge stitches, as below. Following the row numbering, as above, you work the edge stitches (four in this instance), then work the repeated section (here a repeat of nine stitches) until you get to the last few stitches, when you work the other edge stitches (here there are five).

9-stitch heart repeat

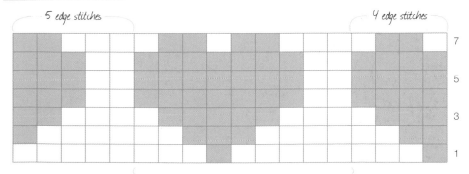

5 edge stitches   *4 edge stitches*

7

5

3

1

9-stitch repeat

CHARTED AND
KNITTED SHAPES

A problem that can arise with charts is that they are often shown on squared graph paper, and the shape of a knitted stitch is rectangular—it's wider that it is deep—so the chart won't accurately show you what the motif will look like. The actual knitted motif will be wider and shorter than the chart.

Motif charts are much better shown on knitter's graph paper, which has rectangular boxes that reflect the shape of a knitted stitch. If you compare this squared paper chart with this knitter's grid chart (below, right) and the knitted sample on page 115, you'll see that the knitter's grid shows the final motif much more accurately than the squared grid.

Square-grid charts aren't a problem—just a bit annoying—if you are copying a motif from a book, but if you want to design your own motifs, then you either have to add in rows to compensate for the distortion or, much easier, work on knitter's graph paper yourself. There are websites you can download and print this paper from (see Resources, page 218).

Square grid heart

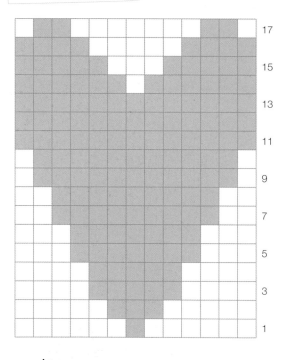

Knitter's grid heart

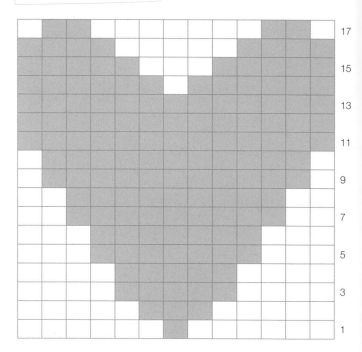

Knitting notes

There are various ways to keep track of where you are in a pattern, but whichever you use, do try to resist the temptation to permanently mark a chart in a pattern book: If you decide to knit the pattern again the previous marks will be dreadfully confusing.

If you have a color photocopier or a scanner, you can make a color copy of the chart and cross off rows as you work them. Or you can use a sticky note and move it up every time you complete a row. You can also buy a special ruler—sometimes with a built-in magnifying strip—that moves over the chart without slipping about.

YARN BOBBINS

One of the trickiest things in color knitting is managing the yarns. If you use the whole balls then within just a few rows you will have a tangle to untwist. The answer is to use bobbins. You can buy a variety of different bobbins and wind yarn onto them, or you can quickly and easily make your own.

1 To establish how much of a color of yarn to wind into a bobbin, count roughly how many stitches are in that area of the motif, then twist the yarn around a knitting needle that number of times (for lots of stitches, say a hundred, twist it around ten times then measure out ten times the twisted length). Space the twists at about the width of knitted stitches and don't pull the yarn tight. Add a bit extra for safety and for sewing in the ends (see page 76), and that's your bobbin quantity.

2 Lay the tail end of the yarn in the middle of your palm, then wrap the yarn in a figure eight around your thumb and little finger, as shown.

3 When you have wrapped all the yarn, take the bobbin off your fingers and wind the tail end (the end that was in the middle of your palm) tightly around the middle and tuck the end under the wraps. Pull gently on the loose end to pull out the yarn from the center of the bobbin.

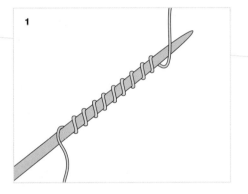

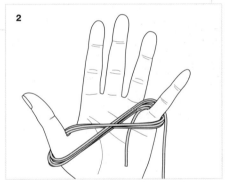

Knitting notes

You need to make a bobbin for each separate area of color (see page 118). So if there are two groups of green stitches on a row, then you need two green bobbins. Pull out just a small amount of yarn at a time so that the bobbins are hanging from short lengths; this will help to stop them tangling. If one color area is just a few stitches, then don't twist that yarn into a bobbin, just leave it dangling and it'll easily pull free of any tangles.

For ideas on how to manage multiple balls or bobbins of yarn, turn to page 77.

WORKING A MOTIF

As discussed, you need to make a bobbin for every separate area of color in a motif, and this can mean more bobbins that you might think. You need to evaluate a chart carefully and work out the maximum numbers of separate areas of color on a single row and make that many bobbins.

For this motif you will need five bobbins—three of the background color and two of the heart color; the highlighted row shows the different areas. If you can work out which bobbins need which amount of yarn, then you can be very precise in making them up. This isn't always simple to do and rather than spending hours agonizing over a chart when you could be knitting it, you can just make up large bobbins and then use any leftovers on another project.

The chart ends on a knit row, so the first row once the motif is complete will be a purl row and this will use the background yarn on the left side of the heart as you look at the chart. Therefore any knitting above the motif will be using that yarn, so you might choose to use a ball instead of a bobbin for that area.

The central background area between the lobes of the heart is only 15 stitches, so you could just use a cut length that isn't wound into a bobbin for that.

Similarly, the lobes of the heart split on row 14, a purl row, so you will be introducing the second heart-color yarn for the right-hand lobe of the heart. This is only 17 stitches, so another cut length would be fine.

This boxed row (row 15) contains the maximum number of separate areas of color in the chart, each of which will need a separate bobbin of yarn.

Bobbin heart

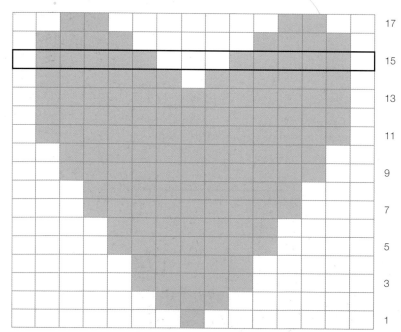

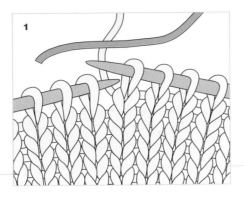

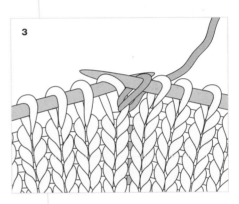

JOINING IN A NEW COLOR YARN

Unlike striping (see Chapter 4, pages 72–93) and stranded knitting (see Chapter 7, pages 136–57), in intarsia you have to join in new yarns within a row, not at the end.

On a knit row:

1 At the change in color, with the tail end of the yarn to the left, lay the new color yarn over the old color yarn.

2 Twist the new color under the old color, bringing it around into the right position to knit with.

3 Knit the first stitch in the new color. At the end of the row, pull gently on the tail of yarn to tighten the first stitch. When the knitting is complete you will need to darn these loose tails in (see page 76).

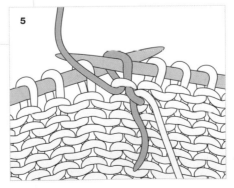

On a purl row:

4 At the change in color, with the tail end of the yarn to the left, lay the new color yarn over the old color yarn and make one complete twist, as shown.

5 Purl the first stitch in the new color. Tighten stitches and darn in ends as for a knit row.

Knitting notes

There are two reasons for making this little twist when joining in a new color yarn: The end of the yarn is anchored just enough to help you tension the first stitch, and the stitch will be made with the yarn going around the needle in the right direction, so the stitch itself won't be twisted. If you just loop the yarn over the needle as when joining in at the end of a row (see page 75), the chances are that the stitch will twist and this will show in the knitting.

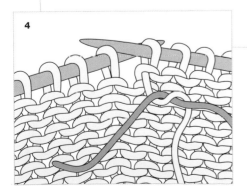

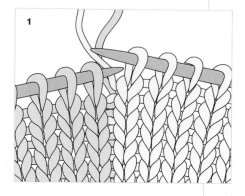

CHANGING COLOR IN A STRAIGHT VERTICAL LINE

Obviously, to change color in a straight horizontal line, you just knit a stripe, or part of one (see page 74). When it comes to vertical lines you need to perfect the art of twisting the colors together properly in order to avoid holes or bumps in your knitting.

On a knit row:

1 At the change in color, bring the new color under the old color and up ready to knit with. Drop the old color and knit with the new color.

On a purl row:

2 At the change in color, bring the new color under and around the old color from left to right, as shown. Drop the old color and purl with the new color.

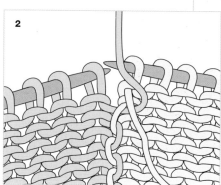

Knitting notes

Resist the temptation to knit the first stitch in a new color as firmly as possible. The stitch is linked to the last stitch in that color on the previous row, not the stitch you last knitted on the current row, and pulling the yarn too tight will just distort the previous stitch. Aim for an even gauge throughout and you can adjust any uneven stitches when the knitting is complete (see page 123).

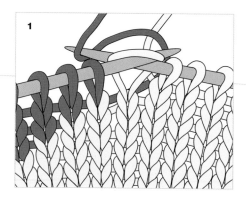

CHANGING COLORS ON A RIGHT-SIDE DIAGONAL SLOPE TO THE RIGHT

This is done in a slightly different way on a diagonal, because the color change is moving rather than staying in the same place as it does in a straight line color change (see above). Note that the diagonal will slope to the left on the wrong side.

On a knit row:

1 At the change in color, bring the new color under the old color and up ready to knit with. Drop the old color and knit with the new color.

CHANGING COLORS ON A RIGHT-SIDE DIAGONAL SLOPE TO THE LEFT

Here, the diagonal will be moving to the right on the wrong side purl rows.

On a knit row:

1 At the change in color, bring the new color under the old color and up ready to knit with. Drop the old color and knit with the new color.

On a purl row:

2 At the change in color, bring the new color under the old color and around ready to purl with. Drop the old color and purl with the new color.

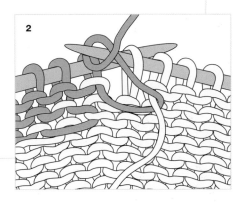

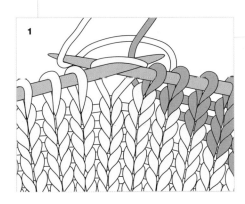

Knitting notes

When you practice these twisting techniques, start with two yarns of the same type in very different colors so that you don't have to worry about gauge and so you can see exactly how the yarns are twisting around one another. Work slowly, and if you make a mistake, unpick and correct it so that you understand where and how you went wrong. It really is worth getting twisting the yarns completely right before embarking on your first intarsia project.

On a purl row:

2 At the color change, bring the new color across and purl with it. Here you are not actually interlinking the yarns, but as the colors are moving across by one stitch, a hole won't form. Having said that, if you find it easier—and prefer the neater look on the wrong side—to always interlink the yarns, then bring the new color under and around the old color from left to right.

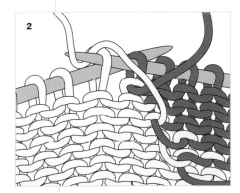

CARRYING A COLOR ACROSS THE BACK

You may sometimes find that you need to carry a color farther along a row from where it is last used, so that it is in the right position on the next row. The best way to do this is to weave the yarn into the back of the working yarn as for stranded knitting (see page 144). However, if the yarns are very different colors and you are worried that the weaving in will show, or if you just forgot to weave in, you can use this method.

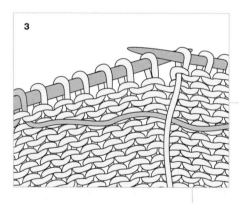

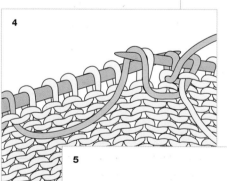

On a knit row:

1 Bring the new color yarn across the back of the stitches to where it is needed. Keep the strand of yarn quite loose. Knit the first required stitch with the new color.

2 You need to catch in the loose strand as you knit across the row: This is done the same way on a purl row and you may find those illustrations clearer (see below). Put the tip of the right-hand needle knitwise into the next stitch and then under the loose strand. Knit with the new color, not allowing the strand to come through the stitch. Repeat on every alternate stitch to catch the whole length of the loose strand against the back of the knitting.

On a purl row:

3 Bring the new color across the stitches to where it is needed. Keep the strand of yarn quite loose and take it under the old color. Purl the first required stitch with the new color.

4 You need to catch in the loose strand as you purl across the row. Put the tip of the right-hand needle purlwise into the next stitch and then under the loose strand.

5 Purl with the new color, not allowing the strand to come through the stitch. Repeat on every alternate stitch to catch the whole length of the loose strand against the back of the knitting.

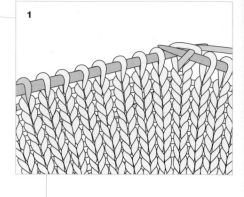

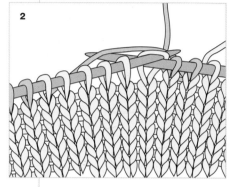

Knitting notes

Although the method described above is perfectly valid, if you are new to color knitting you may find it difficult to judge how loose the strand coming across the back should be: If you don't leave enough yarn then the knitting will pucker up, but if you leave the strand too loose then baggy stitches will appear. So if you can bear it, it's probably better to unpick across the row and reknit, weaving the new color in so that it's in the right place.

Troubleshooting

Even the very best intarsia knitters will have occasional looser or distorted stitches, especially at color changes, but these can be fixed when the knitting is complete.

ADJUSTING STITCHES

When you've finished all the knitting, but before blocking the pieces, lay your work out flat, right side up. At vertical color changes especially there will probably be alternating looser and tighter stitches along the edge. As each stitch is linked to the next one in the same color on the same row, you can distribute any looseness more evenly along the row. Using the blunt tip of a knitter's sewing needle or tapestry needle, carefully ease the adjacent stitch along to a loose one until the loose stitch looks right, then ease the next one along and so on, easing a little less yarn along each time, until the looseness has vanished and all the stitches look even. This usually only takes a few stitches to achieve.

Alternatively, ease the looseness into the interlocking strands on the back, then stretch the knitting gently to even out the gauge. If the stitches are very loose, you can try easing the looseness into the interlocking strands on the back, then using a separate length of yarn to stretch these across the back of the knitting and sew them to the back of an area that is the same color. However, the latter is hard to do neatly and the bulkiness of the fix will probably show in bumps and distorted stitches on the right side.

MISSING TWISTS

If you have missed twisting stitches in one spot and there is now a hole in the knitting, use a tapestry needle and one of the ends left for weaving in, or a new length of the yarn, to carefully sew it closed by taking the yarn through the back of the stitches on either side of the hole.

DISGUISING MISTAKES

Swiss darning (see page 55) can be used to hide any small (and sometimes quite large) mistakes in a knitted color pattern. You can also use this stitch to work single stitches or the tips of points in motifs, both of which, if knitted, can get twisted and look distorted in the finished knitting. For a point, use intarsia to knit to within a few stitches of the final shape, then cut the yarn leaving a long end. Use this end to Swiss darn the missing stitches and then weave it in.

WEAVING IN

Turn to page 76 for advice on weaving in the loose tails of yarn. Where two tails are next to each other and both need weaving in, twist them once around each other and weave each one in, going back along its knitted route to close up any potential holes.

37 Motifs

There are literally thousands and thousands of intarsia motifs designed for the knitter, and it's easy enough to create your own, especially if you work on knitter's graph paper (see page 116). However, before you launch into complex motifs, it's worth knitting swatches with simpler ones, just to practice getting the linking and stitch gauge correct. If you've never worked intarsia before, these motifs are designed to build up your skills, concentrating on one technique at a time.

1 Diagonal stripes will help you learn how to make perfect color changes on the diagonal on knit and purl rows: Just move the stripe across by one stitch on every row. On these stripes the diagonal moves to the left (see page 121), so work in the opposite direction to practice diagonal changes to the right (see page 120). Introducing a new bobbin (see page 117) for each new area of color will help you get to grips with working with multiple yarns.

2 A diamond shape will have you changing colors on the diagonal in both directions on each row. When you are working practice swatches (see page 212) there's no need to buy new yarn; use up any scraps in your stash that are the same weight (see Knitting Notes). In fact, it can be helpful to have yarns in different shades of a color for the background to make it clearer as to how many bobbins are needed and for which areas.

3 A simple square will help you perfect color changes in straight lines (see page 119). It's these that often cause novice knitters the most problems because when the changes are stacked immediately on top of one another, it's almost impossible to keep the first/last stitch in each color even on every row. The solution is to try your best, then fix any very baggy stitches later (see page 123).

4 A circle introduces all the color changes in one simple motif. The motif should be as clear on the back of your knitting as it is on the front; the only difference will be that on the back it is edged with interlocking strands of yarn. If you aim to make the back perfect, the front should be perfect, too.

5 This classic love heart motif is used throughout this book and you'll find a pattern for it on page 114. It uses all the color changes, plus a total of five bobbins—two for the heart and three for the background. (For more on the way to work this heart, turn to page 126.)

Knitting notes

While it's fine to use stash scraps for practice swatches, do pick yarns that are the same weight or you'll just cause yourself even more problems. Trying to achieve an even gauge with one worsted yarn and one sport-weight yarn is impossible. It's also not a great idea to use yarn that's already been knitted and ripped out because the crinkles will make it hard to create even stitches. If you do want to reuse yarn, take the time to wind it smoothly, but not too firmly, around a piece of card, then steam it over a kettle, or with an iron, and leave it to dry and cool. This should get rid of all crinkles, though it can also make a yarn less elastic and forgiving to knit with.

6

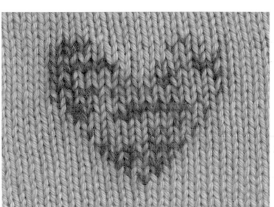

7

 4

5

6 Once you've got to grips with knitting one motif at a time, try working two or three together. For this motif the purple dot in the middle of the heart could be worked in intarsia, or it could be stranded (see page 139), or Swiss darned (see page 55). This would depend a bit on how good you are at each technique, but it's often easier and neater not to work very small areas in intarsia (I stranded this dot).

7 This isn't really intarsia knitting, but it is an easy and effective way of adding a motif to knitting. The whole swatch is knitted in pale pink with a very fine mohair yarn held together with it for the heart stitches only: You simply drop it after the last heart stitch on each row and pick it up again for the first heart stitch on the next row. (For more on knitting with two yarns, turn to Palette 28, page 90.)

38 Color balances in a motif

Intarsia knitting is a great vehicle for experimenting with all aspects of color; in this book we've looked at warm and cool colors (see Palette 3, page 18), complementary and analogous colors (see Palette 4, page 20), and color values (see Palette 5, page 22), and all of those come into play in the swatches in this palette. Using the same motif throughout really emphasizes how much color can affect a design.

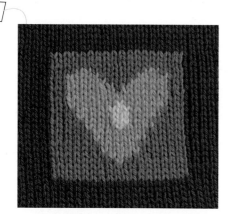

1 This is a palette of warm colors with the darkest value as the background, moving forward to the lightest value as the spot in the center of the heart. Lighter colors are registered by the eye before darker colors, so it's the attention-seeking yellow spot that jumps out first in this swatch. The darker square and background make the lighter-value heart come forward.

2 In this swatch the same colors are reversed, so that the darkest is the central spot and the lightest the background—no color is in the same position as in swatch 1. The overall effect is visually quite three-dimensional, with the heart retreating to look like a shadow-framed picture.

3 This is a cool palette with the two darker colors very similar and the two lighter colors almost identical in value. However, the blue is much more saturated (see Palette 1, page 14) than the pale green, so it dominates it. It's not a color arrangement that's very easy on the eye, as the dark background and frame are very visually heavy against the light heart and spot.

4 Even if you are fairly sure about how you want colors to appear in a motif, it's worth swatching variations as the results can be surprising. Here, using the same palette as swatch 3 but swapping just two colors, the purple and the blue, makes for a much more successful combination. The purple now emphasizes the pale spot and the blue frames the whole design, rather than flattening it.

Knitting notes

All of these swatches are knitted using one yarn collection, which makes the technical aspects of the knitting much easier. I've often found that lots of yarns in a single collection will work very well together colorwise, especially if they are from an artisan producer or small company. The Internet is great here, as you can usually find a shade card showing all the colors in a collection, though if you are very fussy as to shades, it's quite likely that the actual yarn will vary a bit from what you see on the screen.

3

4

5 Unless you have a very good color sense, it's usually best to have a considered plan when putting lots of colors together, or the results can just look a mess. In this big swatch the frame is in dark-value purple and all the central spots are in neutral cream to link the motifs together. The top left motif is complementary green and red, with the warm red heart standing out against the cool green background. The top right motif shifts the colors slightly and flips the roles to make a cool pale green recede on a warm orange background. In the bottom right the colors are both saturated, with the warm yellow heart shining out on the cool blue background. The final bottom left square is a warm and pale pink surrounding a cool and dark purple. So the top left and bottom right motifs balance one another, as do the top right and bottom left motifs, and the overall swatch is colorful and vibrant, but not chaotic.

5

39 Color-effect yarns and stripes

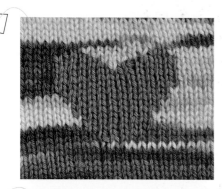

Variegated yarns (see Palette 7, page 32), self-striping yarns (see Palette 8, page 34), and tweed yarns (see Palette 10, page 38) all work well in intarsia, providing extra color for no extra work, although self-patterning yarns (see Palette 9, page 36) are best avoided as the pattern will almost certainly not knit up properly. You can use these yarns as background or motif, although making a self-stripe pattern run smoothly either side of a motif can require a bit of experimentation.

1 A variegated yarn, with quite long areas in each color, is used as the background to a plain heart. I didn't try to make the patterning symmetrical on either side of the heart, and you can see that a blue tint appears on one side, while the other side has more of the brown color. If the yarn is dyed in even-length patches, you can get around this by making up bobbins (see page 117) that start at the same point in the pattern for either side of a motif. If it's an irregular dye pattern, as here, then it's best just to go with the flow as it's almost impossible to make the two sides match.

2 Here the colors are reversed and the motif is in the variegated yarn. As only the top right lobe of the heart needs a separate length of yarn, the asymmetrical color doesn't really register. It's also interesting to see that the solid-color heart in swatch 1 is much bolder on the mottled background than this mottled heart is on the solid background, even though the colors are the same.

3 For this swatch both the motif and the background were worked in color-effect yarns. The background is a marled yarn (see swatch 5, Palette 8, page 35) that changes color very gradually, while the motif is worked in a variegated mohair yarn with a short color change. Do swatch to make sure that you see enough of a color change in a motif, as small motifs and yarns with a long color change just don't make the most of one another. Here, matching bobbins for either side of the heart keep the background consistent.

4 You can exploit long color-change yarns by using them for both background and motif, but working the motifs in a different section of the yarn to the background color at any point. This is a tweed self-striping yarn and the background is worked using one end of the ball, while the motif uses the other end. As in swatch 3, matching bobbins for the background keep it consistent.

5 This heart is knitted in a heather-mix tweed yarn (see swatch 2, Palette 10, page 38) with two plain background yarns, one that complements a color in the tweed and one that matches a color in it. Picking colors in this way can make for interesting intarsia designs, but do be careful that the plains don't dominate a subtle tweed (see swatch 4, Palette 10, page 38).

5

6 A striped background is another way of adding a bit more to a simple intarsia motif, though you are doubling the number of ends that need to be darned in—something to consider if that's a job you hate. In this swatch, and swatch 7, the heart has been shortened by one row to fit it neatly into the two-row stripe pattern, and it's clear how taking out just one row makes it so much squatter in shape.

6

7 In this swatch the roles are reversed and the heart is striped, but it made the motif much harder to work neatly. The stripes didn't help when it came to tensioning stitches either side of the color change (this was a problem in swatch 6 as well), and sewing in all the ends made the fabric very lumpy around the heart. An idea to be used with great caution.

7

Knitting notes

As always with color-effect yarns, careful swatching (see page 212) across the full width of the background or motif, as appropriate, is needed to make sure that the yarn pattern is going to work well. And, even then, you might need to be flexible and put up with some slightly discordant color changes where new bobbins come in and out, though this will, of course, depend on the complexity of the motif. For most color-effect yarns, a simpler motif will be best.

40 Textured yarns

If you've read previous palettes on textured yarns, then you might think that they're not going to work that well with intarsia, but as long as the motifs are graphic and simple, you can use quite heavily textured yarns to good effect. The main problem can come when you try to sew in the ends (see Knitting Notes). Another problem can be weight and needle size, as textured yarns sometimes need quite large needles to knit them up to best advantage, so even if you use quite a chunky yarn for the background, it can be hard to maintain an even gauge across background and motif. However, the good news is that texture is completely brilliant at hiding baggy and uneven stitches.

1 In this swatch the background is a smooth wool yarn and the motif a bouclé yarn (see swatch 3, Palette 12, page 42). The textured yarn makes the knitting easier in that it really does hide any baggy stitches around the edge of the heart (not that I'm admitting there are any), but the fluff does stick to the smooth wool quite a bit, making the motif a bit blurred and untidy. Pulling fluff off can damage the bouclé coils, so repeated careful trimming would be the answer if the fluff bothered you.

2 Here the roles are reversed and the texture is the background, although this time it's a mohair yarn that is the same weight as the smooth 4-ply used for the motif. As with swatch 1, the texture disguises stitch irregularity, this time in the background, of course. Using a monochromatic palette (see Palette 2, page 16) of texture and smooth yarns can create lovely subtle effects; this heart looks debossed.

3 Working both the motif and the background in textured yarns solves the problem of maintaining gauge and offers some disguise for baggy stitches everywhere. If you are using fairly lightly textured yarns, like the mohairs used here, then knitting with them isn't a problem and this might be an answer for you if you are really struggling to get your stitches even.

4 This swatch is worked with a quite chunky bouclé yarn as the background and heart. This is tricky to work with as it's not only quite stiff to knit, but the yarns don't slip smoothly when you interlock them at the joins, so it's harder than ever to maintain even stitches. Having said that, the texture is so dense that it does hide all the problems it has created.

5 It is possible to balance up the weights of different yarns by doubling up a thinner one to match a thicker one. Here, the background is a 4-ply alpaca and the motif a very fine mohair used double. You need to be a little careful to slip the needle through both loops of the doubled yarn on each stitch, but any missed single loops can be pushed through to the back if need be.

6 You can use smaller amounts of background texture by working a frame around a motif. In this swatch it's a simple square around the heart, but the frame could be shaped to complement the motif. A project with multiple motifs could have some motifs framed in texture and others worked in texture to create a very tactile surface.

7 Following on from swatch 6, using texture in different areas of a design can tie elements of color and pattern together. Be aware that thin outlines or borders of two or three stitches can be tricky to work neatly in intarsia, so it can be best to strand them (see pages 138–45); experiment with swatching to see what works best. In this swatch the top and bottom bars of the border are intarsia but the vertical bars are stranded.

8 Even very heavy texture can be effective in intarsia, if the shape is simple enough. In this swatch the heart is just about discernable, but spots would be clearer, and quite good fun against a smooth background.

Knitting notes

When it comes to sewing in the ends of yarn on the back of an intarsia motif, finer textured yarns, such as mohair, don't present a problem. You do need to sew them into the back of a section that's the same color, as the fluff can work its way through to the front, but you should be doing that anyway. However, thicker yarns or those with a heavy or very uneven texture can be tricky to finish neatly. Try using very sharp embroidery scissors to trim the "lashes" off eyelash yarn, after which you can sew in the core strand. But be careful the core doesn't unravel once it is trimmed: Experiment with trimming a scrap piece before potentially damaging your project. Bouclé yarns (see swatch 3, Palette 12, page 42) can usually be carefully "unpicked" to divide them into separate smooth plies that are easier to sew in.

41 Stitch patterns

Introducing stitch patterns into intarsia motifs can be trickier than you might at first think. Not altogether surprisingly, the problems will mainly come at the color joins, with the changes in stitch conflicting with the changes in color. However, with a bit of tweaking you can eliminate this problem, and the results can both look good and can sometimes help disguise any uneven stitches.

1 This is a reverse stockinette stitch heart on a stockinette stitch background, and the problem is immediately obvious around the edges of the heart. Where the stitches and colors both change at the same time, the outline of the heart is blurred by the colors splitting across the purl stitches.

2 The answer is to work the edge stitches of the heart in stockinette, changing to reverse stockinette for the central stitches. So, on a knit row, work the first and last stitches of the heart as knit stitches and the others in the row as purl stitches, and on a purl row work the first and last stitches as purls and the others as knit. Staggering the changes of stitches and colors in this way creates a smooth outline, and the flat stitches barely show on the finished swatch.

3 The same principle applies to most stitch patterns. Here, the heart is knitted in seed stitch on a stockinette stitch background. Due to the knit one, purl one pattern of the seed stitch, sometimes the color change is smooth (where the first and last heart stitches happen to be knit), and sometimes it isn't. You can see the irregular bumps where the color splits across purl stitches on alternate rows on the edge of the heart.

4 Again, the answer is to work all edge stitches as stockinette, and then start to work the pattern. In seed stitch the extra stockinette stitches hardly show, and certainly the overall effect is better than the irregular outline in swatch 3. However, if the flatter stitches do bother you, then when you are sewing in the ends, work small straight stitches over the base of them to create "purl bumps"; no-one will ever spot them as fakes.

Knitting notes

Elements that will be deciding factors in choosing stitch patterns for intarsia are scale and the complexity of the motif outline. A large-scale pattern in a small motif just won't work. A small-scale pattern in a large motif might look a bit busy, but it'll probably be okay. As long as the outline of the motif is fairly simple, you can use all sorts of patterns, although getting a textured check pattern to work well within an organic shape might be a challenge. Where you will run into problems is when the motifs shapes are both small and intricate: Detailed flower petals or animals faces will not be easy to apply a texture pattern to without rendering them indiscernible. If you are desperate to use texture in your design, either confine it to larger areas or the background, or use a lightly textured yarn for some elements (see Palette 40, page 130).

5

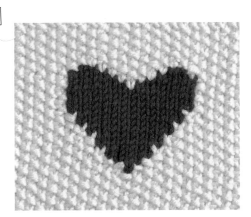

6

5 Here the stitches are reversed and it's the background that's in seed stitch. Again, you need to employ extra knit stitches around the heart to keep the edges of the motif clear. One advantage of using texture in this way—and as in swatch 4—is that the natural irregularity of the seed stitch pattern does hide any uneven stitches the intarsia knitting might produce.

6 Some planning—I find it easiest to do this on graph paper—will allow you to work more complicated stitch patterns, and to work both a background and motif in different textured stitch patterns. In this swatch the heart is in seed stitch and the background in a textured vertical stripe pattern of five stitches garter stitch and five stitches stockinette stitch. I planned the background pattern so that the edges of the heart have at least one smooth stockinette stitch to separate the columns of ridged garter stitch from the seed texture, as without that the two were rather jumbled together. All edge stitches of the heart are in stockinette to keep the color outline smooth.

42 Beads and embroidery

Swiss darning is often used in conjunction with intarsia because it's ideal for working tiny elements of a design that would otherwise be very tricky. But you can also use other embroidery stitches to good effect, both purely decoratively and to disguise any distorted stitches. Beads are also lovely embellishments in intarsia, either as additional decoration or as an integral part of a motif.

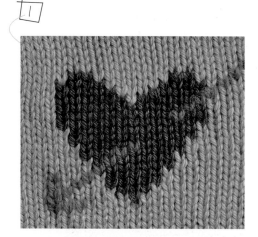

| 1 | This swatch shows a classic use of Swiss darning (see page 55) on an intarsia motif. The heart is worked in intarsia and the arrow is added in Swiss darning once the knitting is complete. I prefer to block any knitting before embroidering it, and then lightly steam or spritz the embroidered area (depending on the yarn fiber) to finish it. Blocking the embroidery, especially if you are pressing it, can overly flatten the stitches and make the fabric lumpy.

| 2 | If your intarsia knitting really hasn't worked out as you hoped and the edge stitches are distorted, you can just cover them up with an embroidered outline. This outline is worked in chain stitch (see page 57), which is chunky enough to cover stitches and yet is still pretty. To keep the stitching symmetrical, it starts at top center and goes around to the lower point. Then a new line is started, again at top center and curving around the other side of the heart.

| 3 | Use embroidery to add detail to simple motifs: This lazy daisy flower with a French knot center (see page 57) is stitched to fit neatly into the lower part of an intarsia heart. While you don't need to plan every stitch in advance, if you know that you are going to use embroidery, then it's worth thinking about stitches before you start. Maybe plot the basic elements on graph paper, just so there are no nasty surprises once all the knitting is complete.

| 4 | Fancy yarns and threads can make even the simplest stitches a bit more interesting. The loops around this heart are just running stitches (see page 56) in a bouclé thread, spaced so that the large loops are on the right side of the knitting. The lines within the heart are running stitches made with three strands of different mohair yarns in the needle.

3

4

5 It can be a bit tricky to judge where to place beads in an intarsia motif using the slip stitch method because the beads sit so low on the stitch; safest to use the knitted-in technique (see page 52). Work out the positions of the beads on graph paper before you start knitting, keeping them away from the edge stitches of a motif as adding a bead AND tensioning the new color stitch correctly can be difficult.

6 This border of beads is worked using the slip stitch method (see page 52), and—despite planning positions on graph paper first—I did have to unravel and move the bead positions at the top of the heart twice before I was happy with how they were sitting. If you want to use this method, a full swatch is a must (see page 212).

5

6

Knitting notes

With embroidery on knitting using fancy or artisan threads, it's a good idea to test for colorfastness and shrinkage (see page 214). Even if you are using standard commercial threads you should work a swatch (see page 212) to check that the threads sit on the yarn as you intended and that you are happy with how all the stitches work. If something doesn't look right, it's better to try again on a different part of the swatch so that you can compare the two stitches and see what improvement came about from working the stitch again, or working it a different way.

Chapter

7 Stranded knitting

Strictly speaking, stranded knitting is the name for all types of color knitting in which strands—or floats—of yarn are carried across the back of the fabric. For most people this means Fair Isle knitting, but Fair Isle is actually just one type of stranded knitting. It comes from the eponymous island in the Shetland archipelago, off the coast of Scotland. Traditionally Fair Isle knitting uses just two colors of yarn at a time, with maybe four to six colors used in total, and the motifs used include "peeries," small flecks of color between the main motifs in a band. Some classic Fair Isle garments use very sophisticated color patterning within the limited palette, with background and motif colors swapping and changing up the knitting.

Nordic knitting is the other classic stranded knitting style and it comes from Scandinavia. Traditional Nordic patterns use larger motifs such as *frostrosen* or "frostflowers," which are snowflake-like flower patterns, worked in only two colors throughout. There is a form of Nordic knitting called *bohus* that originates from Sweden and that keeps the color-patterning confined to the yoke, but the patterning is so spectacular that a small amount of it is all that's needed to make a garment special.

What these knitting traditions have in common is that the floats of yarn on the back of the work are not just a byproduct of placing color, they are there to make the fabric double-thickness and so keep you warm: The Shetlands and Scandinavia are both cold.

Stranded knitting

For many knitters this is the most complex form of color knitting, because you have to work with two, or sometimes more, colors in a single row. There are three ways of doing this: you can work with one yarn at a time, dropping the one/s not in use; you can hold two yarns in one hand, the right or left hand; or you can hold one, or more, yarns in each hand. All three techniques are shown here using two yarns and you will need to experiment to see which suits you best. Whichever you choose, it's probably going to feel awkward at first and your stitches may well be uneven, but practice will soon have everything feeling more comfortable and looking better. So do plan on working quite a few samples before starting a project, and then swatching every pattern before you knit it.

The secret of success in stranded knitting is getting the tension on the floats—the strands of yarn lying across the back of the knitting—right. If they are too tight then the knitting will be puckered, too loose and the stitches will be baggy. The best way to get this right is to spread out the stitches on the right-hand needle every time you are about to change color, then bring the new color across the back and work the first stitch with it. Don't be tempted to work this stitch as firmly as possible to "anchor" the new color, just try to make it the same as the previous stitch.

WORKING A CHART IN THE ROUND

Working stranded knitting in the round is an easier option for a lot of knitters because working just with knit stitch allows them to keep the yarns tensioned more evenly and so the knitting is smoother.

It is possible to work any chart in the round; you just knit every row from right to left, because every row is now a right-side row. However, to make sure the yarns are always in the right position to be picked up n the next row, large single motif charts—such as the heart on page 114—would have to have the main color yarn stranded across the back of the motif, and the motif color stranded across the background. This can be done, but the stranded colors will show through the knitting (see pages 144–145), so these motifs are best reserved for intarsia designs worked in rows (see Chapter 6, pages 112–135).

Small, repeated motifs, such as this heart repeat, are best for stranded knitting in the round. To keep the pattern continuous you need to cast on the right number of stitches so that the edge stitches join to make a complete motif; for this chart you would need to cast on a multiple of nine stitches to accommodate the nine-stitch pattern repeat, and the four edge stitches at one end and five edge stitches at the other end of the chart.

9-stitch heart repeat

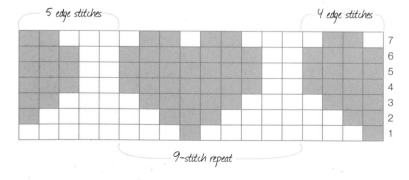

5 edge stitches

4 edge stitches

9-stitch repeat

You would need to weave in the background color yarn just once across the back of each heart motif.

HOLDING YARNS ONE AT A TIME

As you are only holding one yarn at a time with this method, it is the simplest method of stranded knitting but it is also the slowest.

On a knit row:

Start knitting with the first color yarn.

1 At the color change, drop the old color and pick up the new color, bringing it across the back and over the old color. Knit with the new color.

2 At the next color change, repeat the process but bring the new color across and under the old color. Continue alternating the yarns over and under one another at each color change so that they interlace on the back.

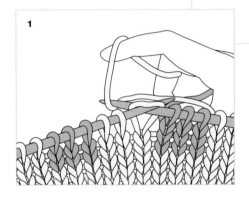

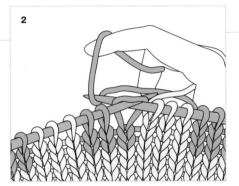

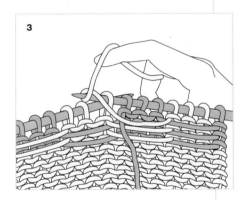

On a purl row:

Start purling with the first color yarn.

3 The principle is the same on purl rows. At one color change bring the new yarn over the old yarn.

4 At the next color change, bring the new yarn under the old yarn.

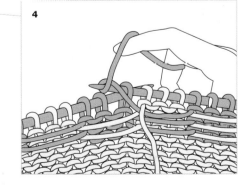

Knitting notes

When you start stranded knitting for the first time, you will probably find this method easiest and you can concentrate on getting the stitch and float gauges right rather than worrying about what's going on with your hands. But if you decide that you like stranded color knitting and want to progress and do more of it, it is worth learning a faster technique.

HOLDING BOTH YARNS IN YOUR RIGHT HAND

This method takes a bit more dexterity than using one yarn at a time, but once you get the rhythm of it, it is much quicker. You'll need to practice to get the stitch and float tension more or less equal with both yarns (see Knitting Notes).

On a knit row:

Place the yarn that appears more often over your index finger and that which appears less often over your middle finger. If it is a regular check pattern, as here, then place the color used first over your index finger.

1 Put the tip of the right-hand needle into the stitch and, using the appropriate finger, knit the number of stitches required in that color yarn.

2 Using your middle finger, knit the stitches in the second color. Make sure that the second yarn comes up from under the first yarn.

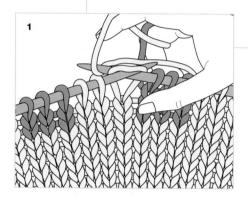

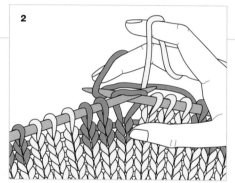

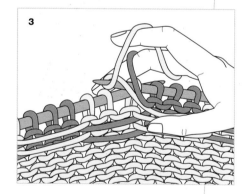

On a purl row:

Hold the yarns as for a knit row.

3 Purl the stitches in the first color.

4 Take the second color across and over the first color to knit stitches with the other finger.

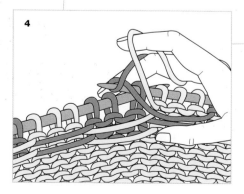

HOLDING YARNS
IN YOUR LEFT HAND

If you knit Continental style, you will probably prefer to try stranding with both yarns in your left hand. The principles are the same as for holding the yarns in your right hand, but because the needles approach the yarn from a different angle, there are two ways you might hold the yarns.

1 Hold one yarn over your index finger and the other over your middle finger, as described for holding yarns in the right hand (see opposite).

2 Hold both yarns over your index finger, with the yarn used more often—or used first—closer to the end of your finger.

3 You can also try wearing a knitting thimble on your index finger: There are various types of these, but they all act to keep two (or more) yarns spaced apart on your finger, making it easier to pick up one with the tip of the needle.

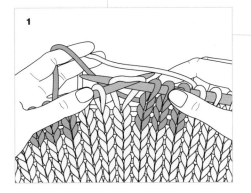

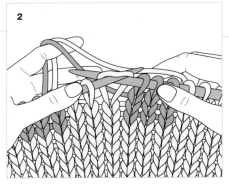

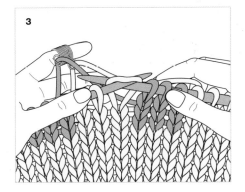

Knitting notes

It's well worth spending quite a lot of time practicing holding and using the yarns in stranded knitting before you start a project. If you just rush straight into the project, then as you get used to the actions needed and improve your technique your stranding will get better, and the difference will really show in the finished knitting: A sweater can end up with very distinct "good" and "bad" sides.

HOLDING YARNS
IN BOTH HANDS

If you can hold one yarn in each hand, then you will, after some practice, be able to knit stranded work quickly and with an even gauge. Most people have one dominant hand and will find it difficult to control the yarn in the other, but if you make yourself work only with your nondominant hand for a while, you will get better at controlling the yarn with it.

On a knit row:

Place the yarn that appears more often—or first—in your dominant hand and that which appears less often—or second—in your other hand.

1 Knit the first color stitches.

2 When the second color yarn is needed, work with the other hand. Holding the yarns like this means that the colors will automatically interlace tidily on the back.

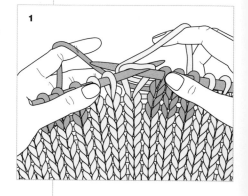

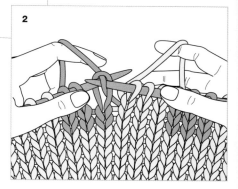

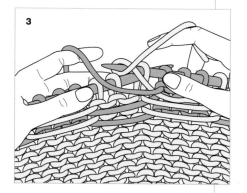

On a purl row:

The principle is exactly the same on a purl row, though you may have to adjust the position of your fingers to catch the yarn with the needle.

3 Purl the first color, controlling the yarn with one hand.

4 Purl the second color with the other hand. You can see here how, with a yarn in each hand, the strands interlace neatly on the back of the knitting.

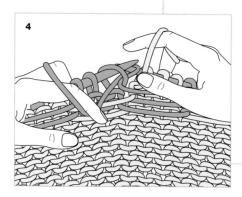

Knitting notes

Even the best stranded knitters will tend to have slightly different gauges with the two yarns, but if you assess the pattern first and always work with the main color in your dominant hand and the subsidiary one in the other hand, then the difference can be unnoticeable.

CATCHING IN FLOATS

If there are five or more stitches between colors, then you need to hold the floats against the back of the knitting as you work or they will snag when you wear or use the item. The simple way of doing this is just to trap them with the working yarn against the back of the middle stitch in the group. If you haven't yet mastered stranding with both hands (see opposite), this is probably the method to use.

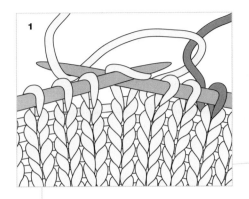

On a knit row:

Catch the yarn into every second or third stitch.

1 Insert the right-hand needle into the stitch. Lay the yarn to be caught in over the working yarn, then knit the stitch. Make sure the contrast yarn does not appear through the stitch; it should just be held firmly against the back of it.

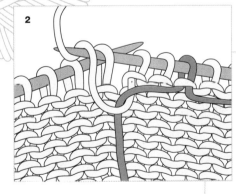

On a purl row:

Again, catch the yarn into every second or third stitch.

1 Insert the right-hand needle into the stitch. Lay the yarn to be caught in over the working yarn, then purl the stitch.

WEAVING IN FLOATS WITH YARNS IN BOTH HANDS

Weaving in the floats more firmly is a good idea on a garment or other item that will get quite a lot of wear. If you can use both hands to work stranded knitting (see page 142), then hold the yarns the same way to weave the floats in.

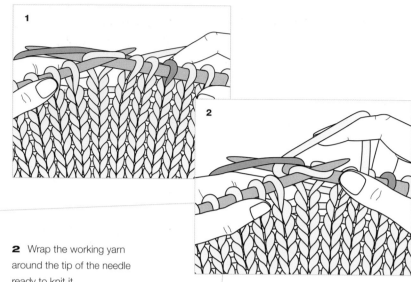

On a knit row:

Hold the yarn you are knitting with in your dominant hand and the yarn to be woven in in your other hand.

1 Insert the right-hand needle into the middle stitch of the group. Lay the yarn to be woven in over the tip of the needle.

2 Wrap the working yarn around the tip of the needle ready to knit it.

3 Bring the working yarn through the stitch on the leftt-hand needle, making sure the woven yarn doesn't come through at the same time. Knitting the next stitch will lock the float in place.

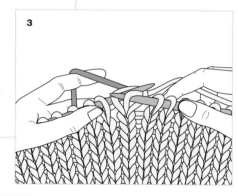

On a purl row:

Hold the yarns as for a knit row.

4 Insert the right-hand needle into the middle stitch of the group. Lay the yarn to be woven in over the tip of the needle.

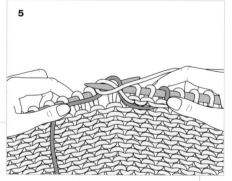

5 Wrap the working yarn around the tip of the needle and purl it, making sure the woven yarn doesn't come through at the same time. Purling the next stitch will lock the float in place.

Knitting notes

When weaving in yarn, make an effort not to catch it into the back of the same stitches on every row as this will create ridges that will show on the front of the knitting. If you wove into the third stitch of a group of five on one row, weave into the second stitch or fourth stitch of that group on the next row.

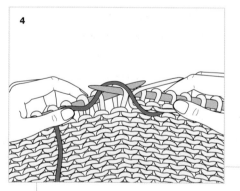

CONTINUOUS WEAVING IN

You can make very thick, cozy knitted fabric by weaving the floats above or below on the back of every stitch. However, this does tend to show through on the front of the knitting (see Knitting Notes).

On a knit row:

The yarns will weave above and below alternate stitches.

1 To weave the yarn over a stitch, insert the right-hand needle into the stitch. Lay the yarn to be woven in over the tip of the needle. Then knit the stitch with the working yarn, bringing it under the yarn being woven.

2 To weave the yarn below the next stitch in the row, knit the stitch with the working yarn, bringing that yarn over the woven yarn.

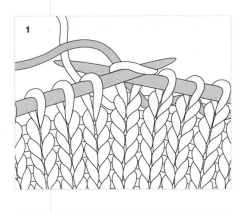

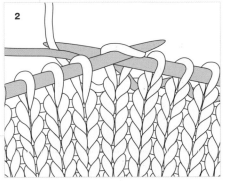

On a purl row:

The same actions apply on a purl row.

3 To weave the yarn over a stitch, insert the right-hand needle into the stitch. Lay the yarn to be woven in over the tip of the needle. Then purl the stitch with the working yarn, bringing it under the yarn being woven.

4 To weave the yarn below the next stitch in the row, just purl the stitch with the working yarn, bringing that yarn over the woven yarn.

Knitting notes

Whenever you weave or catch one yarn against the back of knitting in another yarn, the chances are that a fleck of color of the woven yarn will show on the front of the knitting. However, this may not be a disadvantage if the main yarn is variegated or is a tweed, as the woven-in yarn can just blend into the overall coloring (see swatch 5, Palette 46, page 153). If the show-through is not a problem, then continuous weaving in does make for a very stable and thick fabric.

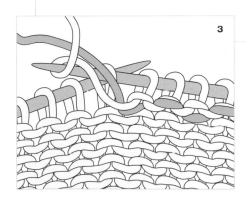

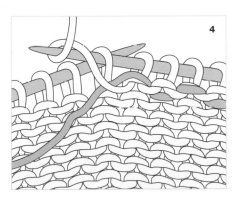

43 Traditional colors and patterns

Both the Fair Isle and Nordic knitting traditions have long roots that include classic motifs and color palettes. These colors originate from before the advent of commercial dyes, so the colors of natural sheep wools and those shades that could be obtained from ancient dye recipes were used. Today there are artisan dyers and spinners who make yarns according to these traditions, but their relative rarity and cost put these yarns beyond the reach of most knitters. However, if you want to knit a traditional motif in a traditional color palette, there are plenty of mainstream yarn options that will give you the right look.

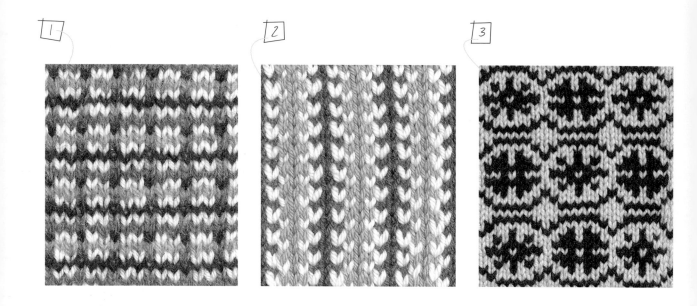

1 Soft, heathery colors are found in traditional Fair Isle designs; colors were made with plant-based dyes. Designs tend to work from a limited palette, such as this red/mauve collection, set against natural cream. This small-scale pattern with its shifting bands of color is a good starting pattern for a Fair Isle novice as not every row involves a color change.

2 A blue-based palette is another classic option; again, the colors should be muted and the whole palette softly harmonious. This pattern has an old-fashioned feel, but three colors are used on every row rather than just the two found in strictly traditional Fair Isle patterns. Controlling three colors successfully takes some skill, so start out with two-color patterns and move on once you have mastered those.

3 Cream or ecru and brown are natural colors of sheep fleece and feature heavily in classic Fair Isles. In this swatch all the motifs have been worked in one shade, but you could use three or four colors, swapping them in and out as the motifs progress. If you wanted to have only two colors in use at a time, you would need to chart the pattern and color repeats carefully, because parts of the curving lines and top and bottom edges of the motifs are on the same rows.

4

5

4 When selecting yarns for a Fair Isle pattern, don't get too carried away by the idea of a gorgeously harmonious palette. A collection of yarns that in the ball look wonderfully subtle together might in fact be so subtle that once knitted into a pattern they just get lost. This swatch contains three shades of gray yarn, but you have to peer hard to spot them. A monochromatic vision is best kept for something simpler, such as stripes (see swatch 5, Palette 29, page 93).

5 There are myriad frostflower patterns of varying degrees of complexity to choose from if you want to knit a Nordic-style pattern. These are sometimes quite small and can be repeated in a band in a similar way to a Fair Isle pattern, or they can be large and you might just position one on each front of a cardigan. If you are female, consider frostflower positions carefully, as one on each breast will just look unfortunate.

6 Nordic knitting is often worked in just black and white, sometimes with a splash of one vibrant hue, such as this red. Rather than the bands of color and pattern that Fair Isle motifs establish, Nordic knits can have quite large areas of a garment filled with just one all-over pattern, creating a bold effect that translates well into contemporary fashion.

6

Knitting notes

If you want to knit a project that is very faithful to either the Fair Isle or Nordic traditions, then the Internet is your friend. Just a little searching will find knitting blogs written by true enthusiasts and then you'll discover a wealth of patterns and artisan yarns that will allow you to recreate all sorts of traditional designs. However, it's undoubtedly worth perfecting the techniques required with commercial yarns before straying into this potentially expensive specialist world.

Contemporary colors

Changing the color scheme of a classic stranded knitting pattern can instantly freshen it and bring it right into the 21st century—this versatility is one reason why the traditional patterns are still so popular today. There are as many options to choose from as there are colors multiplied by one another, so that's more options that you could knit in a lifetime, but usually you'll want a balanced palette with colors in a range of values (see Palette 5, page 22). Do swatch a chosen pattern and palette, placing the yarns in different parts of the pattern to judge the effects (see also Palette 45, page 150).

On these pages the patterns knitted in the previous palette are reknitted in more contemporary color palettes so that you can easily see the difference colors can make.

As you can easily see by looking at Palettes 43 and 44, changing colors really can affect a pattern in sometimes unexpected ways. If you want to knit a large project but change the colors, it's a really good idea to buy just one ball of each of your proposed colors and do some concentrated swatching before committing to the expense of all the yarn needed and then discovering your palette doesn't work in the pattern you have chosen. If your local yarn store doesn't offer the service of setting aside the number of balls you need in a single dye lot, then swatching in tapestry yarns and matching the colors is a good way of avoiding expensive mistakes.

|1| Bold colors of similar values can work successfully, if quite busily, in an all-over pattern if there's a neutral to give them some space (see Palette 24, page 82). Here the red and green have almost identical values and the blue is darker (see Palette 5, page 22), but because the red is a warm color (see Palette 3, page 18) it dominates the cool green and blue, meaning that it's the green that ends up looking weakest. Without the cream this palette would be unbearably dense.

|2| Choosing a dark, rich color for the background immediately throws patterning forward, and the effect can be enhanced by making the lighter colors of similar value (see Palette 5, page 22). All the colors in this swatch are analogous, but the teal and lilac have almost identical values so they are particularly happy together.

|1|

|2|

3 | Neutrals are great background colors for intricate Fair Isle motifs and here a deep, warm red on a cool gray (see Palette 3, page 18) creates a design that's striking and contemporary, and has a minimalist appeal despite the intricacy of the pattern. This is partly to do with the choice of yarn as well as the colors: Modern yarns also come in chunkier weights not available to the original stranding knitters. Scaling up patterns by the simple expedient of knitting them in a thicker yarn can give them a less fussy feel.

4 | A bright background can make delicate patterning into an also-ran feature. This whole palette is warm (see Palette 3, page 18) and although the values vary quite a lot (see Palette 5, page 22), with the orange and yellow of the patterning being lighter and the red darker than the background, it's the saturated orange (see Palette 1, page 14) that completely dominates.

5 | Larger-scale designs can be worked in colors in the same family (see Palette 1, page 14) without losing detail, as long as the values are not too similar. A darker background with a lighter motif gives a nod to traditional color relationships in Nordic knitting, but this swatch would be equally successful with the colors reversed.

6 | While the classic black-and-white palette of traditional Nordic designs is still hugely popular and relevant to today's fashions, it's interesting to see how the designs are affected by a change of colors. This graphic, rather masculine pattern does become gentler worked in pinks, although you have to ask how much this is due to western cultural values assigning the color pink to a notion of femininity as it is to the warmth and color values of the hue (see Palette 3, page 18, and Palette 5, page 22).

45 Color balances in a palette

A fascinating experiment is to knit swatches of one pattern in a single color palette, but swap the colors around within the design. This pattern has five elements—the three stripes that make up the background and the two linear motifs—so I chose five palettes and knitted five swatches, with each color featuring in each area. But beware: If you do the math (or ask a mathematically minded friend, as I did), you'll realize that there are a potential 120 variations, and that's a lot of knitting and a lot of yarn if you want to explore them all. I chose a palette with a range of values (see Palette 5, page 22)—a dark color (purple), a light color (yellow), and three different mid-tones (blue, pink, green)—and there are two warm colors (pink and yellow) and three cool ones (green, blue, and purple) for a good overall balance (see Palette 3, page 18). Also, there are both analogous and complementary colors (see Palette 4, page 20), so overall there's the possibility of lots of interesting color relationships.

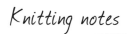

Knitting notes

To save you a huge amount of time and knitting, I suggest graphing out possible color combinations and then knitting just those that look most successful. If you have a computer and charting software then this is easy, as once you've charted the design, you can just swap the colors. There are quite a few charting programs available, mainly designed for cross-stitch but fine for knitting as long as you take stitch shape into consideration (see page 116).

1 Placing the darkest-value color and the most saturated color (pink) in the middle makes the stripiness of the pattern very prominent at the expense of the linear motifs. Even though the latter are worked in the lightest two colors and the yellow is warm against the purple, it's the central bands that draw the eye first.

2 The warm outer band frames the design and the hot pink makes the long motifs very dominant, so there is an overall balance in this combination. The dark central stripe sets off the pale smaller motifs effectively and, as the whole central striped section is cool, it recedes to give an interesting, slightly three-dimensional effect.

3 Having the background light and the linear motifs dark and hot might seem an obvious way of making the thin lines stand out, but the result is very unbalanced. The yellow is confined to such a small area that it gets lost in the pale green and is ineffective, so the overall look is too cool and the long motifs are very harsh against the background.

4 This is a generally very balanced version, the only issue being that the vertical line of the longer motifs is a bit lost against the pale green central bands; making this green just a tiny bit darker would solve this problem. The yellow and purple are analogous, with the yellow being much warmer than the purple, so the ends of the motifs are clearly defined.

5 Having the hot pink as the outer area draws the eye away from the central, and most important, part of the design, and the green and yellow rather blend together in the central band. The mid-tone blue is comfortable enough against the cool central section, but isn't strong enough to make the ends of the long motifs stand out against the pink.

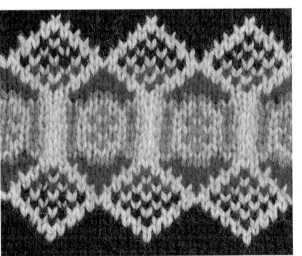

Color-effect yarns

Variegated and self-striping yarns (see Palette 7, page 32, and Palette 8, page 34) can be used to good effect in stranded knitting and provide a way of introducing more color variations without having to handle more strands of yarn. As always when using these yarns, the results can be a bit unpredictable, but swatching across the full width of the project will help you get the effect you want (see page 212).

One potential benefit of using color-effect yarns is that as there are intentional color changes within an area, the eye accepts any flecks of color created by stranding (see pages 144–45) more happily, especially if the color-effect yarn has frequent changes, and the plain colors are not too dissimilar to some of those changing colors.

3

1 In this swatch a red self-striping yarn with a long color-change is used as the background. The effect is great, and you only have two yarns to handle throughout the whole swatch. A neutral plain color such as this gray is a good choice with color-effect yarns if you want the motifs to be clear and the overall effect to be as simple as possible.

2 Here, the roles are reversed and the color-effect yarn is used for the motifs while the plain neutral makes the background. In the smaller area the color transitions are less obvious, but still effective. The floats are woven in frequently (see Knitting Notes), which does give the gray an overall rosy glow, but it's uniform, doesn't fight the neutral, and, as it picks up the motif color, it's not jarring on the eye.

3 Many color-effect yarns are lightweight—really designed for knitting socks—and so they don't make a great fabric for larger projects. However, you can find thicker versions if you hunt (the Internet will be your friend here), even going up to chunky weights, as here. If the color changes are quite short, then keep the pattern simple to avoid too much visual confusion.

[4]

[5]

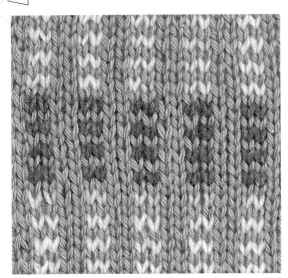

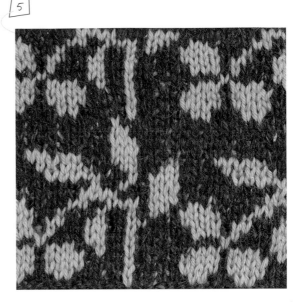

[4] Self-striping yarns that change color over long lengths can be used to make stripes of motifs that at first glance can look as though different color yarns were used to knit them. This is a super-simple pattern of flecks knitted in one yarn that changes from red to white, though it was chance that had the colors changing more or less at the ends of rows rather than in the middle of them.

[5] Tweed yarns (see Palette 10, page 38) are a common element in traditional Fair Isle designs and have one great advantage for novice stranded yarn knitters: The flecks in the tweed disguise flecks from woven-in floats (see page 145) really brilliantly. This red tweed has pink flecks in it, and you just can't tell which are flecks in the yarn and which are flecks from floats. Anything that makes starting out in color knitting easier is great.

[6] Picking out plain colors that match or echo colors in self striping yarns can let you create quite complex-looking effects relatively simply. The stripes in this swatch are the natural product of the yarn, while the spots are knitted in plain yarns. Just the sections where the spots lie are stranded, but the yarns are lightweight so the areas of additional bulk are not very noticeable.

Knitting notes

Many color-effect yarns are lightweight, usually designed for knitting socks. This doesn't make them completely unsuitable for larger projects, but bear in mind that they'll take a long time to knit and the fabric will be thin. Weaving in the floats on every alternate stitch (see page 122) has two advantages and one disadvantage: The advantages are that as the first stitch in each color is better supported than it would be by having longer floats leading to it, it is less likely to be distorted; in addition the knitted fabric is satisfyingly thick. The disadvantage is that the woven-in floats will undoubtedly show to some extent as flecks on the right side of the knitting. If you find this unattractive, you can get around it by working in short-color change yarns or tweed yarns (see swatch 5).

[6]

47 Textured yarns and stitch patterns

As much stranded knitting relies on small detail it might at first seem as though knitting it in a texture—whether it be a yarn or a stitch pattern—is just a mistake, and indeed, this idea does need to be approached with caution. The first thing to accept is that this won't work on intricate patterns; only simple patterns and larger-scale patterns, such as those common to the Nordic tradition (see page 146), really work. And only lightly textured yarns, such as mohair, cabled yarns, and short eyelash yarns, are suitable; any heavier textures just obliterate the shapes you are knitting.

Knitting notes

One element of stranded knitting that really doesn't work well with fluffy textured yarns is weaving in the floats. Strands of fluff or fur will creep out between the stitches and present themselves distractingly on the front of the knitting. The simple answer is to only choose patterns with stitch groups so close together that you don't need to weave in between them.

1 A simple chevron pattern worked in mohair yarn is effective, and though sadly you can't feel this swatch, it's deliciously thick and soft. The mohair had to be used doubled up to match the weight of the plain brown yarn: It's better to have one slightly thicker yarn than a very thin one in a piece of stranded knitting.

2 This swatch reminds me of a flock of crows against the sky; the short eyelashes look like the birds' untidy feathers and are reminiscent of their erratic flight. Another benefit of a yarn like to this to a beginner stranded knitter is that the texture will hide a multitude of slightly uneven stitches, although it's a nightmare when it comes to weaving in floats (see Knitting Notes).

3 The most straightforward way to use stitch patterns is to work bands of them between rows of motifs; here there are bands of seed stitch. To avoid colors interlacing across stitch bumps, you'll need to work a plain knit or purl row (depending on whether you are on the wrong or right side) before and after every motif. The same principles apply to bands of any stitch texture.

1

2

3

4

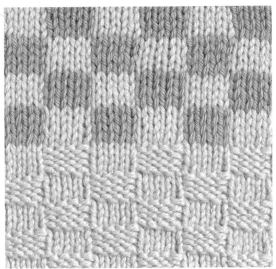

4 You can use a stitch pattern to reflect a color-patterned area, as in this swatch. Note that the color blocks and the texture blocks are both four stitches by four rows, but because of the way a purl stitch is formed, the textured blocks look shallower: To make the shapes match up a bit better you would need to add another row to each textured repeat, though the reverse stockinette blocks will always look a bit wider than the stockinette ones.

5 Trying to knit a stranded pattern in a textured stitch pattern just doesn't really work. Even with quite a simple pattern such as this zigzag, the interlacing stitch bumps muddle the edges of the shapes, and where you are working purl stitches you run into problems with stranding the yarns on the back.

6 However, knitting the same pattern but substituting reverse stockinette texture for a contrast color does create an interesting effect, although you've now moved completely away from stranded knitting and are looking at stitchwork (see Chapter 9, pages 184–211). You could knit a gorgeous project in which color stranded knitting and the same pattern worked in texture reflected each other.

5

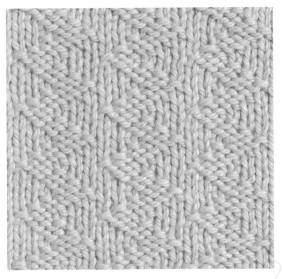

6

48 Beads and embroidery

Classic stranded patterns can be given a fresh twist with just a little embroidery, or you can use stitches to jazz up elements that are a bit less interesting than you hoped, or to disguise some irregular or baggy stitches that you haven't managed to completely fix (see page 123). Similarly, beads can add a bit more to a pattern, or you can use them to replace color stitches in a design.

1 This is a straightforward checkerboard design that's been given a bit of extra interest with a single Swiss-darned stitch (see page 55) in the center of each square. Of course, these could have been knitted and stranded, but then you would have to deal with three yarns on those rows, and single stitches can be tricky to tension beautifully in stranded knitting. The embroidery just goes from one stitch to the next with the thread lying in floats on the back at the same gauge as the knitted floats.

2 There isn't actually any stranded knitting in this swatch, it's a stripe pattern detailed with Swiss darning. The knitted stripes are, two rows white, two green, two white, seven rows green, two rows white, two green, two white. The crenellations in the border are white Swiss darning stitches on the central narrow green stripe, as are the diagonal lines on the wide green stripe.

3 Simple rows of chain stitches (see page 57) divide this chevron stranded pattern. Picking a bright accent color both highlights the stitches, and lifts the overall color palette. These are quite long chain stitches—they follow the spacing set by the knitted pattern—so it's really important to tension them carefully so that they don't pull in the knitting, or become baggy over time.

4 As long as you stick to the laundering rules (see page 214), you can use all sorts of yarns or threads to highlight stranded patterns. This swatch its knitted with a stripe-and-square pattern and the blocks are embellished with cross-stitches in (top to bottom) crewel wool, eyelash embroidery thread, chenille embroidery thread, and fine woolen yarn. As with swatch 1, on the back the threads are floated between stitches at the same gauge as the knitted floats.

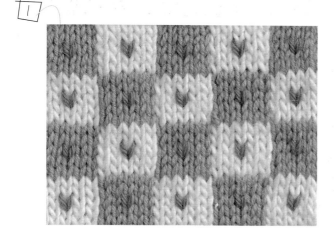

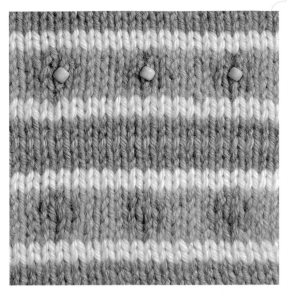

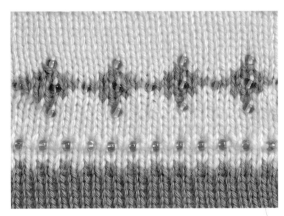

Knitting notes

The secrets of perfect Swiss darning
are the right yarn and a gentle stitch
gauge. It's ideal if you can use the
same brand of yarn as was used to
work the knitting, but if that isn't
possible, it must certainly be the
same weight. If it's too thick then the
stitches will be proud and lumpy; if
it's too thin then the Swiss darning
won't cover the knitted stitches and
the effect won't work.

5 You can use colored beads
instead of single color stitches in a
stranded design. In this swatch the
single stitches in the bottom row of
motifs are Swiss-darned (easier than
stranding and knitting them in) and in
the top row those stitches are
replaced with beads placed using the
knitted-in method (see page 52). The
important thing with beading
stranded knitting is to be very clear
as to which bobbin of yarn you need
to thread the beads onto.

6 Thickly beading an entire
stranded garment might well make it
too heavy (remember that the fabric is
already double thickness), but beads in
just one or two parts of a design can be
a lovely detail. Here, all the beads are
threaded onto the cream yarn—the
green beads threaded on first (used
last), before the blue beads. The blue
beads are placed using the slip stitch
method (see page 52), while the green
ones use the knitted-in method.

8 Aran knitting

There is a certain amount of (usually good-natured) argument over the history of Aran knitting, but it's certain that "ganseys," knitted, textured jumpers (not sweaters), have been produced in the islands off the coast of Ireland for centuries. What is now popularly known as Aran knitting is certainly linked to the eponymous islands, and no matter which name you give them, the traditional patterns carry a lot of history in their stitches; some have cultural and religious meanings as well.

The patterns were originally used to knit sweaters for fishermen, and different fishing families had their own design of intricate patterning for their men's garments. The heavy patterning made the garments very thick and helped protect the men from injury, and—rather more morbidly—if they were drowned at sea, the distinct family patterns helped identify a washed-up body that had been in the water for a while. Arans are traditionally worked in cream yarn because they were once made from sheep fleece that was left unscoured to keep the water-resistant lanolin in the yarn.

Aran techniques

Beginner knitters tend to view Aran patterns with trepidation; all those crossing and looping stitches can look ridiculously complicated to knit. But although it's true that the more intricate patterns need a lot of attention paying to them, the actual techniques involved really aren't difficult to master. Cables involve moving one set of stitches across another set with the help of a little cable needle, and bobbles involve increasing and decreasing. Other techniques need you to knit the second stitch on a needle before the first, but while that requires a bit of manipulation, it's not hard to do. So don't be afraid of Aran knitting, it's actually one of those great techniques that produce a wonderful effect for not too much work.

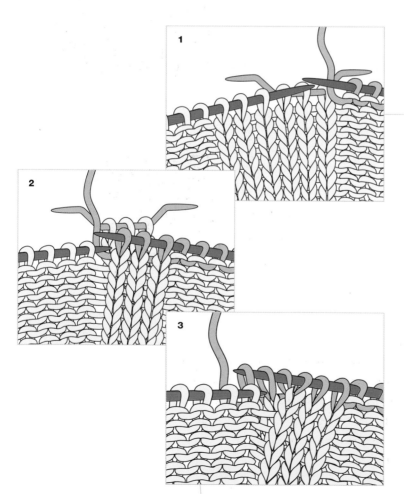

CABLE

The mainstay of most Aran patterns, cables are are all worked following the same basic method, though different numbers of stitches are used. The number of stitches always refers to the whole number in the cable, not the number you slip onto the cable needle. So in C6B (cable six back), the six-stitch cable shown here, you slip three stitches onto the cable needle to cross them in front of the other three. For C4B (cable four back), two stitches would slipped onto the cable needle to be crossed behind the other two making up the cable. These types of cables are sometimes called rope cables.

Cable six back (C6B):

For a back cable you hold the cable needle at the back of the knitting and the twist will go to the right.

1 Work to the position of the cable. Slip the first three of the cable stitches from the left-hand needle onto the cable needle. Leave this at the back of the knitting.

2 Knit the next three stitches (the remaining three cable stitches) from the left-hand needle, going in front of the cable needle to do so.

3 Knit the three stitches that are held on the cable needle to complete the cable six back.

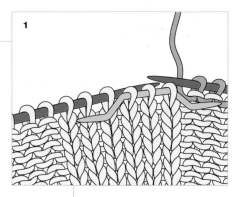

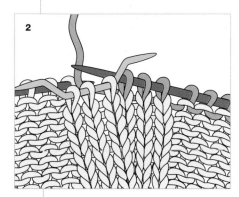

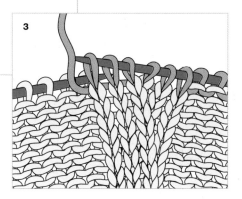

Cable six front (C6F):

A front cable means that you
hold the cable needle at the front
of the work and the twist will
go to the left.

1 Work to the position of the cable.
Slip the first three of the cable stitches
from the left-hand needle onto the
cable needle. Leave this at the front of
the knitting.

2 Knit the next three stitches (the
remaining three cable stitches) from the
left-hand needle, going behind the
cable needle to do so.

3 Knit the three stitches that are held
on the cable needle to complete the
cable six front.

Knitting notes

When you cast on for a cabled piece, cast on only half the number of stitches
needed for the actual cables (so, for each C6B, cast on three stitches). On the
first row increase into each cable stitch to create the number needed. This
prevents the cast-on edge flaring out at the base of the cable. When you bind
off, knit two stitches together across the top of the cable, binding off as you
go, to prevent the top edge flaring.

TWIST STITCHES

Worked using the same principle as cables, twist stitches move stitches across a background to make a wandering cable, rather than over another group of stitches to produce a rope cable (see page 160). As with cables, this technique can be used with different numbers of stitches.

Twist three back (T3B):

This twist will move two stitches in stockinette across to the right on a background of reverse stockinette.

1 Work to one stitch before the stitches you are going to move. Slip the next stitch onto the cable needle, slipping it purlwise if the background is reverse stockinette stitch. Leave this at the back of the knitting.

2 Knit the next two stitches (the ones that will move) from the left-hand needle.

3 Purl the stitch that is held on the cable needle to complete the twist three back.

Knitting notes

Use a bent or "U"-shaped cable needle when you first start cabling; these make it very difficult for the stitches being held to fall off and so give you one less thing to worry about.

Many knitters find that the first purled background stitch after the cable is baggy, especially on the twist rows. Purling into the back of this stitch will help to tighten it and stop the stitches looking stretched.

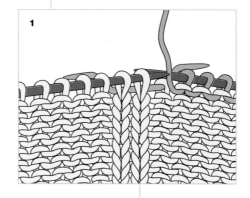

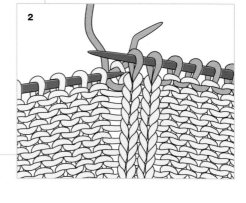

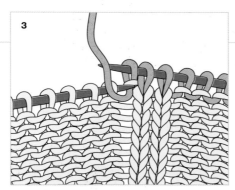

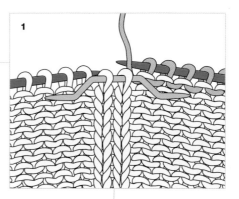

Twist three front (T3F):

This twist will move two stitches in stockinette across to the left.

1 Work to the two stitches you are going to move and slip them onto the cable needle. Leave this at the front of the knitting.

2 Purl the next stitch on the left-hand needle.

3 Knit the two stitches that are held on the cable needle to complete the twist three front.

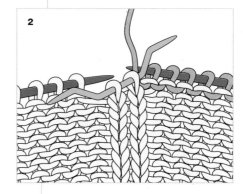

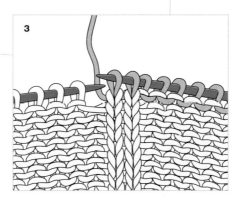

CROSSED STITCHES

You don't need a cable needle to move just one stitch. Crossed stitches move a single stitch across a background worked in the same stitch. Moving the same stitch on every knit row creates a wandering line; moving the same stitch position creates a band of light texture.

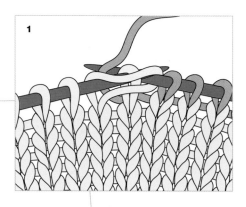

Cross two right (C2R):

This cross moves a single stitch to the right and is sometimes called cross two back (C2B).

1 Work to one stitch before the stitch you are going to move. Put the right-hand needle knitwise into the second stitch on the left-hand needle and knit it, but do not drop the original stitch off the left-hand needle.

2 Put the right-hand needle knitwise into the first stitch on the left-hand needle. Knit this stitch, then drop both original stitches off the left-hand needle.

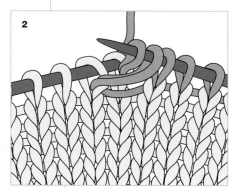

Knitting notes

You can move stitches across any stitch pattern background— just be careful to maintain the correct arrangement of knit and purl stitches. The background stitch might be worked differently to how it would have been if left in place, so it's best to look at the stitch next to it in its new position, rather than judging it by the stitch that came before it.

Cross two left (C2L):

This cross moves a single stitch to the left, and is sometimes called cross two front (C2F)

1 Work to the stitch you are going to move. Put the right-hand needle into the back of the second stitch on the left-hand needle and knit it, but do not drop the original stitch off the left-hand needle.

2 Put the right-hand needle knitwise into the first stitch on the left-hand needle. Knit this stitch, then drop both original stitches off the left-hand needle.

Knitting notes

When working crossed stitches, try not to stretch the two stitches you are moving too much. A little stretching is inevitable, but if you overstretch then the crossed stitch will be baggy. If you are struggling to move one stitch neatly, you can always use a cable needle in the same way as for twist stitches (see page 162).

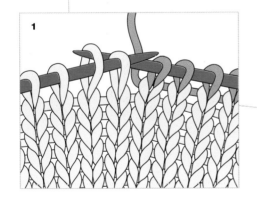

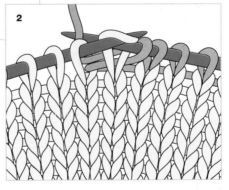

TWISTED STITCHES

Twisted stitches use the same principles as crossed stitches to move a single stitch knitted in one stitch pattern (usually stockinette) across a background knitted in a different stitch pattern (usually reverse stockinette stitch).

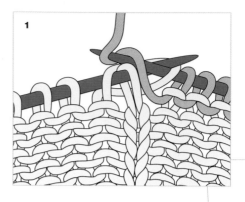

Twist two right (T2R):

This twist moves a single stitch to the right, and is sometimes called twist two back (T2B).

1 Work to one stitch before the stitch you are going to move. Put the right-hand needle knitwise into the second stitch on the left-hand needle and knit it, but do not drop the original stitch off the left-hand needle.

2 Bring the yarn between the needles to the front of the work and purl the first stitch on the left-hand needle, then drop both original stitches off the left-hand needle.

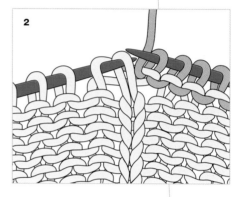

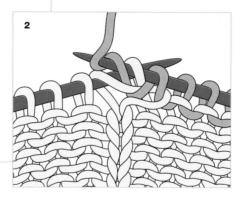

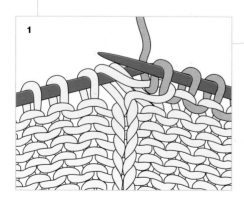

Knitting notes

Be aware that the abbreviations for twisted stitches and twist stitches (see page 162) aren't standardized, so do check which is being referred to in a pattern you are knitting.

WORKING FROM A CHART

As with color patterns (see page 114) Aran patterns can also be presented as charts. This isn't as common as it is for color knitting, but some knitters find charts offer a much clearer view of the overall pattern than written instructions do.

Aran patterns use symbols to describe the stitches and sadly these aren't universal, so you do need to check what's what in any chart you follow. In this chart the short horizontal lines mean "purl on right-side rows and knit on wrong-side rows" (reverse stockinette stitch), and the short vertical lines mean "knit on right-side rows and purl on wrong-side rows" (stockinette stitch).

The diagonal lines mean "C6B" (cable six back). So what this chart is describing is a C6B (see also page 160), over six rows on a background of reverse stockinette stitch. If this pattern were written out it would read as follows:

Panel of 6 sts on background
of rev st st.
Row 1 (RS): K6.
Row 2: P6.
Row 3: C6B.
Row 4: As row 2.
Rows 5–6: As rows 1–2.
Rep these 6 rows.

The reverse stockinette background is not included in the written pattern as it can be whatever width you desire.

Twist 2 front (T2L):

This twist moves a single stitch to the left and is sometimes called twist 2 front (T2F)

1 Work to the stitch you are going to move. Purl the second stitch on the left-hand needle through the back of the loop, but do not drop the original stitch off the left-hand needle.

2 Move the right-hand needle in front of the left-hand needle and take the yarn between the needles to the back of the work. Knit the first stitch on the left-hand needle, then drop both original stitches off the left-hand needle.

Cable chart

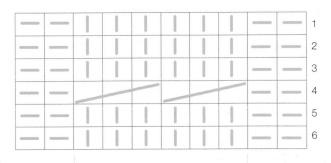

6 stitches

p on RS: k on WS

k on RS: p on WS

C6B

BOBBLES

Bobbles are another key ingredient of many Aran patterns, and there are many versions of them. The three versions shown here are different sizes and are worked in different ways, and most bobble patterns you encounter will be similar to one or another of these.

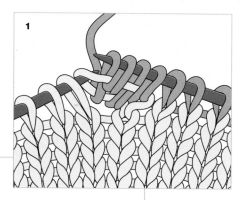

Knot:

These knots are just small bumps in the knitted fabric and are sometimes called popcorn bobbles.

1 Work to the position of the bobble. Increase twice into the next stitch (knit into the front, then the back, the front again, and then the back again), then slip the original stitch off the left-hand needle. You have made four stitches out of one.

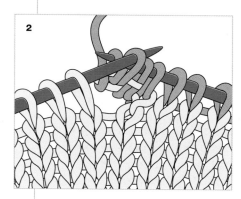

2 Insert the tip of the left-hand needle into the second stitch on the right-hand needle and lift that stitch over the first one.

3 In the same way, lift the third and fourth stitches in turn over the first one, to be left with one stitch and a completed knot.

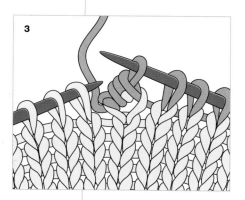

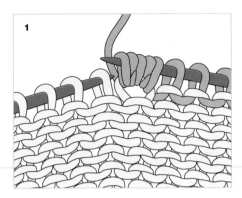

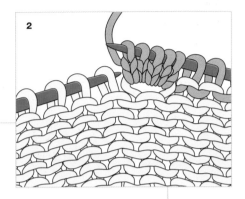

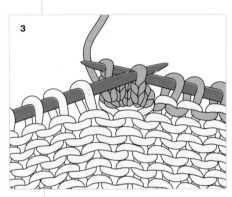

Small bobble:

This bobble uses yarnovers (see pages 188–189) to increase the number of stitches.

1 Work to the position of the bobble. Knit into the next stitch, but do not drop it off the left-hand needle; make a yarnover, knit into the stitch again without dropping it, make a second yarnover, then knit into the stitch for a third time and drop it off the left-hand needle. You have made five stitches out of one.

2 Turn the knitting (just swap the needles in your hands) and purl the five bobble stitches. Turn the knitting again and knit the five stitches.

3 Turn the knitting and p2tog (see page 192), purl one stitch, then p2tog again to make three stitches. Turn the knitting and sk2po (see page 193) to be left with one stitch and a completed bobble.

Knitting notes

These bobbles are all stockinette stitch, and the knot is worked on stockinette, while the small bobble and large bobble (see page 170) are worked on reverse stockinette. But bobbles can also be worked in stitch patterns and on stitch-patterned backgrounds to create even more texture. Try working the large bobble in seed stitch or garter stitch on a stockinette background, or work it in stockinette on a seed stitch background. Once you're familiar with making bobbles (and have picked a favorite—most knitters have a favorite bobble), you can experiment with different stitches and colors (see swatch 6, Palette 51, page 177).

Large bobble:

This bobble will be large and firm, so very prominent on the knitting.

1 Work to the position of the bobble. Increase twice into the next stitch (knit into the front, then the back, the front again, and then the back again), then slip the original stitch off the left-hand needle. You have made four stitches out of one.

2 Turn the knitting (just swap the needles in your hands) and purl the four bobble stitches. Turn the knitting again and knit the four stitches. Turn the knitting yet again and purl the four stitches.

3 Turn the knitting for a final time. Slip the first two stitches knitwise (see page 96) onto the right-hand needle, k2tog (see page 191) then pass the two slipped stitches over the knitted one to be left with one stitch and a completed bobble.

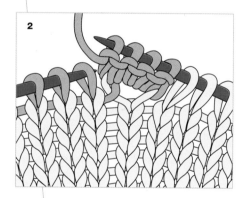

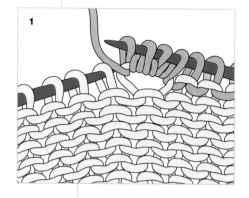

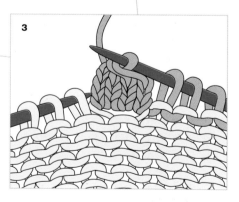

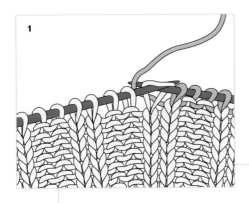

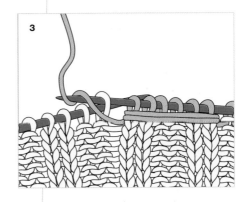

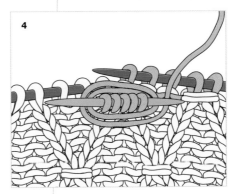

BOUND STITCHES

You can bind groups of stitches together to create a smocked effect. Here, the knitting is a double rib fabric and two knit, two purl, and two knit stitches are bound together, but the stitch pattern and the number of stitches being bound can vary.

1 Work to the six stitches to be bound, then work those stitches in pattern.

2 Slip the six stitches onto a cable needle. Take the working yarn between the cable needle and the left-hand needle to the front, then wrap it counterclockwise twice around the stitches on the cable needle. Wrap it quite loosely at this stage.

3 Slip the bound stitches back onto the right-hand needle. Gently pull the yarn and adjust the wraps to bunch the stitches as tightly together as you wish, then continue to knit along the row.

4 Stitches can be bound into columns or into a diamond pattern as here, or use a combination of both to make the most of the smocked effect.

49 Aran patterns

There are literally dozens and dozens of Aran stitch patterns to choose from, including cables, bobbles, panels, and all-over patterns. Any good stitch directory will offer plenty of choice, and indeed, if you develop a passion for this style of knitting there are Aran-only directories to explore. Here is a selection of popular patterns, worked in classic, worsted-weight cream yarn that shows up shadows well to make the most of the depths of the textures.

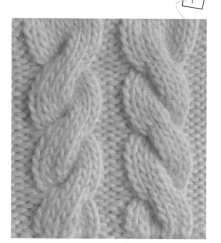

1 This is a classic rope-twist cable pattern. The cable on the right is a C8F and that on the left is a C8B (see page 160), and they twist on every eighth row. Using mirrored cables in a pattern is a very easy way to refine a simple design just a little: The twists can move toward one another, as here, or swap their positions and have them twisting away from one another.

2 This is a slightly more complex cable pattern, though it uses nothing more than the straightforward front and back cables of the previous swatch. It's a nine-stitch panel on a reverse stockinette fabric with a 20-row repeat, so it needs to appear over quite a long length for the best effect.

3 Ring cables are a staple of many Aran designs. These are quite large rings and the middles of them are stockinette, making this a very quick and easy pattern to work. Again, at this scale it's a pattern best worked over quite a large area, though there are smaller variations that work well on little projects, such as caps and mittens.

4 OXO cables, sometimes called "noughts and crosses" cables, are a personal favorite. They are as easy to work as any other cable pattern, but look charmingly complex. Many stitch dictionaries will have versions of these cables worked over different numbers of rows to change the scale.

5 In the original Aran sweaters every part of the knitting was patterned, including the rib. This is a simple double-rib pattern in which groups of stitches are bound at various intervals (see page 171) to pull them together in a smocked effect. The rib loses some elasticity because of this, but is still stretchy enough to perform its function around the bottom of a sweater.

6 Some all-over Aran patterns work the opposite way to most in that they look quite simple, but are tricky to work, and this is one such. None of the actions are in themselves difficult, but there are twisted stitches (see page 166) as well as cable crosses to keep abreast of. The fabric produced is quite stiff, and these patterns generally made up narrow panels in traditional designs.

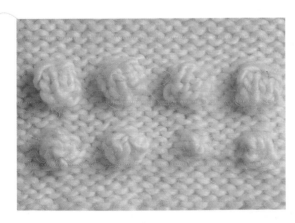

7 Bobbles are an easy-to-work staple of lots of Aran designs, either standing alone, integrated into an all-over pattern, or nestling in the twists and turns of a cable. They can be worked in different sizes, and when there are no turning bobble rows—just increases and immediate decreases—bobbles are often called "knots." All the samples here are worked over four stitches and the bobbles on the top row are worked over four rows: From the right they are a stockinette bobble, a reverse stockinette, a seed, and another stockinette bobble. On the bottom row from the right they are a stockinette knot, a reverse stockinette knot, then a stockinette and a reverse stockinette small bobble.

50 Aran in color

Although Aran patterns are lovely in traditional cream, just because something is traditional doesn't make it infallible, and Aran patterns can look magnificent in color. It can give them an immediate contemporary twist, allowing you to follow a vintage pattern and go out in a garment that is inspiringly modern while still acknowledging its retro roots.

Generally, lighter colors make more of the shadows the stitch patterns create, while darker colors that obscure those shadows visually flatten the patterns, but the impact of the color can be enough to compensate for any lost subtlety. As an Aran sweater can involve many weeks of painstaking knitting, it is a very good idea indeed to swatch (see page 212) every pattern element you intend to use to make sure you like it in the color you are planning. You might find that you need to substitute a bolder cable or make a bobble bigger in order for it to hold its own in the design. The swatches shown below are all variations of the patterns in Palette 49 (see page 172), so that you can easily appreciate the differences color brings to them.

2 Although this is not a dark color, it is a strong, warm one, and it doesn't do a lot for this more complex cable. Often you can find an Aran pattern that can be worked over different numbers of rows, and this is the same basic design as swatch 2 of Palette 49, but with a shorter row repeat, and worked in a finer yarn. The very bright yellow allows for some shadows, but is just too powerful for what is now quite a subtle pattern. Lost in a sea of yellow, the eye skims over the little cable twists.

3 This is exactly the same pattern as swatch 3 in the previous palette, but it is worked in a thinner yarn, to a firm gauge, and the background is worked in stockinette rather than reverse stockinette. When a cable is as raised as this, you can get away with using a stockinette background without the stitch pattern disappearing into it, as long as the gauge is not too loose. This looks good and also gets around the problem of baggy stitches after the cable (see Knitting Notes, page 162). Because this is such a raised cable it can take quite a strong color and still be attractively clear. The orange is a modern shade—well away from the tangerine notes of the '50s and '60s and the earthy oranges of earlier decades—and yet the time-honored pattern sits happily with it.

1 Here are the classic cables again, but worked in deep red. The cable on the right is a C8F and that on the left is a C8B (see page 160), and they twist on every eighth row, as before, but the yarn is a sport-weight rather than an Aran weight, so as well as actually being smaller, they also look less bulky—a bit more refined. As this is a simple, strong pattern, it survives well in a deep color; the twists may not be well-defined by their shadows, but they are still perfectly clear.

1

2

3

4

5

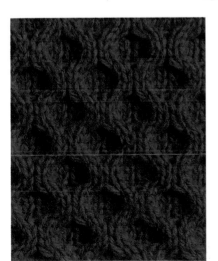

6

7

4 If you want to add just a little color to an Aran design, then pastels are the way to go. This pale primrose yellow is only a few degrees stronger than the traditional cream, but is quite definitely a color. The defining shadows are as strong as on swatch 4 on page 172 and this pattern loses nothing through the introduction of color. The pattern is the classic OXO, but worked in a finer yarn like this it would be great on a child's garment: The chunky scale of Aran patterns in heavy yarn can swamp a little person.

5 This variation of the wrapped stitch pattern (swatch 5) in the previous palette is lovely in this firm-twist, color-dappled yarn. The color variation is very slight and doesn't in any way detract from the pattern (see Palette 52, page 178, for ideas on working Aran patterns in color-effect yarns), and the overall tone is bright and light enough to avoid visually flattening the shadows needed to define the columns. As an added twist, the intervals between the wraps vary in this version to make the overall pattern a bit more dynamic.

6 This is another all-over pattern and one that has a very strongly raised and indented surface. Such patterns revel in strong vibrant color; they loose nothing and the addition of color hauls them happily into the front line of contemporary knitting. This pattern is worked in a sport-weight yarn and to a firm gauge to keep the rings as pronounced as possible, and so the fabric is quite stiff. It wouldn't be great for a sweater, but would be absolutely ideal as a bag or a pillow.

7 As mentioned on page 159, Aran patterns were traditionally made up of combinations of stitch patterns and the combinations were unique to each family in a small community. There are too many of us now for anyone to have a unique combination, but you can make your Aran project stand out with the simple addition of color. This lovely yellow is light enough to let the shadows develop, but bright enough to make a statement, and it complements the collection of cables, bobbles, and all-over pattern beautifully.

51 Multicolor Aran

Palettes 49 and 50 (see pages 172 and 174) look at how and why different single colors affect Aran patterns, but you can use more than one color to knit an Aran design. You need to be a decent intarsia knitter (see pages 112–35 for techniques), and be prepared to darn in lots of ends, but the effects you can achieve are well worth the effort involved (and in many instances, the patterns look more impressively complicated than they actually are).

1. As long as you work out the cable twist repeat and the stripe repeat carefully, classic stripes can add a lot to a basic cable. This is a C6F cable (see page 160 for cable techniques) with the twist made every eight rows: the stripes are eight rows wide and sit over the twists to highlight them. An added bonus of striping conventional cables is that if you join in the new color on a right-side row, you get a different edge to the stripes on the reverse stockinette background and stockinette cable.

2. Contrast cables are knitted using the intarsia technique for changing colors in a straight line (see page 119). Do NOT be tempted to strand the yarn across the back of the cable (see pages 139–42) as it's both hard to keep the gauge even across such a narrow strip, and it causes problems when you twist the cable. This cable is made by working C4B and C4F next to each other on every sixth row. Another feature of working contrast color cables is that you can knit the whole piece in stockinette stitch as the color—rather than the reverse stockinette background—frames the cable. The darker cable color doesn't allow shadows to highlight the pattern, but it does make for a dramatic textured stripe.

3. A two-color contrast cable looks complex, but is actually quite easy to work. Use the intarsia method again and manage the bobbins carefully to avoid tangles (see page 117). This is a C6B cable with each cable color worked across three stitches and the candy-stick twists work really well on the strongly colored background. As with swatch 2, the whole piece is knitted in stockinette stitch: This solves the problem for those who always end up with baggy background stitches on the left of their cables.

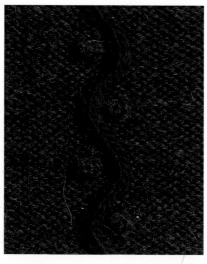

4 You can also knit wandering cables in a contrast color. For this narrow T3B/T3F (see page 162–63) zigzag, it's fine to strand the background yarn across the back of the two contrast stitches (see pages 134–139). However, contrast bobbles (see swatch 6) don't work neatly on a reverse stockinette fabric as you get flecks of the background color in the bobble. Instead, these bobbles are worked in stockinette stitch to give them a bit more emphasis.

5 Bobbles—as well as cables— work well with stripes, but you will need to swatch (see page 212) to get the position right. This is a three-row bobble (see page 169) and, like all bobbles, it sits low on its row, so the stripe needs to be wider at the bottom to accommodate it. These are four-row stripes starting with a knit row, and the bobble is worked on the third row. Pronounced bobbles work well with stronger colors, so you can work bold stripes.

6 Contrast bobbles are a cute way to add accent color, but they do require a lot of ends darning in—two ends for each bobble. You need to work a foundation stitch in the bobble color in the row before the bobble. This is so that when you twist the foundation stitch to knit into the front and back of it, no flecks of the background color appear in the base of the bobble. So work out where the bobble will be on the purl row before it, then knit a single stitch in the bobble color in the right place: You can cut a length of yarn (12in/30cm is usually ample), to work with rather than joining in a whole ball. When the bobble is complete and you have worked a few more rows, pull on the tails of contrast yarn to tighten and neaten the bobble, before sewing the ends in.

5

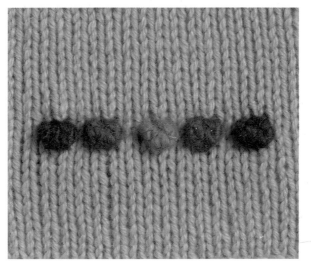

6

Knitting notes

If you are so inclined, you can knit very complicated Aran patterns in multicolors: Choose one color for the background, another for twist cables, a third for wandering cables, a fourth for inserts in diamond cables, and a fifth color for bobbles. If you are undertaking such an ambitious enterprise, it is well worth writing out the pattern repeat adding in A, B, C, etc. for the different colors before you start.

52 | Aran in color-effect yarns

This really is pushing the concept of Aran designs in color as far as it can go, and the results are a bit hit-and-miss. But without experimentation you never know how something will turn out, and some of the results are lovely. I'm absolutely sure that I don't need to remind you that it'll be essential to buy just one ball of a yarn and work a swatch (see page 212) before buying all the balls needed for a project (especially as color-effect yarns can be so expensive), but I am going to mention it in case this is the first bit of this book that you have read.

1 This gently variegated (see Palette 7, page 32) green yarn is subtle enough, and has an overall tone that is light enough, not to overwhelm what is quite a detailed Aran pattern. As the yarn is also quite fine, the definition of the seed stitch within each V shape is lost, but you can see it as texture and so the effect is not entirely spoiled. Variegated yarns like this have a distressed, well-worn effect that works well with vintage patterns, and so can complement a classic Aran design if you want it to hark back to a previous era.

2 As tweed yarns and Aran patterns are both Celtic in origin, one naively and fondly imagines that they might work well together. In real life such line-ups rarely work out, but here it does work out, and rather beautifully. As long as the overall color is fairly light (see Palette 50, page 174), the gentle color variations of tweeds (see Palette 10, page 38) don't detract unduly from the twists and turns of the Aran patterns. This is a heather-mix tweed, but flecked tweeds work, too.

3 In many ways this swatch just doesn't work—the multicolored variegated yarn, the reverse stockinette background, and the intricate cable pattern all add up to far too much; but it does have charm. The brightness of the colors and wriggles of the pattern are lively and fun and the flecked background does make the Aran pattern stand out. This would be too much on a large scale, but if you were working a project in a yarn like this, a single panel or a detail in this pattern might be a cute touch.

1

2

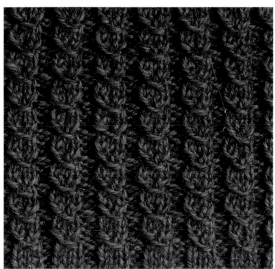

4 This tweedy, multicolored self-striping yarn combines fairly well with this all-over Aran pattern. The pattern is not very bold to start with, and the brighter pink sections of yarn visually flatten it a bit, but the color transition section is especially successful, and the overall textured effect is comfortable on the eye. Again, you probably wouldn't work this over a whole project, but it would make a very good panel in a stockinette project.

5 This is a fairly intricate pattern at the best of times; a wrapped 4 x 2 rib (see page 171), but worked in a two-color-ply self-striping yarn it just becomes a blur of color. The colors are harmonious, but all detail is entirely lost. This yarn is made from two plies of different colors that both change color, but do so at different intervals; to see what a similar yarn looks like in stockinette, look at swatch 1 in Palette 7, page 32.

6 This is such a lovely yarn, but it doesn't help this branching cable pattern at all. The yarn is fluffy as well as self-striping, and (unsurprisingly if you have looked at Palette 12, page 42, or Palette 14, page 46), texture of any kind doesn't work well with Aran patterns. Save this yarn for a gorgeous stockinette project where there is no oddly lumpy texture to distract from its loveliness.

53 Embellishing Aran patterns

Although they are already decorative in their own right, you can embellish Aran patterns further by adding beads and trims. Beads need to be knitted in as you work, so it's best to either write the placement into your pattern or graph the positions before you start. Many trims can be sewn on after the knitting is complete if you feel that it's looking a bit plainer than you hoped.

Do consider the elasticity of the knitting when sewing on a trim: Even if the trim you are using stretches, the stitches holding it on won't and that will be a problem around, for example, cuffs that need to stretch in order to get the garment on. I sewed on all these trims with polyester sewing thread, other than the buttons, which I sewed on with crewel wool.

1 Beads on this wandering cable were placed using the slip stitch method (see page 52). It's a six-stitch cable (see page 160) and they sit across the middle stitch of the upper section, placed between the twist rows. You can bead rope cables just as easily, but the beads tend to look as though they are sitting in diagonal lines rather than emphasizing the twists.

2 Beaded bobbles can be fun (see page 168 for bobble technique). The bottom bobble on this swatch has a small bead knitted in (see page 52) on every stitch after the increases and before the decreases. The top bobble has a single large bead placed in the middle of it using the slip stitch method (see page 52).

3 For me, the spaces in looping cable patterns are just crying out to have something put in them. There are all sorts of little trims commercially available that might suit your project: ribbon flowers, myriad beads, small charms, a sprinkling of beads… This swatch has a sparkly pom-pom in the lowest loop, a stack of sequins topped with a bead in the next one, and a button in the top loop. All three together are a bit much, but one or two at random in a cable pattern would be lovely.

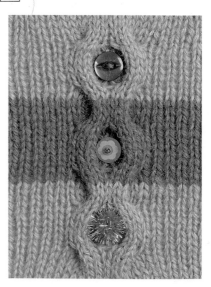

4

5

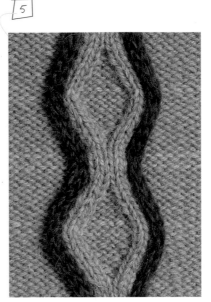

4 You can arrange Aran shapes to be part of an embellished motif; this owl has Aran ring eyes with mismatched buttons in them, and his ears and beak are worked using the intarsia technique (see page 119–23). There are a few straight embroidery stitches along the edge of his ears. Combining different decorative techniques can produce lively and original motifs.

5 You can add emphasis to part of a cable pattern by outlining it in a stronger or contrast color. You can knit I-cords or use (as I did) a chunky yarn— although don't use a very loosely plied one as it won't wear well: This yarn is actually a tube knitted from very fine yarn; effectively a very long I-cord.

6 If you take the last swatch a step further, you can do away with the knitted Aran patterns and create facsimiles with I-cord or yarn. The bobble in the middle of this "cable" is a large French knot (see page 57). While these fake cables will never be mistaken for the real thing, they can be a fun way of adding texture to a project that hasn't turned out as interesting as you hoped.

Knitting notes

The usual issues of laundering apply to embellished knitting. Beads need to be able to be washed by hand (generally, machine-washing beads isn't a great idea), and trims should ideally be made of the same fiber as the yarn in case of any slight shrinkage, although careful hand-washing will usually be okay. Sew a scrap of the proposed trim to your gauge swatch and wash it to check that it doesn't shrink or spoil in any way (see also page 214).

6

54 Aran patterns and embroidery

Generally embroidery can be added once a project is complete, if you think it needs a bit more embellishment, though in some instances you might need to plan spacing to accommodate stitches (see swatch 3). Bear in mind the laundering rules (see page 214) and that embroidery stitches can prevent knitting stretching. It's also best to embroider each motif separately, darning the ends of thread into the back of the stitches, rather than having strands of thread running between motifs: Strands can snap if the knitting is stretched and can snag on fingers or other garments.

1 Chain stitch (see page 57) is particularly complementary to knitting as the shape of the embroidery stitch reflects the shapes of a knitted stitch. In this swatch a simple C6B cable (see page 160) is embroidered with lines of chain stitch that follow the twists of the pattern. Fine crewel wool is used and where the plain section of the cable twists over the embroidered section, the stitches are secured just under the twist and the yarn taken through to the back to emerge and start stitching again where needed.

2 If you work a cable with a stockinette background (see also swatch 3, Palette 50, page 174), you can use embroidery to edge and define the cable twists. Here, tapestry wools are used to embroider rows of running stitches (see page 56) that then have a different-colored wool weaved in and out of them to create curving lines that complement the shape of the cable.

3 Bobbles (see pages 168–70) and embroidery stitches can work beautifully together. In this swatch, from the bottom up, the first bobble has strands of two different-weight yarns brought up through it and then around and through to the back. This bobble is topped with a French knot (see page 57). The next bobble has a coil of chain stitch (see page 57) curling around its base: You might need to plan and leave space for this. The next bobble is completely covered in French knots worked in two shades of orange crewel wool; this makes the bobble very firm indeed. The top bobble is the center of a lazy daisy flower (see page 57); again you'd probably need to plan for this because you'll need quite a bit of space to fit in the petals.

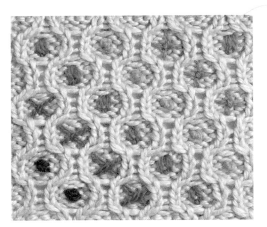

4 You might not want to embroider every divot in an all-over Aran pattern, but tiny motifs in a few of them add splashes of color. Here there are French knots (see page 57), detached chain stitches (see page 57), and vertical and diagonal cross-stitches (see page 56). Bear in mind that connected areas of embroidery will stop knitting stretching, so don't leave long strands of thread from one stitch to another on the back of the work.

5 You can also use embroidery stitches to completely fill in areas. This swatch is the same pattern as swatch 1 of Palette 53, but the snaking curve of the cable is further emphasized by filling in parts of it with closely packed rows of chain stitches. Filling in like this does make the fabric firm and inelastic, so it needs to be used with caution.

Knitting notes

If you are working with traditional-weight yarns for an Aran design, then you will need quite a chunky embroidery yarn to prevent the stitches from disappearing into the knitted texture. Tapestry wools are available in a huge variety of colors and work well with worsted-weight yarns. If you want a thicker embroidery yarn, look for rug wool that can be bought in cones and skeins.

9 Stitchwork

There are only two basic stitches in knitting, the knit stitch and the purl stitch, yet with just these you can create hundreds of different texture patterns. Novice knitters are sometimes put off trying these patterns because they look complex, but the actual techniques aren't difficult—it's keeping track of where you are in a pattern and getting the stitch gauge right that can be tricky, sometimes even for skilled knitters. However, once you've practiced a pattern a couple of times you'll be more familiar with the repeats and can concentrate on perfecting the stitches rather than worrying about what comes next in a row.

Stitchwork patterns do change the gauge and drape of a fabric, so you can't just substitute one pattern for another in a project. However, you can include panels and single motifs quite easily as long as you work a gauge swatch (see page 212) first, and these are great ways of adding a bit of texture and detail to plain knitting.

This chapter explores lace patterns and knit and purl texture patterns. If you are interested in Aran knitting turn to Chapter 8 (see pages 158–83), and for slip stitch textures turn to Chapter 5, Palette 7 (see pages 108–109).

Stitchwork technique

Other than knit and purl stitches, the techniques you need to know to create texture stitch patterns are mainly increases and decreases, as it's adding and taking away stitches that shapes so many of these patterns. Yarnovers can be used to add a stitch as well as create an eyelet in lace patterns. As with so many knitting techniques, nothing here is actually hard to do; just read the instructions carefully and practice on a swatch before embarking on a project.

YARNOVERS

These are formed by taking the yarn over the right-hand needle before working the next stitch, leaving a loop that can be worked into as a stitch on the next row. Exactly how this is done depends on the combination of knit and purl stitches either side of the yarnover. In the USA all these types of loops are just called "yarnover," but in the UK each has a different name and it's necessary to understand the differences between them in order to work them properly.

Yarn forward (yfwd):

This is how to work a yarnover between two knit stitches.

1 Bring the yarn forward between the tips of the needles.

2 Take the yarn over the right-hand needle to the back of the knitting and knit the next stitch.

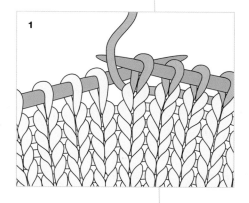

Knitting notes

All yarnovers will produce a small hole or eyelet, which can be part of a lace pattern, or works well as a buttonhole or drawstring hole. If you work a two-stitch decrease (see page 190) immediately before or after the yarnover, the hole will remain but the number of stitches won't increase. You can reinforce the edge of an eyelet with embroidery stitches (see Palette 19, page 66), which is decorative and practical for buttonholes or drawstring holes.

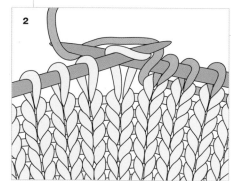

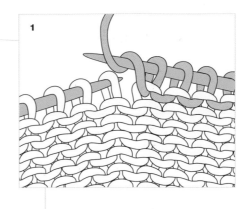

Yarn round needle (yrn):

This is how to work a yarnover between two purl stitches.

1 Take the yarn over and right around the right-hand needle so that it comes between the tips of the needles to the front again.

2 Purl the next stitch.

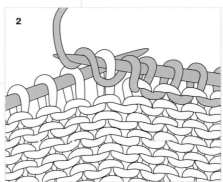

Yarn forward round needle (yfrn):

This is how to work a yarnover after a knit stitch and before a purl stitch.

1 After the knit stitch, bring the yarn forward between the tips of the needles, then take it over and right around the right-hand needle so that it comes between the tips of the needles to the front again.

2 Purl the next stitch.

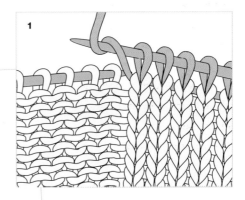

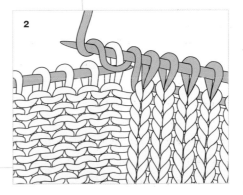

Yarn over needle (yon):

This is how to work a yarnover after a purl stitch and before a knit stitch.

1 After the purl stitch, put the tip of the right-hand needle knitwise into the next stitch.

2 Take the yarn over the right-hand needle to the back of the knitting and knit the next stitch.

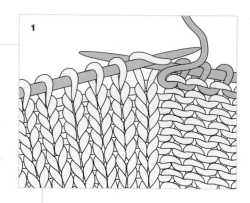

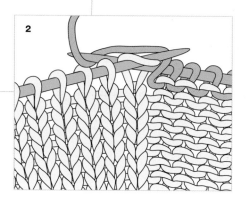

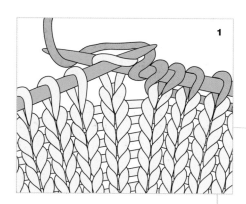

The same principle applies for all types of yarnover; just wrap the yarn twice around the needle instead of once.

Multiple yarnovers:

You can wrap the yarn around the needle more than once, then on the next row work into one of the yarnover loops and drop the other one off the needle. This will create a larger eyelet than a single yarnover will.

1 This is a double yarn forward yarnover, worked between two knit stitches. Bring the yarn forward and take it over the right-hand needle to the back, then bring it forward again and over the needle again, so that you have made two new loops. Knit the next stitch.

Yarnover at the start of a knit row:

Where yarnovers are needed at the start of a row you need to work them properly to make the extra loop that can be worked into on the next row. This is how to work a yarnover before a first knit stitch.

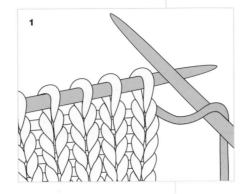

1 Drape the yarn loosely over the right-hand needle.

2 Insert the right-hand needle knitwise into the first stitch, bring the yarn around to the back, and knit the stitch, tightening the yarnover as you do so.

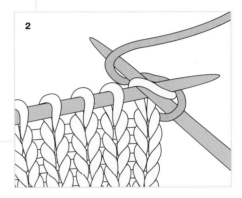

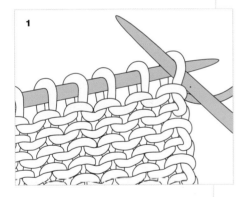

Yarnover at the start of a purl row:

This is how to work a yarnover before a first purl stitch.

1 With the yarn held to the back, insert the right-hand needle purlwise into the first stitch.

2 Bring the yarn up and over the tip of the left-hand needle then under the tip of the right-hand needle. Purl the stitch, being careful to pull the new stitch through the original stitch only, not through the yarnover loop as well.

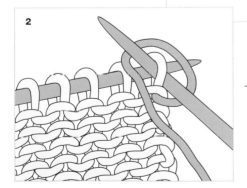

Knitting notes

When you are working back along a row that has a yarnover at the start, be careful not to drop the yarnover; the loops are a bit floppy and can easily slide unnoticed off the needle. Be particularly careful if you are working in the round on double-pointed needles and have a yarn over the first stitch on a needle.

DECREASES

These involve reducing the number of stitches—usually making two stitches into one—and the various ways of doing this create slightly different effects in the knitted fabric. Some decreases slant to the left and some to the right, and using the right one can make a visible difference to a stitch pattern.

Knitting notes

If you have to decrease at each end of a row, working mirrored decreases will give your knitting a professional look. On right side rows work skpo or ssk at the start of the row, and k2tog at the end of the row, then the decreases will slant toward one another. This effect can be decorative, so you can work the decreases a couple of stitches in from an edge so that they are visible when the project is sewn up—these are known as fully fashioned decreases.

The other decreases given here can also be used in this way.

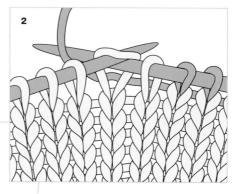

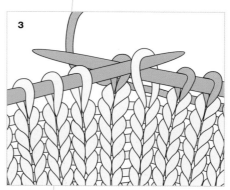

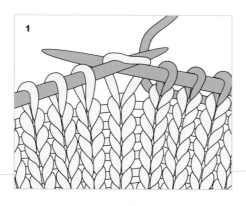

Slip one, knit one, pass the slipped stitch over (skpo):

This decrease slants to the left on stockinette stitch.

1 Slip the first stitch of the decrease knitwise onto the right-hand needle (see page 96).

2 Knit the next stitch, the second one of the decrease stitches.

3 Without stretching the slipped stitch, put the tip of the left-hand needle into the front of it and lift it over the stitch just knitted and drop it off the needle.

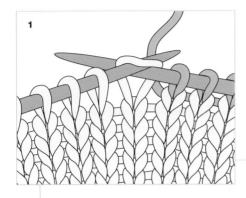

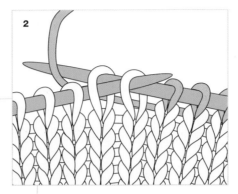

Slip, slip, knit (ssk):

This decrease slants to the left on stockinette and is neat and flat.

1 One at a time, slip the first and then the second of the decrease stitches knitwise (see page 96) onto the right-hand needle.

2 From the left, insert the left-hand needle into the fronts of these stitches and then knit them together. You are effectively knitting the slipped stitches together through the back loops, but having twisted them first.

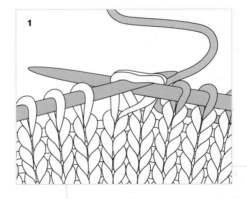

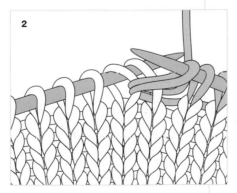

Knit two stitches together (k2tog):

This decrease slants to the right on stockinette.

1 From left to right, insert the right-hand needle through both decrease stitches.

2 Knit the two stitches together as if they were one.

Purl two stitches together (p2tog):

Used on a purl row, this decrease slants to the right on stockinette.

1 Insert the right-hand needle purlwise through both of the decrease stitches.

2 Purl the two stitches together as one.

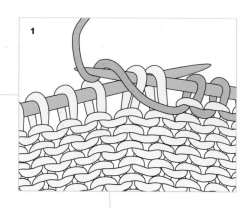

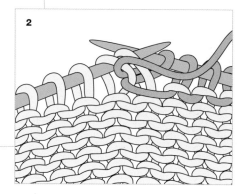

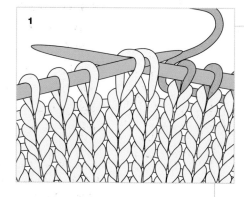

Knit two stitches together through the backs of the loops (k2togtbl):

As the two stitches have been twisted, this decrease slants to the left on stockinette.

1 Insert the right-hand needle through the back loops of both decrease stitches, then knit them together as one.

Purl two stitches together through the backs of the loops (p2tog tbl):

As the two stitches have been twisted, when used on a purl row this decrease slants to the left on stockinette.

1 From left to right, insert the right-hand needle through the back loops of both decrease stitches. This can be fiddly to do as you have to twist the needles around. If the stitches are tight and it's hard to get the needle through them, put the needle into the fronts of the stitches first and stretch them just a bit, then try again. Purl the two stitches together as one.

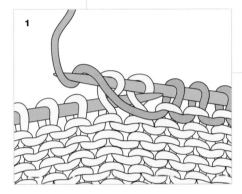

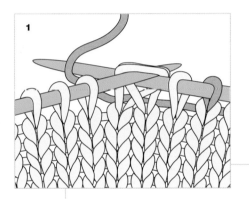

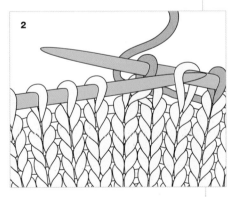

Slip one, knit two together, pass the slipped stitch over (sk2po):

This decrease turns three stitches into one, with the outer stitches sloping towards the central one on stockinette stitch.

1 Slip the first decrease stitch knitwise (see page 96). Knit the following two decrease stitches together (see page 191).

2 Without stretching the slipped stitch, put the tip of the left-hand needle into the front of it and lift it over the stitches just knitted together, then drop it off the needle.

Knitting notes

If you want to decrease by more than two stitches at a time on an edge, don't work multiple decreases next to one another as the knitting won't lie flat. Instead, bind off the number of stitches you want to decrease by at the start of each row.

INCREASES

These involve adding to the number of stitches, and as with decreases (see pages 190–193), there are various ways of doing this, which will create different effects in the knitted fabric.

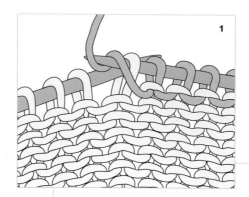

Increasing one knitwise (inc):

This increase has a visible small bar across the increased stitch and slants to the left on stockinette.

1 Knit into the stitch to be increased in the usual way, but do not slip the original stitch off the left-hand needle.

2 Insert the right-hand needle into the back of the same stitch on the left-hand needle and knit it again, then slip the original stitch off the left-hand needle.

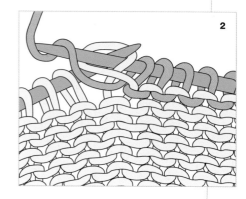

Increasing purlwise (inc):

This increase has a visible small bar across the increased stitch and slants to the right on stockinette.

1 Purl into the stitch to be increased in the usual way, but do not slip the original stitch off the left-hand needle.

2 Insert the right-hand needle into the back of the same stitch on the left-hand needle; you will need to tip the left-hand needle toward you a bit to do this. Purl the stitch again, then slip the original stitch off the left-hand needle.

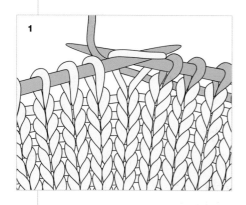

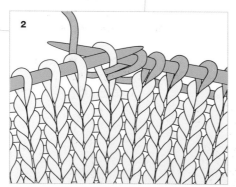

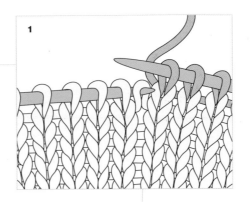

Make one right (M1R):

This increase slants to the right
on stockinette.

1 From the back, slip the tip of the
left-hand needle under the strand
running between the stitch just knitted
and the next stitch.

2 Turn the left-hand needle so that
you can knit into the front of the lifted
strand on the left-hand needle to make
an extra stitch.

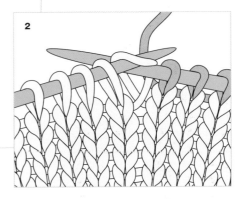

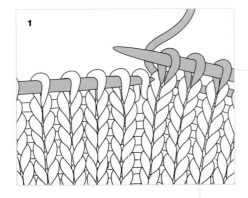

Make one left (M1L):

This increase slants to the left
on stockinette.

1 From the front, slip the tip of the
left-hand needle under the strand
running between the stitch just
knitted and the next stitch.

2 Knit into the back of the lifted
strand to make an extra stitch.

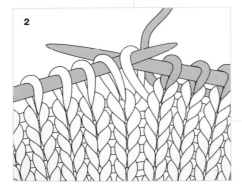

Make one on a purl row:

The same principles apply to making a stitch on a purl row.

1 Lift the strand from the back and purl into the front of it for an increase that slants to the right on stockinette.

2 Lift the strand from the front and purl into the back of it for an increase that slants to the left on stockinette.

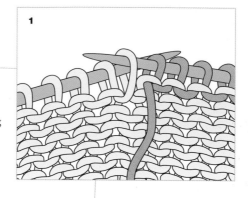

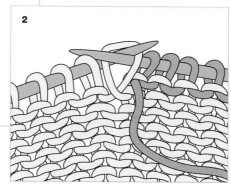

Lifted increase left on knit row:

This increase slants to the left on stockinette.

1 From the front, insert the left-hand needle into the top of the stitch below the stitch just knitted.

2 Knit this stitch.

Lifted increase right on knit row:

This increase slants to the right on stockinette.

1 From the front, insert the right-hand needle into the top of the back of the stitch directly below the next stitch on the left-hand needle. Knit this stitch, then knit the next stitch in the usual way.

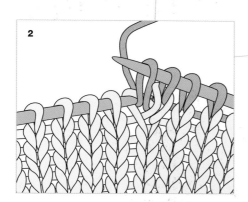

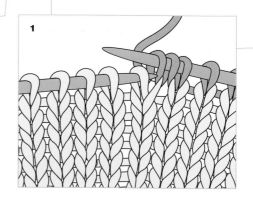

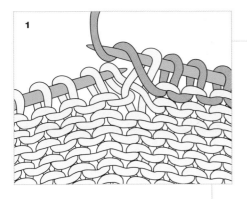

Lifted increase on purl row:

The same principles apply for making a lifted increase on a purl row.

1 From the back, purl through the top of the stitch directly below the next stitch on the left-hand needle, as shown, for an increase that slants to the left on stockinette. Purl through the top of the stitch below the stitch just purled for an increase that slants to the right.

Knitting notes

As with decreases (see pages 190–93), increases can be worked a few stitches in from an edge to provide a decorative feature. Note that increases and decreases don't exactly mirror one another in shape, but the overall effect works well.

BOUND STITCHES

Yarnovers (see pages 186–89) can also be used to bind three stitches together. This effect is quite delicate; if you want the bunching to be more obvious, use the wrapping technique (see page 171).

1 With the yarn at the back, slip the first of the three stitches to be bound together purlwise onto the right-hand needle (see page 96).

2 Knit the next stitch, then bring the yarn forward and make a yarnover (see page 186) before knitting the final stitch of the three.

3 Use the tip of the left-hand needle to lift the slipped stitch over the first knitted stitch, the yarnover and the second knitted stitch, then drop it off the needle.

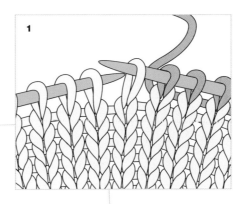

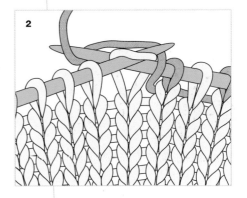

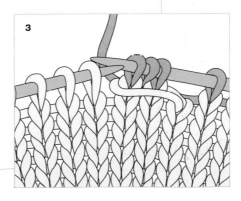

LOOPS

Loop knitting is both very yarn hungry and time-consuming to work, but it does make a lovely trim for edgings and cuffs (see swatch 3, Palette 57, page 204). There are two methods of working loops, one on right-side rows and the other on wrong-side rows, though the loops will appear on the right side with both techniques.

Single loop:

In this method the single loops are made on the right side of the knitting. Once you have finished them you can cut through the ends to produce stranded fur if you want to.

1 Knit the stitch before the loop position, but do not drop the original stitch off the left-hand needle. Bring the yarn forward between the tips of the needles. Hold your left thumb in front of the knitting and wrap the yarn under and around it (see Knitting Notes page 116).

2 Keeping your thumb in position, take the yarn back between the tips of the needles.

3 Knit the same stitch through the front loop again, then drop the original stitch off the left-hand needle. Now you can take your thumb out of the loop.

4 Insert the left-hand needle through the front of the two stitches just made and knit them together to secure the loop.

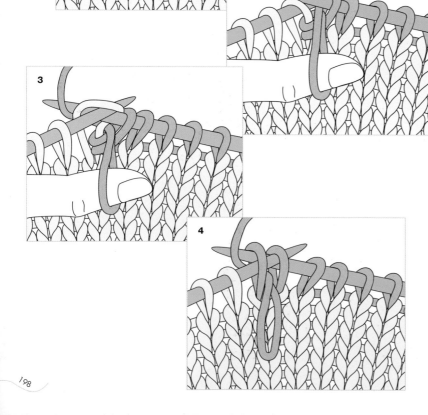

Knitting notes

Most knitters find it easiest to grip the right-hand needle in the palm of their hand with the ring and little fingers and use the other fingers to wrap the yarn around the left thumb, but as long as you don't stretch the stitches too much, you can hold the needles however is most comfortable for you.

When you have finished a loop row and the row above, slip a knitting needle through all the loops and pull down gently to even them out and tighten the tops.

Clustered loops:

These loops are worked on wrong-side rows, but the loops themselves hang down on the right side of the fabric. You should not cut these loops as the individual strands will pull out.

1 Where you want a cluster of loops, take the yarn between the tips of the needles to the back of the work and insert the right-hand needle knitwise into the next stitch. Stretch out two or three fingers (depending on how long you want the loops to be) of your left hand behind the right-hand needle. Wind the yarn over and around the fingers, and over the end of the right-hand needle at the same time, three times.

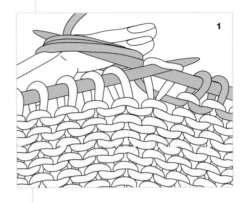

2 Draw the right-hand needle with the ends of the loops on it through the stitch, but do not drop the original stitch off the left-hand needle. Take your fingers out of the loops.

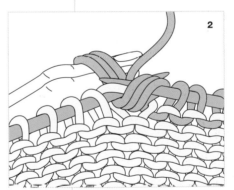

3 Slip the ends of the loops onto the left-hand needle and knit them together with the original stitch through the back loops. Pull the loops firmly on the right side of the work to tighten the stitches.

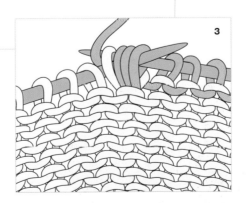

55 Lace knitting

The principle techniques for lace knitting are yarnovers (see pages 186–89) and basic decreases (see pages 190–93). Other than those, lace knitting is essentially just knit and purl stitches, no matter how complex the pattern looks. And lace is very versatile—it's not only for intricate baby shawls and fussy bed jackets; lace edgings can turn plain projects into boho masterpieces, and panels or motifs can add simple yet interesting detail. The regular structure and defined holes of simpler lace patterns mean that they work well in colors of different values and saturation (see Palette 1, page 14, and Palette 5, page 22), so you do have great freedom of choice. Worked in bold colors and chunky yarns lace can be modern and cool, both in terms of temperature and style.

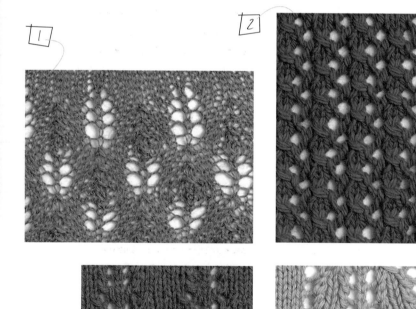

1 │ Is this what you think of when you hear the words "knitted lace"? A ridiculously fine yarn knitted into a complicated pattern is the traditional form of knitted lace, which was originally used to imitate very expensive knotted lace; what we think of as "real lace." Although this type of lace has its place, and many fans, it is just one interpretation of what knitted lace can be.

2 │ A simple repeat pattern knitted in a worsted-weight yarn in a saturated color is also lace. If you are new to lace knitting then look for patterns that have short repeats—maybe only four rows—and with wrong-side rows that are just purled. Patterns like this aren't difficult to follow, and if you need to unpick, you can just go carefully back to the last plain purl row.

3 │ A slightly more complex lace might have motifs composed of groups of holes scattered between areas of plain stockinette. Establishing the first few rows of a pattern can be the trickiest bit; once it starts to grow it's easy to see how the pattern of holes is formed and it becomes obvious if you lose track and make a mistake. Areas of stockinette give you something to unpick back to if need be.

4 │ Lace panels or inserts can be very useful for adding a bit of interest to a plain project. If they are worked over just a few stitches they can usually be added in without affecting gauge or drape too much. To check this, work a gauge swatch (see page 212) as stated in the pattern, then work a section of the lace panel you'd like to use. On the plain swatch, mark out the number of stitches used in the panel, then measure the panel and the marked-out section and compare the results. If the panel is too wide you may be able to compensate by taking out a couple of plain stitches from the project.

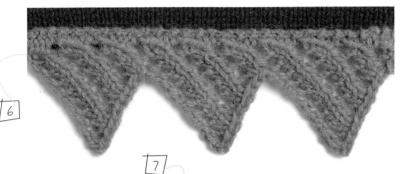

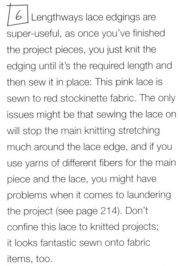

Knitting notes

An excellent way of keeping track of where you are in a more complex lace pattern is to use stitch markers. Thread a ring marker onto the needle between every set of stitch repeats (or two sets, whichever suits you), and every time you finish a row repeat, clip a stitch marker to the edge of the last row. If you're really worried about making a mistake and having to unpick, then you can periodically use a tapestry needle to thread a length of scrap yarn through the stitches on the needle to create a lifeline. If you have to unravel, then you can just pull the yarn out down to the last the lifeline, which will hold those stitches safe for you to put them back on the needles.

5 Lace edgings can be worked in three ways: from the bottom up, from the top down, and lengthways. This is a bottom-up edging, so once you've worked the lace pattern rows, you just embark on the rest of the project. (Top-down patterns are knitted at the end of the main knitting.) As long as your gauge swatch (see page 212) shows that the lace doesn't pull the knitting in too much (these patterns do tend to do this), you can just add a favorite edging to the bottom of a plain project.

6 Lengthways lace edgings are super-useful, as once you've finished the project pieces, you just knit the edging until it's the required length and then sew it in place: This pink lace is sewn to red stockinette fabric. The only issues might be that sewing the lace on will stop the main knitting stretching much around the lace edge, and if you use yarns of different fibers for the main piece and the lace, you might have problems when it comes to laundering the project (see page 214). Don't confine this lace to knitted projects; it looks fantastic sewn onto fabric items, too.

7 Single lace motifs offer another useful way of adding a bit of lace detail to an existing project without affecting gauge or drape too much. Work gauge swatches as described in swatch 4 to check that the motif won't create any major problems, and then just pop one into your pattern (if you're a new knitter then it's probably best to be a bit more considered and write out the pattern rows where the lace motif will be).

8 Lace braids can be used in a similar way to edgings (see swatches 5 and 6), or they can be sewn onto a knitted or woven fabric so that the background color shows through the holes in the lace. Alternatively, treat them as panels and add as many stitches either side as are needed for your project.

56 Stitch patterns

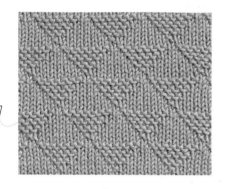

Here is just a tiny sampling of the hundreds of stitch patterns available to the knitter. The choice of yarn fiber and weight, as well as color, has a great influence on stitchwork as it relies on sometimes quite subtle or small-scale textures to create the effects. And if you have a naturally quite loose or especially tight tension, you may well find you need to change needle sizes to make the most of some of these patterns (see also Swatching, page 212).

1 Very smooth yarn with a slight sheen is excellent for knitting stitchwork as the smoothness defines the stitches clearly and the sheen allows the light to reflect off the surface and emphasize texture further. Mercerized cotton yarns were the traditional choice for these patterns, but new yarns such as bamboo and soya can also work very well. Mid-tone value colors (see Palette 5, page 22) that allow shadows to show will also help make the most of subtle patterns.

2 There are lots of patterns based on simple checks, and the regularity and comparative clarity of the shapes mean that checks work well in matte yarns and saturated colors (see Palette 1, page 14), though it's still best to stick to lighter values (see Palette 5, page 22) for best effect.

3 You can scale up patterns just by working them in chunky yarn. As the individual stitches become so much larger they also become more visible, so you need quite defined textures to prevent the eye getting lost in the plain stitches. And be aware of how many repeats you can fit in—often a pattern will need several to establish the textures and be effective. A word of warning: More delicate, intricate patterns just tend to look clunky knitted in thick yarn.

4 Many texture patterns use both knit and purl stitches on the right side and so, worked as a border, they look equally good set against stockinette or reverse stockinette as the main fabric. The lower part of this swatch shows the texture running straight off stockinette stitch. In the upper part there is a single row of stockinette between the main reverse stockinette fabric and the texture pattern: This creates a clean line so that the edge of the texture doesn't blur into the main fabric.

5 Do you usually just work single rib, with an occasional foray into double rib if you're feeling brave? Shame on you. There are many different rib patterns to choose from that can add a subtle but effective twist to a simple project. Be aware that not many rib patterns will stretch as much as single rib, and indeed, some are barely stretchy at all.

6 As with lace (see swatch 4, Palette 55, page 200), some stitch patterns work as panels and can be added to existing plain projects without affecting gauge or drape too much. However, it is worth swatching a panel pattern and checking it against a plain swatch to make sure that you can replace one with the other (see swatch 4, Palette 55, page 200).

Knitting notes

Do consider stitch patterns as borders and bands as well as over-all texture. Changing to a texture is an effective way of highlighting part of a project, though you do have to swatch to check whether the patterning draws the knitting in. Even if it does, this might work as a feature; a textured band at the top of a bag that draws in the plain stockinette below it will add shaping as well as a design detail.

7 This pattern features rows of elongated stitches made by wrapping the yarn twice around the needle when you knit, then dropping one of the loops when you work back across the row. Patterns with elongated stitches aren't suitable for projects for babies or small children as tiny fingers easily get caught in the loose stitches: This can damage the fingers and the knitting.

8 Again as with lace (see swatch 7, Palette 55, page 200), you can knit single textural motifs into plain stockinette without problems. As always, a swatch is a good idea (see page 212), but it'll rarely be an issue to work just one motif into a sweater as a permanent brooch, or onto a pocket as a simple but effective feature.

57 Color-effect yarns

Lace and stitch patterns are usually knitted in one color to keep the focus on the texture, and because having both knit and purl stitches on the right side makes it tricky to join in new colors attractively. However, color-effect yarns solve the latter problem while tweed and self-striping yarns with a long color change can add lovely color variation without confusing the eye.

1 Variegated yarns are usually too much with even the simplest lace patterns. This is a lovely yarn and the pattern is regular and well-defined, but the pattern doesn't display the yarn to best effect and the yarn overwhelms the pattern texture. Not ugly, but also not a successful combination.

2 This is a self-striping yarn with a long and gradual color change and it works beautifully with this check texture pattern. The stitches show up a bit better in the light section than they do in the darker part, but it's easy for the eye to establish the regularity of the pattern throughout and so register the overall checks.

3 Self-stripers with a short-length color change do come into their own when it comes to loop knitting: The effect is maybe a little riotous, but great fun. This swatch is knitted in garter stitch so the interlacing stitch bumps exaggerate the striping, and the furry edging is a small explosion of color.

Knitting notes

The issues with knitting self-striping swatches in plain stockinette (see Palette 8, page 34) apply to using these yarns for texture patterns: In fact, it's even more important to work a full-width swatch as the change of color can have a considerable effect on the pattern (see swatch 6). If one color does obscure a pattern, but at full width it turns out to be just a couple of rows wide, then it won't be a problem, but if you'd knitted a standard gauge swatch in which that color covered a whole pattern repeat then you just wouldn't know that your yarn was in fact fine for the project.

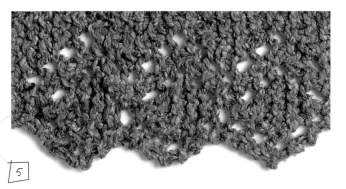

 Here, a tweed yarn is knitted into a herringbone pattern and the nature of the yarn and lines of the pattern create a knitted fabric that is very reminiscent of traditional twill fabric weaves. The texture of this stitch pattern is light and subtle and the tweed does muddle it a little bit, but the general effect is good, partly because this yarn is quite light in overall color value (see Palette 5, page 22).

5 Although heather-mix tweed yarns have color changes, they are uniformly scattered and don't intrude on a lace pattern. In this swatch the issue isn't the color, it's the weight of the yarn. It's relatively heavy and the individual stitches look a bit clumsy and rather detract from what should be a delicate pattern.

6 The distinct stripes this yarn creates are clear despite the lace pattern; in fact, so clear as to be rather distracting. The eye sees the stripes before registering the texture, and the fact that the holes show up better on some colors than on others just adds to the overall confusion.

7 Long color-change self-striping yarns can look great in lace edgings. If you matched one of the colors to the main yarn color then the effect would be interesting once the lace was sewn on. Many self-stripers are lightweight yarns designed for sock knitting, and so are also an ideal weight for lace.

58 Textured yarns

The relative subtlety of stitch texture does not on the whole work well with textured yarns, but if you really want to add more texture to an already textured pattern, there are some options open to you. Swatching (see page 212) is a must and you may well need to try various needle sizes to come up with what works best for the yarn (which might like quite a large needle to show off its texture) and for the pattern (which might prefer a smaller needle to create well-defined stitches).

1 Even a really simple pattern of garter stitch stripes on stockinette fabric gets lost if knitted in eyelash yarn, even when that yarn has relatively short eyelashes. If you peer hard you can see the ridges of knit stitches, but is the effect worth even the tiny amount of effort involved in changing stitch pattern?

2 As this yarn is such a pale color value (see Palette 5, page 22), the check stitch pattern does stand a fighting chance of showing through the fuzz, but it's still little more than an impression of what might have been. You can use an electric beard trimmer to shave some of the fuzziness off finished knitting, but you need to be very careful not to snag and cut any stitches, and surely it would be better to use a more suitable yarn in the first place than to make a lovely (and maybe expensive) mohair yarn bald.

3 A chunky yarn with a knitted texture (it's a bit like I-cord) copes well with a grid stitch pattern, though the darkness of the color (see Palette 5, page 22) doesn't help the stitch definition. Generally stitch patterns work well in yarns up to a worsted weight, but with weights above that the stitches can start to look clumsy and can detract from the overall look of the knitting.

4 Mohair can be interesting in ghosted effects (see also swatch 7, Palette 37, page 124). On the bottom part of this swatch it's knitted together with a plain yarn to create a background for looped stitches in just the plain yarn (you simply abandon the mohair when making a looped stitch and then pick it up again for the next knitted stitch). The middle of the swatch has texture checks with both yarns used for the stockinette and the plain yarn only for the garter stitch (the mohair is stranded across the back of the garter stitch, see pages 138–45). At the top the checks are all in stockinette, some in both yarns and the others in just the plain yarn.

1

2

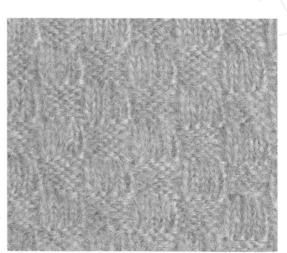

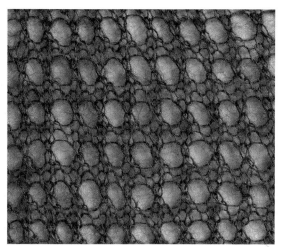

Knitting notes

Textured yarns do offer quite a good disguise for uneven gauge or the odd discrepancy in a pattern repeat. So, if you can make a yarn work with a stitch pattern then you won't have to concentrate as much on finessing the fabric as you would if you were using smooth, shiny yarn that showed up every miniscule imperfection in your knitting.

5 This is a slightly fiddly fabric to make, and there are lots of ends to sew in from the single rows of mohair, but it's a nice effect. This is basically the same pattern as swatch 7, Palette 56 (see page 203), but the elongated stitches are knitted in mohair and the rest of the swatch is in a plain yarn. This was a sport-weight mohair and so it didn't need to be used doubled up to match the gauge of the plain yarn. The issue of the ends may well put you off a whole project knitted this way, but a band or two in the middle of plain knitting would be very effective.

6 Lace with large holes and a simple, regular pattern can look delicate and ethereal knitted in fine mohair. The core of the yarn is so thin that the fuzz holds the stitches in shape—stops them flopping loosely—and so the pattern is quite well displayed, even through the fuzzy halo of the yarn.

59 Beads and embroidery

The delicacy of embroidery and beading when worked using fine threads and small beads can be a lovely complement to subtle stitch texture. In addition, patterns can provide a useful grid for placing stitches and the slightly stiffer fabric the changing stitches can produce makes for a firmer background than plain stockinette.

1 This seed stitch diamond pattern offers a good home to individual lazy daisy flowers (see page 57). As taking the embroidery thread (crewel wool was used here) across the knitting between flowers would prevent it stretching, each flower is worked individually. You might not want to embroider as densely as this, but the occasional motif embroidered into a pattern can provide whimsical detail.

2 Embroidery stitches can be practical as well as decorative. Here, the line of chain stitch (see pag 57) is attaching the leaf lace trim to the stockinette as well as being decorative. Running stitch (see page 56) is also useful used like this, although it's advisable to make occasional small backstitches on the wrong side to anchor the stitching and prevent it pulling in the fabric.

3 The holes in a lace pattern are just begging to have things threaded through them… This is ombre ribbon (the color changes shade across its width) and it adds both color and depth to the lace pattern. You need to be careful that the ribbon doesn't pull in the fabric, so anchoring it on the back with tiny stitches in sewing thread is a good idea.

4 Beads can look pretty in lace knitting, but you'll need to swatch (see page 212) to experiment with positioning. In the bottom row of this swatch the beads are placed on the second row above each lace motif using the slip stitch method (see page 52); as the beads drop down quite a bit with this method, they end up sitting at the top of the motif. The next row up has a bead placed in the middle of

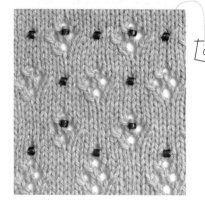

each motif using the knitted-in method (see page 52). The third row of beads is placed between motifs using the slip stitch technique; as before, because these beads drop down they are actually placed on the row above the middle one of the pattern. The top row is a combination of rows two and three, and even though the beads are placed on different rows, they do line up.

5 | Adding beads to loop stitches (see page 198) gives them a lovely weight and swing, and it's easy to do. Just thread them on as usual (see page 50), then slide one along onto each loop as you make it. When the knitting is finished you can push all the beads down to the bottoms of the loops. The light color of the beads also helps to visually separate the dark yarn loops. The bump at the top of each loop stitch can be a bit ugly, but working seed stitch above the loops disguises the bumps very effectively.

6 | Lightweight and delicate, sequins can look gorgeous knitted into lace (see page 54). Here the lace is knitted in mohair that has a metallic sparkle strand in it that complements the way the light reflects off the flower-shaped sequins. One sequin is placed between each motif and others are knitted in randomly in the stockinette above the lace pattern.

7 | To place beads just on the edge of the holes in this lace pattern they are knitted in (see page 52) to the knit stitch of an skpo (see page 190), then tweaked to make sure they sit above the stitch that's passed over. This is a bit painstaking, but doing it this way ensures that the beads don't wriggle through the holes to the back.

8 | You can place beads in single rib using the slip stitch method (see page 52) so that they sit in the purl furrows. This does make the rib slightly less stretchy, but it still functions as rib, and it does look pretty. The color variations in these beads are just how they came, and the changing tones add some liveliness to the uniform pattern.

Knitting notes

You need to be especially careful choosing beads to add into lace knitting as the weight of the beads can pull the pattern out of shape. Fine yarns need small beads or sequins, whereas heavier yarn can support larger beads (see swatch 4). It's vital to swatch (see page 212) to check your beads and yarn suit each other, and remember that beaded items must be hand-washed and that you cannot steam-block sequinned lace.

5

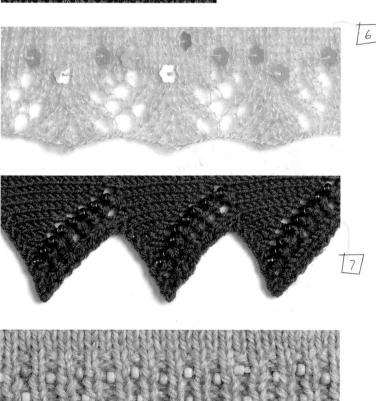

6

7

8

Texture and colorwork

Combining textured stitch patterns with colorwork can take a bit of planning, but the results can look great, and there are some practical advantages, too. The samples here use stripes (see Chapter 4, pages 72–93), intarsia (see Chapter 6, pages 112–35), and stranding techniques (see Chapter 7, pages 135–57); for slip stitch color and texture patterns turn to Chapter 5 (see pages 96–111).

Knitting notes

Working more complex textures than seed stitch is entirely possible, but it is best to write or graph out the pattern (whichever you find easiest to use) before you begin. Then, if the stitch pattern/s you want to use is/are complex and if you are good, knit a swatch (see page 212) for each motif.

1 In this swatch the intarsia motif is knitted in seed stitch on a stockinette background. To keep the edges of the motif clear—without the color-swapping caused by interlacing stitch bumps— you need to work every first stitch in the motif color as a knit stitch (see swatches 3 and 4, Palette 41, page 132). The nature of seed stitch means that this doesn't really show in the finished motif, and if the odd stitch does look wrong, when weaving in the tails you can always use one of them to make a little straight stitch over a knit stitch to make a fake purl bump.

2 You can use quite adventurous stitch patterns if the intarsia motif is large enough and simple enough. Here, loop stitch (see page 198) fills the heart shape, with the loops worked on alternate stitches and positioned so that they always form the edge stitches: In the central dip of the heart this involved making loops on adjacent stitches in a couple of places, but the overall texture is thick enough for this discrepancy not to show.

3 Stripes can be worked in different textures to great effect. You need the first row in a new color to be just knit (or purl if it's a wrong-side row), and if you're working on a large project it's worth checking the gauge of each pattern to be sure that one doesn't pull in the knitting much more than another. (Careful blocking will sort out any small differences in gauge.) Swatch (see page 212) each pattern separately in the right yarn and measure the same number of stitches in each swatch.

3

4
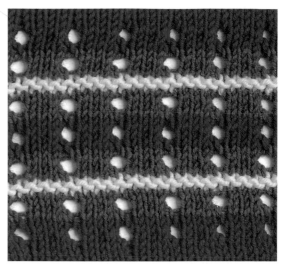

4 You can create stripes of eyelets to sit within color stripes, though you'll need to swatch (see page 212) to establish the right position for the eyelets in relation to the color change; here, they are worked on the third row of a four-row color stripe. The yellow stripes are garter stitch, making ridges to further divide up the fabric.

5 Single stitch dots are placed using stranding within a stitch pattern that gives a quilted effect. The way knit and purl stitches interlace means that the dots do not sit exactly in the middle of the diamonds, though they are in fact placed centrally. The depth of the red against the lightness of the yellow (see Palette 5, page 22) means that the dots draw the eye even though they are so small.

6 Give in to the temptation eyelets offer and add variety to a piece of knitting by threading things through them. Here a ribbon bow decorates a heart motif, but you can experiment with all sorts of trims and notions. Consider laundering (see page 214) and make sure that what you add isn't too heavy for the knitting (which can stretch quickly and alarmingly), but other than that you can be as creative as you like.

5

6

Swatching

If you've read almost any of the palettes in this book, you'll have come across references to swatching. If you've knitted projects from a pattern, then you'll have (hopefully) knitted gauge swatches for them. All swatches are essentially tests to check and establish elements of a knitting pattern before you embark on the actual project. And they are more than just useful: often they are vital.

If you are a confident and experienced knitter, then some of the following isn't aimed at you. But if knitting is a big new adventure for you, then take the time to swatch properly; you really will be able to create better projects as a result.

Gauge swatches

The gauge of a project is the number of rows and stitches that you should have in a square of knitting of a given size, usually 4 x 4in (10 x 10cm). Knitting patterns will tell you the gauge needed to create the project as the designer intended.

Using the yarn and needles given in the gauge instruction, cast on eight stitches more than the number you need to be able to count. Working in the stitch pattern stated, work a piece of knitting that's eight rows more than the number you need to count. Bind off the knitting loosely so that you don't pull the bound-off edge in.

Lay the knitting flat without stretching it. Lay a ruler across the stitches with the 2in (5cm) mark

centered on the knitting, then put a pin in the knitting at the start of the ruler and at the 4in (10cm) mark: The pins should be well away from the edges. Count the number of stitches between the pins, including a half stitch if there is one. Repeat the process across the rows to count the number of rows to 4in.

If you have too few stitches to 4in, then your gauge is too loose. If you have too many stitches, then your gauge is too tight. Either way, you need to get the gauge right before you knit the project, as being just one stitch or row out across 4" will add up to quite a few stitches out across a wider measurement, and then the project you have spent so long knitting won't fit.

Don't just try to knit to a different gauge: You have a "natural" gauge and if you try to knit tighter or looser it won't be consistent and you will simply end up with uneven knitting. To change gauge you need to change the size of your knitting needles. A rule of thumb is that one difference in needle size will create a

The wrapper of a ball of yarn will usually give you the recommended needle size and gauge, but some yarns—such as this fine mohair—can look good knitted up with larger (top) and smaller (above) needles.

difference of one stitch in the gauge: You need to use larger needles to achieve fewer stitches and smaller ones to achieve more stitches. So if you need to achieve 23 stitches to 4in using US 5 (3.75mm) needles but you have 24 stitches in your gauge swatch, then knit it again using US 6 (4mm) needles. And if you only have 22 stitches, then knit a swatch with US 4 (3.5mm) needles. Keep swatching until you've got the gauge asked for.

Yarn swatches

Another good reason for knitting a swatch is to see how a yarn knits up. Conventional smooth yarns rarely hold surprises, but even so, if it's a fiber you've not used before it's worth buying one ball and knitting a swatch to check that you're happy working with it before spending a lot of money on the yarn.

Textured yarns (see Palette 12, page 42) are always worth swatching, because quite often you'll want to try a few needle sizes to see what works best for your project. Using needles too small can compress and flatten texture, or create a very stiff fabric. The latter might be excellent for a bag, but hopeless for a scarf.

Color-effect yarn swatches

It's almost always worth knitting a large swatch of a color-effect yarn, a swatch that is the width of the project (see Palettes 7–10, pages 32–39). This is because a small swatch will only give you the gauge; it won't give you much idea of what

your yarn will look like once it's knitted up into a project. And color-effect yarns can look very tempting in the ball or skein, and be very disappointing once turned into fabric. It's best to buy one ball and work a full-size swatch before investing in all the yarn needed for a large project.

Texture swatches

If you are going to be working a stitch pattern you are unfamiliar with, it can be a good idea to knit a larger swatch to get completely used to the pattern, and to assess how it looks over a large area. Obviously if you are following a pattern then there should be a photo of it and we can assume you like it or you

wouldn't be knitting it, so there's no need for the large swatch if you're confident working the stitches. But if you are picking a pattern from a stitch directory, then it's certainly worth doing the extra work.

Directories often don't show all swatches to the same scale, so it can be hard to assess a pattern from the photo, plus the photo often only shows one or two pattern repeats. Once a pattern is expanded into ten repeats it can look rather different.

Motif swatches

For a project with several different motifs, do spend time swatching them all. You can do this on several small swatches or one big one, whichever you find easiest, but don't just work one motif from a multi-motif design. It's worth spending the extra hour or so swatching all of them to check that you understand any idiosyncrasies and to establish how many bobbins of how much yarn you need to make up before you start the project (see page 118).

Left to right: a variegated yarn knitted in stripes with a plain yarn; a variegated yarn with a short color change; a self-striping yarn with a long color-change.

Bead swatches

There are a couple of good reasons for knitting bead swatches: To check that the beads you've chosen are appropriate for the weight of yarn you are using (see page 50), and to decide on which placing technique to use. A project will usually, but not always, ask for the slip stitch method (see page 52), or maybe the knitted-in method (see page 52), but if it doesn't then you need to work a section of the pattern to determine the technique to use, as they do look quite different.

Embroidery swatches

With any embroidery on knitting it's a good idea to test for colorfastness and shrinkage. Test for colorfastness by dipping the thread in warm water and rubbing it firmly in a scrap of

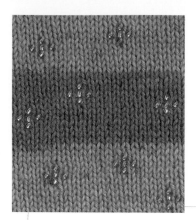

A precise pattern of beads is usually best-placed using the knitted-in method (above right); a more open pattern can use the slip stitch technique (above left).

white cotton cloth. If any of the thread color appears on the cloth, then the thread is not colorfast. You can test for shrinkage by embroidering a swatch and washing it: Measure the swatch carefully before and after washing to see how much it reduces by. Careful hand-washing will get around many laundering issues, but testing threads, especially fancy ones, is never a waste of time.

Laundering swatches

If you've been good and knitted all your swatches, then take the final step and launder them before committing to the project. Some yarns change quite drastically if washed incorrectly (or at all—there are dry-clean only yarns), and it's better to discover that with a swatch than with a whole project. Launder according to the yarn wrapper if that's what you're likely to actually do, but there's no point in hand-washing the swatch if you're most likely to pop the project in the machine.

Many washing machines have woolen or delicate cycles these days, so it can be perfectly viable to machine-wash knitting. I keep an old pillowcase especially for washing swatches. I put them in that and tie the top so that the swatch doesn't get tangled or felted onto anything else.

Functional details, such as eyelet buttonholes (below left), can be highlighted with embroidery, or you can use stitches purely decoratively (below right) to create textural motifs.

Substituting yarn

If you want to use a yarn that's different to the one suggested in a pattern, then you need to do some testing, and then some math to find out how many balls of it to buy.

Choosing a yarn

Unless you are an expert knitter and are good at altering patterns, choose a substitute yarn that is the same weight as the pattern yarn or you'll end up with a project that's an entirely different size to the pattern measurements.

Balls of two different brands of worsted yarn won't necessarily contain the same quantity of yarn, even if the balls weigh the same amount. It's the yardage in a ball, not its weight, that's important.

And different yarn brands may not knit up to the same gauge. The yarn wrapper on the ball you'd like to substitute should tell you a standard gauge for it, and as long as this isn't different from the recommended pattern yarn by more than a stitch or row, or two, you should be able to use different needles to get the right gauge (see page 212).

Before buying a huge amount of a substitute yarn, it's a great idea to buy just one ball and knit a gauge swatch to be absolutely certain that you can get the right gauge with that yarn.

Doing the math

If the substitute yarn has a different yardage per ball to the pattern yarn, then you need to do a sum to work out how much to buy. If you just buy the number of balls given for the pattern yarn you are quite likely to either not have enough to complete the project, or have an annoyingly large amount left over. To do the sum you need to know the yardage of both the pattern yarn and the substitute yarn: This should be on the yarn wrapper.

First, multiply the yardage in one ball of pattern yarn by the number of balls the pattern needs to find out the total yardage needed to make the project.

Then divide the total yardage by the yardage in one ball of the substitute yarn to find out how many balls of that yarn you need to buy.

A sample sum

The pattern yarn contains 109 yards (100m) of yarn in each ball and you need 13 balls to make the project.

109 x 13 = 1,417 yards (1,300m) of yarn needed.

The substitute yarn contains 123 yards (113m) of yarn in each ball.
1,417 ÷ 123 = 11.52.
So you only need to buy 12 balls of the substitute yarn.

Yarns

The yarns used in this book include those listed here. For stockists please check the websites listed on page 218.

Artesano

100% Alpaca 4ply; 100% pure superfine alpaca; 1¾oz (50g); approximately 200yd (183m)

100% Alpaca DK; 100% pure superfine alpaca; 1¾oz (50g); approximately 109yd (100m)

Austermann

Step; 75% superwash virgin wool, 25% nylon; 3½oz (100g); approximately 460yd (420m)

Blue Sky

Alpaca Silk; 50% alpaca, 50% silk; 1¾oz (50g); approximately 146yd (133m)

Brushed Suri: 62% baby suri, 22% merino, 11% bamboo; 1¾oz (50g); approximately 142yd (130m)

Melange; 1005 baby alpaca; 1¾oz (50g); approximately 110yd (100m)

Multi Cotton; 100% organically grown cotton; 2¼oz (67g); approximately 100yd (91m)

Sport-weight; 100% baby alpaca; 1¾oz (50g); approximately 110yd (100m)

Worsted Hand Dyes; 50% royal alpaca, 50% merino; 3½oz (100g); approximately 100yd (91m)

Colinette

Giotto; 50% cotton, 40% rayon, 10% nylon; 3½oz (100g); approximately 153yd (140m)

Crystal Palace Yarns

Cotton Chenille; 100% mercerized cotton; 1¾oz (50g); approximately 98yd (105m)

Debbie Bliss

Angel; 76% super kid mohair, 24% silk; ¾oz (25g); approximately 218yd (200m)

Baby Cashmerino; 55% merino, 33% microfiber, 12% cashmere; 1¾oz (50g); approximately 136yd (125m)

Cashmerino DK; 55% merino, 33% microfiber, 12% cashmere; 1¾oz (50g); approximately 120yd (110m)

Donegal Luxury Tweed; 85% wool, 15% angora; 1¾oz (50g); approximately 96yd (88m)

Fez; 85% extrafine merino, 15% camel; 1¾oz (50g); approximately 109yd (100m)

Paloma; 60% baby alpaca, 40% merino; 1¾oz (50g); approximately 71yd (65m)

Party Angel; 72% super kid mohair, 24% silk, 4% metalized polyester; ¾oz (25g); approximately 218yd (200m)

Rialto 4ply; 100% extrafine merino superwash; 1¾oz (50g); approximately 189yd (173m)

Elle

Sock Wool; 80% pure new wool, 20% nylon; 1¾oz (50g); approximately 220yd (200m)

Ice Yarns

Long Eyelash; 100% polyester; 1¾oz (50g); approximately 38yd (35m)

Mohair Bouclé; 70% mohair, 30% acrylic; 3½oz (100g); approximately 240yd (220m)

Jamieson's

Double Knitting: 100% Shetland wool; ¾oz (25g); approximately 82yd (75m)

Katia

Cancan; 100% polyester; 1¾oz (50g); approximately 46yd (42m)

Lang Yarns

Jawoll Superwash; 75% superwash new wool, 18% nylon, 7% acrylic; 1¾oz (50g); approximately 230yd (210m)

Triple: 100% nylon microfiber; 1¾oz (50g); approximately 120yd (110m)

Louisa Harding

Thistle: 60% merino, 40% baby alpaca; 1¾oz (50g); approximately 98yd (89m)

Malabrigo

Gruesa; 100% pure wool; 3½oz (100g); approximately 65yd (60m)

Manos del Uruguay

Serena: 60% baby alpaca, 40% pima cotton; 1³⁄₄oz (50g); approximately 170yd (155m)

Maxima; 100% extrafine merino; 3¹⁄₂oz (100g); approximately 219yd (200m)

Millamia

Naturally Soft Merino; 100% extrafine merino; 1³⁄₄oz (50g); approximately 136yd (125m)

Noro

Kureyon; 100% wool; 1³⁄₄oz (50g); approximately 109yd (100m)

On Line

Linie 195 Solo; 50% superwash extrafine merino, 50% acrylic; 1³⁄₄oz (50g); approximately 22yd (20m)

Regia

Design Line by Kaffe Fasset; 75% superwash new wool, 25% nylon; 1³⁄₄oz (50g); approximately 230yd (210m)

Extra Twist Merino; 75% superwash merino, 25% nylon; 1³⁄₄oz (50g); approximately 230yd (210m)

Rooster

Almerino Aran; 50% baby alpaca, 50% merino; 1³⁄₄oz (50g); approximately 100yd (91m)

Almerino DK; 50% baby alpaca, 50% merino; 1³⁄₄oz (50g); approximately 124yd (113m)

Rowan

Big Wool; 100% merino; 3¹⁄₂oz (100g); approximately 87yd (80m)

Cashsoft 4ply; 57% extrafine merino, 33% acrylic microfiber, 10% cashmere; 1³⁄₄oz (50g); approximately 175yd (160m)

Cocoon; 80% merino, 20% kid mohair; 3¹⁄₂oz (100g); approximately 126yd (115m)

Felted Tweed DK; 50% merino, 25% alpaca, 25% viscose; 1³⁄₄oz (50g); approximately 191yd (175m)

Fine Lace; 80% baby suri alpaca, 20% merino; 1³⁄₄oz (50g); approximately 437yd (400m)

Kidsilk Haze; 70% super kid mohair, 30% silk; ³⁄₄oz (25g); approximately 229yd (210m)

Kidsilk Haze Stripe; 70% super kid mohair, 30% silk; 1³⁄₄oz (50g); approximately 465yd (425m)

Lima; 84% baby alpaca, 8% merino, 8% nylon; 1³⁄₄oz (50g); approximately 109yd (100m)

Pure Wool 4ply; 100% superwash wool; 1³⁄₄oz (50g); approximately 174yd (160m)

Shimmer; 60% cupro, 40% polyester; ³⁄₄oz (25g); approximately 191yd (175m)

Summer Tweed; 70% silk, 30% cotton; 1³⁄₄oz (50g); approximately 131yd (120m)

Wool Cotton; 50% merino, 50% cotton; 1³⁄₄oz (50g); approximately 123yd (113m)

Schoppell Wolle

Zauberball; 75% wool, 25% nylon; 3¹⁄₂oz (100g); approximately 459yd (420m)

Crazy Zauberball; 75% wool, 25% nylon; 3¹⁄₂oz (100g); approximately 459yd (420m)

Sirdar

Crofter DK; 60% acrylic, 25 cotton, 15% wool; 1³⁄₄oz (50g); approximately 184yd (168m)

Spud & Chloë

Sweater; 55% superwash wool, 45% organic cotton; 3¹⁄₂oz (100g); approximately 160yd (146m)

Fine; 80% superwash wool, 20% silk; 2¹⁄₄oz (65g); approximately 248yd (247m)

Stitch Perfect

Only Fair Extra-fine Mohair; 70% baby mohair, 30% nylon; ³⁄₄oz (25g); approximately 239yd (210m)

The Little Knitting Company

Angora 50; 50% angora, 30%wool, 20% nylon; ³⁄₄oz (25g); approximately 126yd (115m)

Cobra; 41% wool, 41% acrylic, 18% nylon; 1³⁄₄oz (50g); approximately 169yd (155m)

The Natural Dye Studio

Dazzle 4ply/Sock/Sport; 100% British Blue-faced Leicester Wool; 3¹⁄₂oz (100g); approximately 394yd (360m)

Dazzle HT 4ply/Sock/Sport; 100% British Blue-Faced Leicester Wool; 3¹⁄₂oz (100g); approximately 437yd (400m)

Resources

Listed here are the yarn suppliers that I used:
Please visit the websites to find local suppliers
for the yarns. Also here are stores I like, books
that I find useful, and blogs that I read.

Books I find useful

There are lots and lots of knitting books to choose from
and what you'll like depends on personal taste, but for
solid information and technique I turn to:

***Ultimate Knitting Bible* by Sharon Brant**
Lots of techniques clearly explained.

The Harmony Guides
I have the originals and the re-issues and often
consult them for stitch patterns.

***1000 Great Knitting Motifs* by Luise Roberts**
A great source of color pattern inspiration.

Yarn suppliers I used for this book

These are the websites for yarns I used
(see page 216 for yarn info).

Artesano
www.artesanoyarns.co.uk

Austermann
www.austermann-wolle.de

Blue Sky
www.blueskyalpacas.com

Colinette
www.colinette.com

Crystal Palace Yarns
www.straw.com

Debbie Bliss
US: *www.knittingfever.com*
UK/Europe:
www.designeryarns.uk.com

Elle
www.elleyarns.com

Ice Yarns
www.iceyarns.com

Jamieson's
US: *www.simplyshetland.net*
UK/Europe:
www.jamiesonsofshetland.co.uk

Katia
www.katia.com

Lang Yarns
www.langyarns.com

Louisa Harding
US: *www.knittingfever.com*
UK/Europe:
www.designeryarns.uk.com

Malabrigo
www.malabrigoyarn.com

Manos del Uruguay
www.artesanoyarns.co.uk/
'Manos Del Uruguay'

Millamia
www.millamia.com

Noro
US: *www.knittingfever.com*
UK/Europe:
www.designeryarns.uk.com

On Line
www.knittingfever.com

Regia
www.coatscrafts.co.uk

Rooster
www.roosteryarns.com

Rowan
www.knitrowan.com

Schoppell Wolle
www.schoppel-wolle.de

Sirdar
www.sirdar.co.uk

Spud & Chloë
www.spudandchloe.com

Stitch Perfect
www.stitchperfect.co.uk

The Little Knitting Company
www.thelittleknittingcompany.co.uk

The Natural Dye Studio
www.naturaldyecompany.com

Other useful websites

Joann Fabrics
www.joann.com

Michaels Arts & Crafts
www.michaels.com

AC Moore Arts & Crafts
www.acmoore.com

Kaleidoscope Yarns
www.kyarns.com

Halcyon Yarn
www.halcyonyarn.com

Webs: America's Yarn Store
www.yarn.com

Lion Brand Yarn
www.lionbrand.com

Yarn Market
www.yarnmarket.com

Yarn Supplier
www.yarnsupplier.com

Jagger Spun Yarn
www.jaggeryarn.com

Knitting-Warehouse
www.knitting-warehouse.com

Cotton Clouds
www.cottonclouds.com

Patternworks
www.patternworks.com

Knit Picks
www.knitpicks.com

Knitting blogs I read

There are literally hundreds of knitting blogs and too many are badly written, with blurry photos, and full of moans and complaints. But there are stars, too. I like:

The Yarn Harlot
One of the early blogs and still one of the best. Don't think you'll just "visit" for a few minutes; be prepared to spend some time with Stephanie Pearl-McPhee and her well-written and very funny blog, which is also very instructive.
www.yarnharlot.ca

Purl Bee
You can revel in good taste and understated style at this blog; and if you're in striking distance of New York City, the store is a joy.
www.purlbee.com

The Panopticon
Visit Franklin at his blog for some fantastic entertainment, and to find out what a panopticon is.
the-panopticon.blogspot.co.uk

Other blogs I spend too much time looking at

Again, there are just so many out there, but these are the three I call in on regularly.

Male Pattern Boldness
What's not to love about Peter? Nothing; nothing at all.
malepatternboldness.blogspot.co.uk/

That Man Quilts?
A torrent of well-written quilting information: I read it religiously and I don't actually quilt.
quiltfool.blogspot.co.uk/

Stitches and Seams
I'm always inspired by Debbie's fabulous attitude to life, and am in awe of her dressmaking skills.
stitchesandseams.blogspot.co.uk/

Abbreviations

This is a list of abbreviations commonly found in knitting patterns, but do check abbreviations listed in a pattern you are following because different phrases or contractions are sometimes used.

alt	alternate; alternatively
approx	approximately
BC	back cross
beg	begin(s)(ning)
bet	between
BO	bind off
C6B	cable six stitches (or number stated) back
C6F	cable six stitches (or number stated) front
CC	contrast color
cm	centimeter(s)
CN	cable needle
CO	cast on
col	color
cont	continue
cr(oss) 2L	cross two stitches (or number stated) to the left
cr(oss) 2R	cross two stitches (or number stated) to the right
dbl	double
dec(s)	decrease(s)(ing)
DK	double-knitting
dpn	double-pointed needle
FC	front cross
foll(s)	follow(s)(ing)
g(r)	gram
g st	garter stitch

in(s)	inch
inc	increase(s)(ing)
incl	include
k	knit
k1b	knit stitch in row below
k2tog	knit two stitches (or number stated) together
kfb	knit into the front and back of a stitch
ktbl	knit through back of loop
kwise	knitwise
LH	left hand
LT	left twist
m	meters
M1	make one stitch
MB	make bobble
MC	main color
mm	millimeters
oz	ounce(s)
p	purl
p2tog	purl two stitches (or number stated) together
patt(s)	pattern(s)
pfb	purl into the front and back of a stitch
pnso	pass next stitch over
psso	pass the slipped stitch over

ptbl	purl through back of loop
pwise	purlwise
rem	remain(ing)
rep	repeat
rev st st	reverse stockinette stitch
RH	right hand
rnds	rounds
RS	right side
RT	right twist
sk	skip next stitch
sk2	skip next two stitches
skpo	slip one stitch, knit one stitch, pass slipped stitch over
sk2po	slip one stitch, knit two together, pass slipped stitch over
sl	slip
ssk	slip one stitch, slip one stitch, knit slipped stitches together
st st	stockinette stitch
st(s)	stitch(es)
tbl	through back of loop
tog	together
WS	wrong side
wyb	with yarn at the back
wyf	with yarn at the front
yb	yarn back
yf	yarn front
yfrn	yarn forward and round needle
yfwd	yarn forward
yo	yarn over needle
yo2	yarn over needle twice
yon	yarn over needle
yrn	yarn round needle

Yarn standards & conversions

YARN STANDARDS

The Yarn Council of America offers the following system of categorizing yarns, and you might find it useful. However, it really is only a general guide and if you are knitting from a pattern you should use the gauge and needle sizes that suggests, as those are what the designer has worked with to create the fit and drape of the project.

Yarn weight symbol	Yarn category names	Suggested US (metric) needle size	Gauge range in stockinette stitch over 4in (10cm)
0 LACE	fingering, 4-ply, 10-count crochet thread	000–1 (1.5–2.25mm)	33–40 sts
1 SUPER FINE	fingering, 4-ply, sock, baby	1–2 (2.25–3.25mm)	27–32 sts
2 FINE	sport-weight, lightweight double knitting, baby	3–5 (3.25–3.75mm)	23–26 sts
3 LIGHT	lightweight worsted, double knitting	5–7 (3.75–4.5mm)	21–24 sts
4 MEDIUM	worsted, afghan, Aran	7–9 (4.5–5.5mm)	16–20 sts
5 BULKY	chunky, craft, rug	9–11 (5.5–8mm)	12–15 sts
6 SUPER BULKY	bulky, roving, super-chunky	11 and larger (8mm and larger)	6–11 sts

WEIGHTS AND LENGTHS

You can use either the imperial or metric measurement system in a project, but don't mix the two or you'll just get in a muddle. This chart tells you how to convert from one system to another.

ounces	=	grams	x 0.0352
grams	=	ounces	x 28.35
inches	=	centimeters	x 0.3937
centimeters	=	inches	x 2.54
yards	=	meters	x 0.9144
meters	=	yards	x 1.0936

KNITTING NEEDLE SIZES

Slightly confusingly, there are three systems of sizing knitting needles, and not every size exists in every system. This chart gives you the equivalent sizes across the three systems.

Metric	US	old UK & Canadian
25	50	–
19	35	–
15	19	–
10	15	000
9	13	00
8	11	0
7.5	11	1
7	10½	2
6.5	10½	3
6	10	4
5.5	9	5
5	8	6
4.5	7	7
4	6	8
3.75	5	9
3.5	4	–
3.25	3	10
3	2/3	11
2.75	2	12
2.25	1	13
2	0	14
1.75	00	–
1.5	000	–

Index

Abbreviations 220

adjusting stitches 123

analogous colors 20

annotating patterns 116

appliqués 41, 70–71

Aran knitting 108, 159–183

artisan threads 135

Autumn colors 26

beading
  Aran knitting 180
  intarsia knitting 135
  stitchwork 208–209
  stranded knitting 156–157
  swatches 214
  techniques 50–54, 58–63,
    88–89

bias stripes 92

blanket stitch 56, 64, 66

block patterns 102–103

blocking 105, 109

bobbins, yarn 117

bobbles 168–170, 173, 177,
  180, 182, 183

Bohus knitting 137

bouclé yarns 42–43, 130, 131

bound-off edges 59

bound stitches 171, 197

braid-effect yarns 110

bright colors 15, 82, 83

buttonholes 56, 67, 70, 93,
  186, 214

buttons 71, 93, 180

cables 59, 63, 160–161,
  167, 172–177

carrying color across the
  back 122

carrying yarns up the side 75

catching in floats 143

chain stitch 57, 65, 67, 88,
  134, 156, 182, 183, 208

changing colors 120–121

charting programs 150

charts 114–116, 138, 167

check stitch patterns 206

checkerboard designs 156

chenille yarns 44, 110

chevron patterns 79, 154,
  156

chunky yarns 45

color analysis, professional
  24, 26

color balancing 126–127,
  150–151

color-effect yarns
  Aran knitting 178–179
  intarsia knitting 128
  slip stitch knitting
    110–111
  stitch patterns 40–41
  stitchwork 204–205
  stranded knitting 152–153
  stripes 84–85
  swatches 213
  types 31–39

color families 15, 16–17

color-mixing 35, 53, 81,
  90–91

color notebooks 28–29

color pooling 32

color saturation 15, 21, 23

color values 22–23

color wheels 14–15, 18, 20,
  21

color words 15

colorfastness 68, 135, 214

colorwork and texture
  210–211

complementary colors 21

contemporary colors
  148–149

Conversions 221

cool colors 18, 19, 60, 78

cotton perlé 69

crewel wools 69, 88

cross-stitch 56, 64, 88

crossed stitches 164–165

darning in ends 76

decreases 190–193

diamond grid patterns 62

diamond shapes 124

disguising mistakes 55,
  123, 134

Donegal tweed 38

double-rib patterns 173

double seed stitch 41

dressmaker's markers 68

embroidery
  Aran knitting 182–183
  intarsia knitting 134
  stitchwork 208–209
  stranded knitting 156–157
  striping with 88–89
  swatches 214
  techniques 55–57, 65–69

eyelash yarns 43, 44, 131,
  154, 206 see also fur yarns

eyelets 66, 188, 214

Fair Isle knitting 36–37, 64,
  93, 137, 146–147, 149,
  153, 211

flat stockinette stitch 106,
  107

floats 137, 138, 143, 144

fluffy yarns 46

four-row stripe patterns 78,
  84, 90, 91, 177

French knitting 70

French knots 57, 65, 134,
  181, 182, 183

frills 64

frostflowers (frostrosen) 137

fur yarns 43, 44, 46, 154,
  198 see also eyelash yarns

ganseys 159

garter stitch 40, 54, 86–87,
  98, 100, 106, 133, 206

gauges 51, 53, 62, 87, 95,
  207, 212

glass beads 61

grid stitch patterns 206

grids 116

heart motifs 62, 114, 124

herringbone patterns 205

houndstooth check patterns
  100

I-cords 41, 47, 70, 181

increases 194–197

intarsia knitting 45, 64, 76,
  113–135, 210

joining in new yarn 74, 119

knitted-in beading 49,
  52–53, 58, 62, 63, 135, 214

knitter's graph paper 116

knitting needle sizes 43,
  212, 221

lace knitting 200–201, 208

laundering 44, 50, 66, 68,
  70–71, 181, 214

lazy daisy stitch 57, 65, 70,
  134, 182, 183

line patterns 100–101

loop knitting 198–199, 209

markers 68

marled yarns 85

matching self-patterning yarns 36

mathematical sequences, in striping 92

matte beads 61

mistakes *see also* unpicking
beading 51
disguising 55, 123, 134
embroidery 65, 67
Fair Isle 64
yarn types 70, 148

mohair 42, 87, 90, 91, 110, 130, 154, 206, 207

monochromatic designs 16, 93, 130

mosaic patterns 106–107

motifs 114–116, 118, 124–127, 181, 213

multiple yarns 77, 79, 90

needle sizes 43, 212, 221

neutral colors 82, 83

Nordic knitting 137, 147, 149, 154

notebooks for color 28–29

noughts and crosses cables 172

novelty yarns 31, 42, 87 *see also* textured yarns

one-row stripe patterns 78, 79, 80, 84, 85, 89

OXO cables 172, 175

pastels 15, 24, 25, 80–81

pearl threads 69

peeries 137

personal colors 24–27

picot cast-ons/bind-offs 64

pigment color wheels 15

pinstripe effects 111

plaid patterns 88, 100

plain stockinette stitch 11, 31, 33, 42, 70

plain yarns 44–45, 84, 85, 87, 111

pockets 67

pom-poms 35, 41

pooling, of color 32

practice swatches 124–125, 212–214

primary colors 14, 20, 21

purl stitch 40, 41, 54

random stripe patterns 79

resources 218–219

reverse stockinette stitch 40, 47, 84, 86, 87, 89, 92, 103, 132

reversible patterns 104–105

rib stitch 40

ribbon yarns 43, 44, 47

ring cables 172, 174

rope-twist cable 172

round, working in the 138

ruching effects 109

ruffle-effect yarns 43 *see also* ribbon yarns

running stitch 56, 64, 89, 134, 208

saturation of color 15, 21, 23

Scottish Harris tweed 38

secondary colors 14

seed stitch 40, 47, 86, 87, 132, 133, 208, 210

self-patterning yarns 36–37, 40, 41, 84, 128

self-striping yarns
Aran knitting 179
beading 63–64
slip stitch knitting 111
stitchwork 204–205
stranded knitting 152, 153

striping with 84–85
types 34–36

sequins 50, 54, 59, 63, 64, 209

sewing in the ends 131

slip stitch beading 49, 52, 54, 58, 59, 62, 135

slip stitch knitting 95–111

slubbed yarns 42, 47

space-dyed yarns 32
see also variegated yarns

Spring colors 24

squares 124

steam blocking 105

stitch markers 201

stitch patterns 40–41, 46–47, 133, 155, 202–211

stockinette stitch 91, 99, 106, 107, 182

stranded embroidery floss 68

stranded knitting 76, 137–157

stripes 62, 64, 73–93, 124, 210–211

Summer colors 24

swatches 124–125, 212–214

Swiss darning 55, 64, 88, 123, 134, 156, 157

tapestry wools 68, 183

tensioning stitches 55, 75, 101, 138, 142

tertiary colors 14

texture
and colorwork 210–211
patterns 108–109, 133
swatches 213

textured yarns
intarsia knitting 130–131
slip stitch knitting 110–111
and stitch patterns 46–47
and stitchwork 206–207

stranded knitting 154–155
striping with 87

threading, beads 50–51

three-dimensional effects 103, 109

thumb cast-ons 59

traditional colors and patterns 146–147

trims 70–71

tweed patterns 98–99, 205

tweed yarns 38–39, 85, 111, 129, 145, 153, 178

twist stitches 162–163

twisted stitches 166–167

two-row stripe patterns 32, 75, 78, 80, 81, 86

unpicking
beading 51, 58
embroidery 65, 67, 88
lace knitting 200, 201
textured yarns 46, 131
twisting techniques 121
yarn ends 76

variegated yarns 32–33, 84–85, 111, 128, 145, 178, 204

vertical stripe patterns 79

vintage threads 69

warm colors 18, 19, 26, 27, 60, 78

weaving in 123, 144, 145, 153, 154

weight of yarns 33, 55, 73, 91, 125, 131

Winter colors 27

yarn bobbins 117

yarn ends 76

yarnovers 186–189

Acknowledgments

As with all books, this one was a team effort. A big thank you to James Evans for commissioning the book and getting it all started, and to Richard Webb for keeping it all going in the right direction and for his patience with me. My thanks to Lindsey Johns for her creative page design, to Simon Rodway for clear technique illustrations, to Angela Koo for ensuring that my words made sense, and to Andrew Perris for the enormous number of swatch photographs. Sarah and Luise, I really couldn't have done this without you. Many thanks to Jamieson's of Shetland for supplying their double-knit yarn in wonderful colors (for a full range of their yarns go to the website, the address is in Resources on page 218). And many thanks also to Mrs Moon, who let me loose in their lovely yarn shop and subsidised many of the yarns I used in this book (visit them online or in the real world, see Resources for details). And as always, thanks to Philip for the food.